WORDS AFTER SPEECH

WORDS AFTER SPEECH

A Comparative Study of Romanticism and Symbolism

Paul Coates

First published 1986

Published by
THE MACMILLAN PRESS LTD
Houndmills, Basingstoke, Hampshire RG21 2XS
and London
Companies and representatives
throughout the world

Printed in Hong Kong

British Library Cataloguing in Publication Data
Coates, Paul
Words after speech: a comparative study of
romanticism and symbolism.
1. European literature – History and criticism
2. Romanticism   3. Symbolism in literature
I. Title
809′.9145   PN56.R7
ISBN 0–333–39191–8

For my parents

Words, after speech, reach
Into the silence.

(*Burnt Norton*)

Contents

Preface

The following book attempts to document some of the continuities between Romantic, Symbolist and Post-Symbolist poetry in America, Europe and England. Reference to 'England' in this context may raise some eyebrows: the cross-currents flowing between European and American Romanticism and Symbolism have been extensively charted, but both traditionalist and would-be revolutionary English critics view the native tradition in isolationist terms. Wordsworth may have felt it was bliss to be alive in the dawn of revolutionary France, and Coleridge may have sharpened the razor of his intellect on German texts, but both men finally subsided into an Anglican parochialism. The English poetic tradition is often said to have done likewise. If the fading brightness of vision in the later work of these poets is often regretted, one must suspect the mourning critics of crocodile tears; for by and large they endorse an English poetic tradition that has followed a similar path. Simultaneously, as it were, the elements of radical novelty in Romanticism are played down and its continuities with Thomson and Akenside accentuated. The juxtaposition of Wordsworth with Hölderlin, Rilke, Leśmian and Celan (among others) effected by this book aims at bringing out what could be called the *surrealism* of his verse, were not the formulation too provocative. My aim is, as I say, to indicate some of the subsequently suppressed continuities between English and European Romanticism. An 'alternative tradition', as it were, but a tradition nevertheless. And, although the stream of this tradition by now runs rather deep underground, it is instructive to observe its outcrops in the work of the greatest living English poet, Larkin. One may baulk at this: Larkin himself is notoriously indifferent to 'foreign literature', whilst the majority of his exegetes have stressed the suburban particularities of his verse. Poem after poem by Larkin can be seen, however, to be engaged in the paring-away of these particularities; initially exasperated by their clogging dross, working through them to an absolute image. That six-line poem 'As Bad as a Mile' is emblematic of this movement: the final negation of motion, the stillness of the unraised hand, corresponds to Larkin's near-silence, his

ix

commitment to writing only as and when the Muse dictates. And, if the 'alternative tradition' can be seen to have infiltrated work generally deemed a bastion of the poetic establishment, may it not be possible to cherish hopes of that establishment's demise?

Much of the following book utilises a form of what has come to be known among Marxists as 'reflection theory', which in its notorious and classic version postulates the ultimate determination by economic factors of the products of the culture of a particular period. The 'superstructure' is said to mirror 'the base'. The word 'reflection' itself, however, denotes both an exact and automatic material reproduction of an object and the process of an event's turning-over (and overturning) in the mind. I stress this duality because it permits one to formulate critical explanations and exegeses of art-works that are both sociological and anti-sociological, both reductivist and fantastic. The mirror of art, of course, inverts as it reflects; hence no precise one-to-one correspondence between art and event can be established. Moreover, the tracing of remote connections by the critic is, by virtue of its very far-fetchedness, less a diminution of the art-work than a means of attaching to it another art-work, its echo and parody, which is also criticism. This is perhaps the main sense of the modification of 'reflection theory' effected by Benjamin and Adorno. The critical text that confesses its own fictional, speculative status demonstrates its sympathy with the fictions of art itself. Its divided nature, as both art and criticism, itself reflects the consequences of those modernist works that incorporate theory: that render criticism redundant by pre-empting its constructions, and that justify it by emphasising their solidarity with it. To bring art and criticism under one roof is to compel both to forfeit the illusions of their innocence. As each one takes cognisance of the other, it reflects the divisions that persist in the world and the mind.

All the translations contained in the following book are the work of its author, unless otherwise stated. As a rule, I have given prose passages by Hölderlin, Celan and other poets both in their original languages and in English, because of the poetic merits of their prose. Prose extracts from French authors I have left untranslated, with the exceptions of the quotations from 'L'évolution créatrice', which appear by virtue of their philosophical rather than their literary suggestiveness. I have followed

Michael Hamburger's practice in his Penguin selection of Celan translations and avoided the misleading and, in any case, futile attempt to translate the multi-valent titles of the separate volumes of poetry Celan published.

Acknowledgements

The author and publishers should like to thank the following for permission to reprint copyright-material in this book:

The S. Fischer Verlag, for permission to reprint and translate 'Psalm' and 'Tübingen, Jänner' from 'Die Niemandsrose', and the Suhrkamp Verlag for permission to reprint and translate poems from Celan's collections 'Atemwende', 'Fadensonnen', 'Lichtzwang', 'Schneepart' and 'Zeitgehöft'.

Harvard University Press for Emily Dickinson's 'As if the Sea Should Part', which is reprinted by permission of the publishers and Trustees of Amherst College from *The Poems of Emily Dickinson*, edited by Thomas H. Johnson (Cambridge, Mass.: The Belknap Press of Harvard University Press) copyright 1951, © 1955, 1979, 1983 by the President and Fellows of Harvard College. Also, Little Brown and Co., for the same poem (copyright © 1929 by Martha Dickinson Bianchi; copyright © renewed 1957 by Mary L. Hampson), the copyright of which they also control.

The Insel Verlag, for permission to reprint and translate Hugo von Hofmannsthal's 'Manche freilich' and the extract from his 'Erlebnis'.

The Państwowy Instytut Wydawniczy, for permission to print and translate a selection of poems by Bolesław Leśmian, as well as to reprint the extracts from my book *Identyczność i nieidentyczność w twórczości Bolesława Leśmiana* in Chapter 4.

The Insel Verlag, for permission to reprint Rilke's 'Ausgesetzt auf den Bergen des Herzens', and The Hogarth Press and W. W. Norton and Co. Inc., for permission to translate it.

The Otto Müller Verlag, for permission to reprint Georg Trakl's 'Klage' from the *Dichtungen und Briefe* (Salzburg. 1969), and for permission to translate it.

I should also like to thank the editor of *Forum for Modern Language Studies*, for permission to reprint a modified version of my essay 'Transformations of the Mirror in the Poetry of Bolesław Leśmian'.

1 Prologue:
Words after Speech

The essays that comprise this book consider poets from different cultures and historical periods. It may therefore be worthwhile indicating some of the continuities between their work – continuities that serve to justify their juxtaposition, for all their temporal and linguistic heterogeneity – before proceeding to analyse their poems separately. These continuities exist in an area defined by such words as 'inspiration', 'dream', 'authority' and 'negation' (among others).

To begin with 'inspiration'. The writers assembled within this book share the belief that there is a sense in which their works can be said to 'write themselves'. In part this belief is a reflex of the sense of history born in the Romantic era: different types of expression inhabit different historical periods, as Hegel was to stress when tracking the course of the temporal unfolding of Spirit. The logical corollary of this is that works are dictated more by history than authorial intention. The Romantics forgo proprietary rights in their works: outpourings of 'inspiration', they cannot be produced to order; their significances are potentially infinite (different meanings will be ascribed to one and the same text in different cultural situations), and are often invisible to their author. The Romantic text is thus akin to a message in a bottle: its sender cannot foresee its final destination. Very often the Romantic poet will express his or her personal vision, opposed to the fiat of constituted authority, and then fall silent. This silence is often a refusal to identify with the authority that demands allegiance upon expiry of the poet's youth – and his or her poetic licence.

The works generated by 'inspiration' tend to be 'difficult'; once the trance of composition has passed, the poet finds himself in the position of the literary critic attempting to comprehend a work that appears to have been conceived by another person. In this sense, Romanticism founds literary criticism as an hermeneutic discipline: it is surely no accident that the first great English critical text, *Biographia Literaria*, should have arisen in response to the poems of Wordsworth. The Romantic text is

1

often the symptomatic coagulation of the author's self-mystified experience and anguish. It is thus like a dream: with a dream's authority
over the mind. Perhaps as a response to the imminent shrinking of the
world into the global village, the Romantic mind reaches out for an
infinity of possibilities, towards reality as a *totality*: it can never achieve
the point of rest from which to sum up experience. The author can never
formulate an authoritative final statement, for all such statements have
become suspect; hence Romanticism is less the reaction against the
Enlightenment than the logical conclusion of its iconoclasm. The
ideology of democracy which begins to prevail in this period further
invalidates the authoritative posture. The fragmented idiom of the
Romantic makes no secret of its fallibility; it invites the reader to fill in
the gaps, to make good its failings.

I have remarked that the work dictated by 'inspiration' is difficult.
This may be the reason why Wordsworth and Coleridge use a stripped-
down, simplified diction in their *Lyrical Ballads*: to emphasise that the
difficulties are not the result of authorial wilfulness – for the author, after
all, is speaking as plainly as he knows – but of necessity. As the author
relinquishes his authority, the work comes to seem self-generating. Its
words can seem to the artist to be the words of the Other. They thus
acquire the aura of the Sublime. Images of the Sublime are the fruit of a
disavowed violence in their beholder. When the writer terms his work the
result of 'inspiration' effectively he disowns it. This negation is a strategy
that enables the poet – as Bloom puts it – 'to continue to defend himself
against his own created image by disowning it, a defense of *un-naming* it
rather than *naming* it'.[1] Wordsworth's Miltonic and Keats's Spenserian
cadences and references are alibis meant to clear the poet of the
presumption and sin of personal creation: the poem presents itself as the
site of a possession, envious of the authority and prior access to the
language enjoyed by the dead mentor. Thus the Romantic poet is both
genius and medium, and each of his functions aggrandises the other: the
more resounding the claims made on behalf of individuality, the more
passionate the individual's attempt to submerge his own voice in the
voice of the Other when he fears his isolation. Fearful of the violence of
the Sublime, the poet will seek shelter in the womb of the unconscious of
language, in mimicry of folk forms. Another haven is dream, which
functions quasi-independently of the mind from which it issues, and
replaces the authoritative gesture of discursive thought with the humility
of the image, the flash of insight in a 'spot of time'. Dreams speak when
the poet himself would be silent: they mediate between sterility and
plenitude. Perhaps the most seductive of refuges are the

Gesamtkunstwerk and cinema, whose powerful totalisations overwhelm the self. Film production appears to reconcile individual and collectivity. By creating through art the illusion of reality, it seems to fulfil the Romantic dream of the reconciliation of culture and nature, rather than the dominance of one by the other. In actuality, however, film is less the saviour of art than the saviour's parody: the Anti-Christ who appears in the twilight of art.

Romantic poets often view their works as oneiric hieroglyphs. The German Romantics in particular (though one should note here that the term 'Romantic' has very different meanings in English and German criticism: a German would not term Goethe a Romantic) adopted procedures that anticipated the automatic writing of the surrealists. The dream poem is a scandal: a fragment of primary process jutting up out of silence, breaching the borders of darkness and infiltrating the day. It represents those who lie outside the systematised world of authority: the leech-gatherer, the lunatic and the opium-eater. The Romantic period sees a realisation that anyone can be a writer – just as we are all dreamers. If it also saw the evolution of the ideology of the 'genius', this was in part a dialectical reaction against its own collectivist drives, and in part a recognition of the individual's dependence upon that which is other than himself: his 'genius' or attendant spirit. 'Genius' is one of the primal words of the period, for it equivocates between individualism and collectivism (one 'is' a genius, on the one hand; one 'has' one, on the other). It partakes of the dialectical paradoxicality of the isolated individualist who writes ballads (paradox of the *lyrical* ballad).

The stylistics of dream are those of condensation, displacement and discontinuity. These are features of the primary process, and the Romantic would doubtless align them with Imagination, as opposed to Fancy. The dream poem is the work of an individual whose mastery of language and identification with society are intermittent. Rejection of one's own language can be an expression of an Utopian wish to surmount the class structures inscribed in its every intonation. Hence, perhaps, the attraction foreign cultures held for Wordsworth, Coleridge and Hölderlin, or, later, Conrad and Beckett. Where no foreign culture is available, the poet has recourse to archaism (Keats, Hopkins, Leśmian, Tennyson, among others). The fact that the dream poem can be formulated at all, even if it is pilloried by the quarterlies or mocked by the established literary authorities, is a sign that the language of the private individual, of unique experience, and of the traditionally anonymous and declassed, is beginning to be socially acceptable. Romanticism is the beginning of a long revolution. Society makes these concessions to the private language for several reasons. First, because it knows that private language to be an impossibility, and hence ultimately self-defeating: however great the similarities between them, poems and dreams are different things. Also, society prefers symbolic to actual revolution. Nevertheless, it is also aware of the exposed shortcomings of the established language of hierarchy and Reason. The French Revolution had shown that the contradictory components of society, so demurely separated by the binary oppositions of the heroic couplet, could come together, clash and even fuse. (When subject melts into object in Romanticism, symbolic upheaval occurs.) The concessions society made are often idealised as the beginnings of Democracy; and they can legitimately be seen as such. One must remember, however, that so far democracy, like the private language, has proved a contradiction in terms. World-wide, opposed régimes term themselves 'democratic': the word is fetishised because the thing is unattainable.

The literature of dream is not the same as automatic writing, though the word 'automatic' is suggestive. It emphasises that the associative writing instituted by the Romantics generally requires the support of a simple verse structure, usually ballad or blank verse. It must be sufficiently simple to accommodate the moments at which the author slackens the reins of control: at times of authorial near-abeyance, the text must be able to live a ghostly life on the verge of death, to tick over, like music or the breath rhythm of the unconscious man (the breath-rhythm that lies at the heart of modern aesthetics, and dictates its adoption of free verse). The structure need not be a form of versification: in Hölderlin's poems, for instance, it is the semi-automatic alternation of the tones. These simple structures also grant the poet access to the mechanisms that generate myth in the 'collective unconsious': the area designated by this term may be the same as *langue*, and be 'unconsious' in the sense that no individual can achieve complete consciousness of it, since its sole comprehensive map is that of the totality of language in its spatial and historical unfolding. These structures permit the individual his individualism whilst shielding him from some of its worst consequences. Simultaneously, as it were, they provide the basis for an improvisation that questions all structure, lending the mind the illusion of safety it requires in order to roam freely a universe whose endless vistas and Piranesi perspectives would otherwise open up on insanity. The possibility of insanity is held at bay by means of this dialectic of isolation and community. And, just as the communal forms of myth and folk lore buttress the poet, so the length of the poem insulates the reader against the shock of its most powerful moments. The Romantics are not yet prepared to do as Eliot was later to do and simply juxtapose the 'inspired', 'demonic', passages, without any padding.

These moments of shock, I would suggest, often appear in the margins of an oeuvre valued for other characteristics. In fact, they can only manifest themselves at the margin, the limit of the writer's conscious intention, for they are the forces that subvert his intended systems. Buried in the middle of a long poem, such a passage will burn a hole in it, undermining the linearity and discursivity that surround it. Such is the case with the 'spots of time' in *The Prelude*, such as the stolen-boat episode; whilst the exclusion of 'Nutting' from that poem is surely a reflection of the problems it creates for Wordsworth's self-image as Nature's reverencer. Hence the resonance of such works as 'Kubla Khan', 'La Belle Dame sans Merci', Heine's 'Mein Herz, mein Herz ist traurig' (My heart, my heart is sad) – with its devastating final line – or Stefan George's 'Im windes-weben' (In the wind's weavings): all, as it were, by-products of their authors' overriding ambitions. Their peripheral status testifies to the success of the author's self-unknowing – his dream. The result is the frequent massive disproportion between the sections of an oeuvre that are readable and those that are not (think of Blake, Wordsworth, Emily Dickinson, for instance). Where the poet is also a critic, he may attempt to pre-empt this judgement of the extent to which his work is readable (which means: worth reading, not necessarily the same thing as 'easily understood') through a deliberate slimness (Eliot or Coleridge).

One reason for this disparity between the consciously intended massiveness of a body of work and the paucity of readable portions within it is the fatal tendency of the writer's dream structures to become automatic in the most pernicious sense: empty. (As Coleridge was to complain Wordsworth's poems did at certain points.) Simplicity of rhythm is fatally prone to slide into banality. The simplicity of the rhythms expresses the fact that poetry is no longer a learned art. For Wordsworth in particular, *poeta doctus* would be an oxymoron. In this context, Byron emerges as an eighteenth-century poet in hiding, as one might expect given his admiration for Pope: he dons *Knittelvers* or doggerel in order to survive the revolt of the masses, just as the French aristocrats disguised themselves as sans-culottes. In the poetry of Byron the eighteenth century plays dead; it hopes to return once its executioners have departed. In 'The Ancient Mariner' and 'La Belle Dame sans Merci', by way of contrast, the illusion of helplessness is augmented by the fact that the poet really is hypnotised by the simplicity of his rhythms. Simple rhyme schemes can be amulets clutched during the passage across the abyss. It is thus that they function for Coleridge, Keats, the Wordsworth of the 'Lucy' poems – the oneiric effects of which have been described by F. W. Bateson – and Emily Dickinson. The simplicity relaxes the imagination like a drug: a truth drug. It is likely that 'Kubla Khan' was disrupted less by the visit of the person from Porlock than by the imperative to sustain an intricate rhyme scheme (the late fruit of months of despairing Coleridgean exercises in versification), its complexity serving to arrest the somnambulistic drift of dream into language.

I have spoken above of how the poet's deliberate surrender of conscious censorship of his work in this period calls into being the critic, who is needed to sift it for its nuggets: criticism is the necessary corollary of Romanticism. The antagonism between them indicates the degree to which the poem has been infiltrated by the primary process. Another concomitant of the abandonment of the aesthetics of strict rhetorical control is the emergence of the anthology, compiled on quasi-Arnoldian principles and comprising the writer's most intense ('inspired') passages. Like all lasting institutions, the anthology fulfils a dual function. On the one hand, it propagates the ideology of inspiration and so furthers the poet's project, often more effectively than the poet himself (this is one of the senses in which the critic who compiles an anthology must needs be an artist, whilst this partial usurpation of the artistic function gives the actual poet another reason to dislike him); but on the other hand the anthology records the moments at which individual and language coincided in order to gloze over the growing antagonism between them. It thereby recuperates the writer's project for society, insisting on the continued meaningfulness of language. Nevertheless, the extensive areas of non-anthologised writing indicate how inefficient society really was, how little of the individual's energy it was able to channel into language. The extreme rarity of the anthologised work highlights the immensity of the gap between individual and society, speaker and language, *parole* and *langue*. Hence the modernist experience of the negativity of language: its generalised nature defeats the expression of individual experience. The work of Hopkins provides perhaps the completest documentation of the impossibility of linguistic adequation of the pungently individual: his work reveres the unique 'thinginess' of the object, its *haeccitas*, but concludes in the sterility of the 'terrible sonnets', in which individual self-identity reveals itself as a curse: 'God's most deep decree / Bitter would have me taste; my taste was me'. The pursuit of the unique word for the unique thing concludes in obsessive neologism and incomprehensibility, in the creation of such words as 'betweenpie'. The fate of the Romantic quest for the unique – which is a quest for neologism – is depicted with tragic sympathy and humour in the poems of Leśmian.

Both the real dream and the dream text posit an absence of paraphrasable meaning accompanied by an immanence of significance within the text itself. The Romantic poem is to the collectivity as a dream is to the individual. Nevertheless 'the dream text' is finally only a metaphor, though an illuminating one. The meaning of the dream text is an absence, like the meaning of a dream. The fact of its existence indicates the possibility of being at the heart of absence: absence of speech, consciousness and society. Its paradoxical existence at the hub of the void generates the religion of art, which venerates expression as a rare miracle.

The Bible speaks of old men dreaming dreams and young men seeing visions. The crumbling of religious faith from the eighteenth century onwards deprived dreams of their visionary status, and a society shot through with inequality, of the consoling icon of equality after death. The secularised vision became available for deployment as part of the poet's arsenal. The dream poem acts as a mediator that knits up the broken halves of discourse; and, just as the bourgeoisie mediates between the feudal opposition of rich and poor, so the dream text bridges the chasm between the rhetoric of the privileged and the inarticulacy of the dispossessed. The key figure here is Wordsworth, who writes Miltonically but *of the declassed*. The dream poem inhabits a sort of Utopian space, the unattainable 'nowhere' from which the individual is permitted to enunciate his pain in a language the communal nature of which would otherwise preclude adequate rendition of individual suffering: a truth recognised by Cordelia when she says the worst is not so long as we can say 'this is the worst'. The space of the dream poem is the page, the site of writing: it mediates between speech and silence; the marks on the page constitute a system of notation that records a voice, and yet themselves 'say' nothing. The poet's awareness of the evaporation of the audience and his own loss of authority are the preconditions of writing. His words can never find their way back to speech, for he has no patron or forum but the open market, and the multiplicity of meanings his words amass, in an attempt to speak to the largest possible number of readers, precludes the existence of a single auditor situated at a single place in time – and hence in the end precludes the existence of any auditor at all. Perhaps that is why Kleist and Kafka fall into laughing-fits when they attempt to read their works out loud to an audience: they see the absurdity of their own action. If the realm of listening is that of time, the polysemic text – the dream text – knows only space and the spacings of the page. It is an 'image', a configuration of black marks on a white ground.

The freedom of writing, like the freedom of dream, is a negative one. As Adorno notes, at the turn of the century – and, I should wish to maintain, earlier, in Romanticism, too – 'absolute freedom within art – as always, a restricted zone – conflicted with the perennial state of unfreedom in the totality'.[2] This is negative freedom: it achieves liberty through its negation of the pre-existent world, and yet its liberty itself becomes tyrannous through the absolutism of its negativity. It is the negativity of the contemplation of an infinity of possibilities within an imagination sealed off from choice of any single one.

This negative freedom, however, has its positive aspect, as the following remarks in Bergson's *Creative Evolution* reveal:

> What is it to think the object A non-existent? To represent it non-existent cannot consist in withdrawing from the idea of the object A the idea of the attribute 'existence', since, I repeat, the representation of the existence of the object is inseparable from the representation of the object, and indeed is one with it. To represent the object A non-existent can only consist, therefore, in *adding* something to the idea of this object; we add to it, in fact, the idea of an *exclusion* of this particular object by actual reality in general. To think the object A as non-existent is first to think the object and consequently to think it existent; it is then to think that another reality, with which it is incompatible, supplants it. Only, it is useless to represent this latter reality explicitly; we are not concerned with what it is; it is enough for us to know that it drives out the object A, which alone is of interest to us. That is why we think of the expulsion rather than of the cause which expels.[3]

As Bergson describes it, the cause of the expulsion is present only negatively. The non-existent, he argues, consists in the *addition* of something to the original object – an addition that displaces the original. One may feel that the negations found in a Wordsworth or a Leśmian represent responses to a threat to the worlds they describe: rural worlds being corroded by the imminence of industrialisation. The poet himself employs a double negative: by attaching a negative prefix to an adjective or noun, or by writing of the beauty of the object that does not exist, he admits that the world it belongs to is vanishing and cherishes it in the moment of its dematerialisation; and by omitting to depict the thing that displaces it he admits his ignorance concerning that thing – to understand which one needs the sort of specialist knowledge a Balzac will make a show of possessing – and his will to reject it: he sees only its negative aspect as the destroyer of a valued world. But if negation had become a widespread poetic trope by the time of Symbolism, this is more than merely 'a reflection of industrialisation' (though it is that as well): it is testimony to the seductive power and *richness* of the negative. This richness is the co-presence of two objects within the space and time marked out for one: their superimposition is the source of a superabundance of experience. The richness of negativity is of a piece with the Symbolist desire to supersaturate the senses through synaesthesia and the *Gesamtkunstwerk* (total art-work):[4] it is the darkness of the mine in which the Symbolist jewels gleam. The negative, thus, is not 'negative' in the colloquial sense: it combines a sense of loss with an intoxication of excess. It cannot be interpreted, and condemned, as 'pessimistic'. Rather, it is paradoxical: as the coloured disc appears white when it spins fast enough, so the excessiveness of colour and speed in the era of the modern – the excess of *the new* – creates a blur of events the mind perceives as a blank.

2 Archaeology: the Romantic Roots of Symbolism

THE USES OF PROJECTION: BLAKE AND WORDSWORTH

Jerusalem London unreal: the double vision of William Blake

'Without contraries there is no progression. Attraction and repulsion, reason and energy, love and hate, are necessary to human existence.' Thus, at the beginning of *The Marriage of Heaven and Hell*, Blake formulates his doctrine of contraries. The interpenetration of opposites – the marriage of Heaven and Hell – is achieved through projection, which transposes the positions of subject and object. His work often approaches a state of conceptual, and sometimes grammatical, *enantiodromia,* in which everything devolves into its contrary. His most famous conceptual opposition is of course that between innocence and experience, but the dialectic of the contraries blurs the sharpness of the distinction. Thus some of the poems originally assigned to the innocence sequence could be shifted to the experience section: 'Blake eventually discovered that four of the later Songs of Innocence were sufficiently close to being Songs of Experience to merit inclusion in that series.'[1] Similarly, the Tyger both is and is not twin to the Lamb (it may be interesting to note a parallel between this poem and Keller's novel *Der grüne Heinrich* (Green Henry), whose hero in his youth imagines that the illustration of a tiger may represent the distant God of whom he has heard: the Christianity of Keller and Blake, in so far as one can speak of it, is equally unorthodox); 'The Clod and the Pebble' achieves a symmetrical stalemate of innocence and experience. The interdependence of opposites lends a poem such as 'London' the elliptical suggestiveness that was later to be the basis of the Symbolist aesthetic.

> I wander through each chartered street,
> Near where the chartered Thames does flow.
> And mark in every face I meet
> Marks of weakness, marks of woe.
>
> In every cry of every man,
> In every infant's cry of fear,
> In every voice, in every ban,
> The mind-forg'd manacles I hear –
>
> How the chimney-sweeper's cry
> Every blackening church appalls,
> And the hapless soldier's sigh
> Runs in blood down palace walls;
>
> But most through midnight streets I hear
> How the youthful harlot's curse
> Blasts the new-born infant's tear
> And blights with plagues the marriage hearse.

'London' is obviously one of Blake's most remarkable poems. The repetition of the word 'chartered' in the first two lines suggests the inescapability of exploitation: one turns the corner of the chartered street – of the first line – and comes face to face with a chartered river. But the image also contains a derisive irony at man's pretensions to have subjugated nature: a chartered river is a paradox, and hence an impossibility. The repetition creates a sense of nightmare and obsession that is crucial to the poem's critique of reality and the perceiving mind. The repetitions (particularly 'every') thunder oppressively from line to line, evoking the pervasiveness of corruption in this world. Blake's critique of the mind extends to the projecting mind of the poet himself. For 'I mark in every face I meet' can imply that the marks of woe are scored upon the faces of the passers-by by the poet's own imagination: Blake's rage encompasses a criticism of the distorting tendencies of rage itself. The reference to 'marking' can suggest the drawing of a sign upon human faces: it is as if Blake moves through the town as an angel of death, marking out the elect and the damned. This angel of destruction is a *visual artist* – like Blake himself, scoring marks upon his woodcut; and, like the visual artist, he translates words into images or colours (the soldier's sigh runs red down the walls): his London is a multi-sensory nightmare. I have remarked that Blake's critique of London includes criticism of the mind that perceives it (if he used his double vision to transform an old man into a thistle, might he not be guilty of other projections also?). The phrase 'mind-forg'd manacles' neatly catches this ambiguity: it hovers between an admission of the possible guilt of the projecting onlooker, and an enraged protest against mental servitude. Certain phrases have a dream-like condensation that testifies to the co-operation of fantasy in the composition of the poem. 'Every blackening church appalls', for instance, has this dream complexity: the church is a whited sepulchre that discloses its inner darkness through its indifference to the chimney-sweeper's cry; the evident blackness of the sweep appalls a church wishing to conceal its own inner corruption; the chimney-sweeper himself blackens the church by leaning feebly against its walls (sliding down them like the blood of the soldier's sigh: the conjunction of the two phrases within the same verse causes them to interact and fuse with each other). The sigh that turns to blood contains similarly condensed references: it evokes tuberculosis, bloody punishment of the slightest murmur of discontent, the imperviousness to blood of palace walls, the blood-soaked cornerstone of the autocratic régime. The chimney-sweeper and the soldier, like the speaker of the poem, stand outside the edifices of authority: inhabitants of the street, they are outsiders. Only the speaker, however, is able to survive in his exclusion: he draws strength from his aggressive ability to see through palace walls, church walls and passing faces, to the reality below. The reiterated 'every' of the poem is instinct both with the oppressiveness of London and possible paranoia in the speaker. Sultriness is present in the sound patterns too, especially in those of the last two stanzas, which almost choke upon their own discourse: on the recurrent plosives, the *l*s, the repeated flat *a*s. Because the oppressiveness of the city is reflected in the clotted phonetic passages of the poem itself, it reveals itself as truly, and horribly, ineluctable: even the enraged observer can find no point of leverage from which to dislodge this world. (The exasperation felt here may in part stem from the cramped conditions in which Blake wrote the songs – his rage at lack of greater space – using every precious inch of the notebook that had belonged to his brother Robert, who died of consumption in 1787.) The last stanza plays on the duality of 'curse' as an oath heard in one place and a general malediction manifest in the fates of successive generations. The harlot's curse is both uttered over the cradle of the new-born infant and is manifest in a society in which marriage and harlotry are indistinguishable. (This is part of a certain misogynism in Blake: woman is depicted as the destroyer.) Blake's poem begins by referring to 'every face'; it fittingly concludes with an image that draws the full cycle of life within the compass of the curse: the new-born infant is blasted even in its cradle. The cry heard at midnight carries further in the hush than it would during daytime, and so acquires a more terrible resonance. In 'London' the illusive procedures of Symbolist aesthetics enact the mind's derangement by a tentacular evil. Its conceptual and grammatical short-circuits render mental collapse in the face of corrupted being.

Another such study of corruption is 'The Sick Rose'.

> O rose, thou art sick:
> The invisible worm
> That flies in the night
> In the howling storm
>
> Has found out thy bed
> Of crimson joy;
> And his dark secret love
> Does thy life destroy.

If it is possible that Blake's position as an artist illustrating his own works led him to assume that in cases of obscurity the images would clarify the poems (or vice versa), 'The Sick Rose' shows how it is more common for meaning to vanish in the gap between word and image. For the relationship between them is extremely enigmatic. It is as if Blake's verbal imagination was liberated by knowledge of the presence of an imagistic safety set – which freed him to write surreally. The illustration to 'The Sick Rose' shows a closed rose blossom from which a spirit is striving to escape; a caterpillar is chewing one of the rose tree's leaves. The elements of sickness and destruction are common to both image and poem. But what are we to make of the storm, the invisible worm (which of course cannot figure in the illustration), and the night of the poem? Blake's notebooks give an alternative penultimate line, in which 'her' replaces the 'his' of 'his dark secret love' – a strange variant that undermines the common reading of the poem as an obscure enactment of male – female sexual encounter. What possible reason is there for this substitution? 'Rose' is traditionally female; the flight of 'her' invisible worm to her could mean the restoration to her body of the absent phallus. (Its invisibility may however be that of the clitoris; especially since reference to the female sexual organs is implicit in the 'crimson'.) Blake may be writing of the self-impregnating, narcissistic bisexuality of plants, superimposing upon this theme images redolent of human sexuality ('bed', 'crimson' and 'found out' can all connote loss of virginity). The poem poises between the implications of 'rose' and 'crimson', much as Hawthorne's *The Scarlet Letter* balances between 'scarlet' and 'red'. 'Rose' is innocent red, red innocent even of red (not all roses are red); 'crimson' is red stained with culture, impregnated with experience. 'Rose' is to 'crimson' as 'thou' is to 'her'. The poem suggests a mythological narrative in which the invisible god descends in a cloud of darkness to violate his victim in secrecy. But there are also suggestions of Lesbian affection as a form of self-mystified self-love. Critical speculations are the only possible response to a poem so cryptic: speculation is the aura round the poem, but it can never actually coincide with it. The poem may be about the corrosive effects of secrecy – a recurrent theme in Blake. It may be so strongly conscious of these effects because it is itself a secret. The illustration that surrounds it is not a gloss in its margin but another tendril in the thicket that densely entwines it. If the poem deviously hints at a 'bed' that is both the (crimson) flower and the root (where a canker gnaws unseen), the illustration is far more bland and ignores the roots and the secret world of underground. The caterpillar is a merely conventional conceptualisation of the force that destroys the rose – a force that is far more problematic, and resistant to visualisation, the grounds of its being 'invisible', 'dark' and 'secret'. 'The Sick Rose' defiantly shrugs off its illustration.

Another poem from 'Songs of Experience' whose subject is sexuality is the marvellous 'Sunflower':

> Ah, sunflower, weary of time,
> Who countest the steps of the sun,
> Seeking after that sweet golden clime
> Where the traveller's journey is done;
>
> Where the youth pined away with despair
> And the pale virgin shrouded with snow
> Arise from their graves and aspire
> Where my sunflower wishes to go.

The pale virgin and the youth arise from their graves like flowers piercing the soil. The missing verb indicates the impossibility of action to implement desire. By anthropomorphising the sun and granting it steps, Blake as it were deprives both humans and the sunflower of movement: the faculty of motion is projected and cannot be recalled. Like 'The Sick

Rose', 'The Sunflower' is concerned with the way the rootedness of the flower renders it a passive victim of the processes of existence. The youth and the maiden are doubly hindered, for even after they have arisen from their graves they can only aspire – rooted to the spot like the sunflower itself. This aspiration comprises the subterranean self-referentiality of the poem: aspiration is the 'Ah' of the gentle opening aspirate. 'Where the traveller's journey is done' suggests the onset of night as the sun steps down in a blaze of gold; it is also, however, the perpetual noon of Utopia: where the sun takes no steps, where all journeying is 'done', because time has been fulfilled and need no longer progress. The sexuality of the youth and the maiden is pallid and other-worldly. The conventional diction and vocabulary employed to describe it (ll. 5–6) provide an implied criticism of the feebleness of their desire. Even when they rise together from the grave they do not realise their desires but remain transfixed in staring aspiration. Despite the parallels between the youth and the virgin and the legend of Hyperion and Clytie, there is no exact congruence, for in the myth Hyperion (the youth) is the sun and Clytie the scorned lover who pines for her love in the form of a sunflower slavishly following his steps as he crosses the sky. Moreover, in Blake's poem it is the virgin who is scornful ('shrouded in snow' suggests the Petrarchan unattainable lady), whilst the youth 'pines'. The mythical tropes are off-key, like the biblical tropes of the Prophetic Books: the poem is a cluster of possible meanings with no single significance. It thus overwhelms the would-be interpreter and achieves the status of a myth in its own right. This mythical status is problematic, however: if the poem has the semantic density of myth, it lacks the sustaining institutional religious framework that repeats the myth, compels one to return to it, and allows one time to see the unfolding of its various significances. Hence, perhaps, the final unreadability of the Prophetic Books. It is as if the modern poem with the density of myth must of needs be short because it exists in opposition to the official systems of mythology. One cannot, as it were, construct a system upon suggestivity: the aesthetics of suggestion subvert the aspiration to system.

Blake's sunflower is weary of time and yearns for a perpetually sunny 'clime'. The word is wittily apt, for the rhyme with 'climb' reminds one that everywhere the sun has to climb and descend, that there is no place of repose outside the bounds of regulated time. This yearning for timelessness is perhaps the thing that frustrates love in the first place: the youth pines away, the maiden remains virgin, because they refuse to kiss the joy as it dies, to live in eternity's *sunrise* (rather than its sunset). The humans and the sunflower of this poem both are and are not the same:

the comparison between them is problematic (just as all the dualities of Blake–word and image, subject and object–are problematic). This eerie interplay of identity and non-identity prefigures the regress of archetypes who both are and are not alike in the Prophetic Books. The experience of likeness that is also unlikeness is central to Blake's heretical inflection of the Bible. A heretic both is and is not a Christian: his belief in the validity of the myths persuades him to retain their terminology, whilst his disbelief prompts him to alter the sacred texts. The regress of relationship between Blake and Los and Los and Urizen is typical of this sameness in difference.[2] The whole of Blake's work can be seen to attempt to comprehend this relationship, which is one of *projection*: the form of the self is imposed upon that of the other. The necessity of the other is, however, problematic to an artist with Blake's strength of will. Yet he knows that without contraries there is no progression.

'Strange fits of Passion': the horse–man

The figure of the horseman dominates Romantic poetry–from Byron's *The Giaour* to Goethe's 'Willkommen und Abschied' (Welcome and Farewell) and Słowacki's *Mazepa*. He often comes from afar and departs in a whirlwind. The horse is of course a creature of warfare, but in this period of revolutionary war the horseman also has a revolutionary connotation: that of the individual's freedom to make his way through pathless wastes, or to step up to seize the reins of power. In *Mazepa* the page-boy is strapped to a horse which eventually bears him to the rank of king in the Ukraine: association with the horse brings about his rise in social status. Nevertheless, the figure of Mazepa also expresses a certain fear of the (libidinal) forces one has to control, ride or survive if one is to achieve power. Horse plus rider constitutes a double being, a centaur-like man–beast. The man who follows the animal in himself may suffer a bestial loss of consciousness or conscience: he may also race in imagination like a beast because unable to do so in reality as a man (in the case of Byron, the step onto the horse's back conceals one's own lameness). The symbolic reverberations of the relationship between rider and horse is the theme of Wordsworth's 'Strange fits of passion', in which the teleological nature of the horse–man's desire is first embodied and then rejected. Wordsworth's empathy with the mineral world reveals itself to be part of a reality in which fear has *petrified* the human being on the edge of transgression.

Strange fits of passion have I known:
　　And I will dare to tell
But in the Lover's ear alone
　　What once to me befell.

When she I loved looked every day
　　Fresh as a rose in June,
I to her cottage bent my way,
　　Beneath an evening moon.

Upon the moon I fixed my eye,
　　All over the wide lea;
With quickening pace my horse drew nigh
　　Those paths so dear to me.

And now we reached the orchard plot;
　　And, as we climbed the hill,
The sinking moon to Lucy's cot
　　Came near, and nearer still.

In one of those sweet dreams I slept,
　　Kind Nature's gentlest boon!
And all the while my eyes I kept
　　On the descending moon.

My horse moved on, hoof after hoof
　　He raised, and never stopped:
When down behind the cottage roof,
　　At once, the bright moon dropped.

What fond and wayward thoughts will slide
　　Into a Lover's head!
'O mercy!' to myself I cried,
　　'If Lucy should be dead!'

The rarity with which horses appear in Wordsworth's work can be correlated with a rejection of his own revolutionary youth, of passion and travel (Annette and France), in favour of the sedentary wise passiveness of the stoic. In this poem the horse initially moves 'with quickening pace' towards Lucy's cottage: the horse's movement expresses the rider's desire to see her. But this symbiosis of man and beast, summed up in the 'we' the poet applies to them both (a dangerous pairing that interposes the rider–horse relationship in front of the relationship with Lucy, thus paving the way for her final imperilment), has the corollary that when the rider slips into a dream state, a state in which hidden wishes surface, the horse's tread matches his desire. 'Hoof after hoof' lets one see each step as if the horse's tread slows – unlike the earlier blur of the 'quickening pace'. The revocation of 'quickening' may also imply a substitution of the dead for the living (the quick). Moon and horse approach the cottage simultaneously, as if acting in concert: when the rider turns his thoughts away from Lucy (distracted by her likeness, the lucent moon?), he as it were wills her death. The equivalence established between moon and cottage as the former slides down the sky is a displacement and replacement of the ideal. The moment the ideal touches the earth it evaporates. The frame-analysis of the hoof-steps is in part an attempt to postpone the inevitable simultaneity of satisfaction and death. The moon stands for the chaste unattainable female, for Diana–Dorothy perhaps? The averting of the gaze from the symbol of the object of desire (the cottage comes before the moon to censor it, even as Wordsworth desires a failure of the censoring instance) is perhaps an indication of the forbidden, incestuous nature of this desire. Wordsworth preserves himself from violation of the incest taboo by stopping short of the cottage. Does he realise that in yearning for Dorothy he is 'wishing for the moon'? The power to quicken ascribed to the horse's tread indicates the strength of the libidinal desire arrested by the super-ego. As the film of the gallop slows into frames, the poet ages in the course of the poem: he was 'the Lover' but is so no longer. He will only speak to the Lover – that is, to himself (memory addresses its previous self) – because his secret is too scandalous to be shared with anyone except a fellow culprit. Sublimation supplants desire as conscience awakens at the end and the teleology of narrative snaps to leave only a fragment: the poem becomes a palimpsest, semi-symptomatic. Fearful of the beast he rides, of the power of his desire, the poet mentally halts: the imagined, feared, wished-for death of Lucy is punishment for, and consummation of, his hubris in choosing to mount the horse, thinking he could rein in desires. The poet substitutes imaginative alchemy for real action, breaking the trajectory of the ballad and subverting it into a lyric: a 'lyrical ballad'. Instead of Byron, the revolutionary horseman, one has the poet as spectator, with no power of locomotion. But what Wordsworth loses in reality he gains in the imagination: the abysses of his verse echo on to anticipate the praxis of Trakl or Celan.

Mental borders: the mechanisms of projection

The image of the horse presented in 'Strange fits of passion' may recall the
sleeping horse with 'Mane, ears, and tail, as lifeless as the trunk / That
had no stir of breath' described in a fragment from 1804, which was
never incorporated into *The Prelude*. Jonathan Wordsworth has written
of the importance for Wordsworth's verse of such 'border-states' as that
of this pony, asleep on his feet, or of the leech-gatherer, who is described
as 'not all alive nor dead'.[3] What Jonathan Wordsworth terms the
'border-state' involves the intersection of several types of border: the
border between wilderness and civilisation symbolised by the sparsely-
populated Lakeland districts that provide the primal scenes of the
poetry; the space between night and day (hence the frequency of walking
in moonlight); and of course the border between waking and sleep, the
marginal zone from which so many of Wordsworth's greatest passages –
such as 'Strange fits of passion' – can be seen to have issued.
Wordsworth employs blank verse and simple balladic forms because
they allow a certain automatism of progression – there are no complicated rhyme schemes to sustain – which acts as a midwife to the
unconscious. The sleep-walking rhythms can, however, induce a feeling
that reality is perpetually beyond the grasp. Take for instance the
following fragment from the second book of *The Prelude:*

> the soul,
> Remembering how she felt, but what she felt
> Remembering not, retains an obscure sense
> Of possible sublimity, at which
> With growing faculties she doth aspire,
> With faculties still growing, feeling still
> That whatsoever point they gain, there still
> Is something to pursue.

There is a great deal of repetition in this passage: 'Remembering',
'With', 'growing' and the three occurrences of 'still'. It creates a sense of
frustrated groping for the unattainable, the aspiration of which the
passage itself writes, rather as when one tries to move in a dream but
remains rooted to the spot. The placement of 'With' at the start of two
successive lines, and of 'still' at the end of two lines, reinforces this sense
of marking time, as does the present participle. The triple 'still' contains
the meanings both of persistence and of immobility. The fusion of
obstinacy and frustration yields a very Wordsworthian mood. It

reappears in a different context in the following famous passage.

> The immeasurable height
> Of woods decaying, never to be decayed,
> The stationary blasts of waterfalls,
> And everywhere along the hollow rent
> Winds thwarting winds, bewildered and forlorn,
> The torrents shooting from the clear blue sky,
> The rocks that muttered close upon our ears –
> Black drizzling crags that spake by the wayside
> As if a voice were in them – the sick sight
> And giddy prospect of a raving stream,
> The unfettered clouds and region of the heavens,
> Tumult and peace, the darkness and the light,
> Were all like workings of one mind, the features
> On the same face, blossoms upon one tree,
> Characters of the great apocalypse,
> The types and symbols of eternity,
> Of first, and last, and midst, and without end.

Wordsworth writes here of 'Winds thwarting winds', of woods that are decaying yet 'never to be decayed', of 'the stationary blasts of waterfalls'. These paradoxes and crossed currents evoke a state of deadlock. This in turn provokes irritation in the author: the components of the scene are assembled mutteringly, in a dismissive, blustering list. Coleridge's phrase 'mental bombast' might well be applicable here. The exasperation culminates in the nausea and distaste felt for that which is 'giddy' and 'raving'. It is Wordsworth's impatience with tumult and multiplicity, his wish to drive through events to the unifying principle behind them: it is he himself who feels sick and giddy in the face of their variety. If the speaking crags are almost grotesque, the touch of caricature is of a piece with Wordsworth's irritation with natural objects that refuse to reveal the Nature behind them. The mood is reminiscent of that of 'Nutting', in which the sense of absence pervading the natural scene provokes boyish aggression against nature. There is an angry straining for a revelation that remains obstinately in abeyance. Wordsworth works off his anger on the scene by imposing upon it the unity it refuses to disclose of its own accord: the abstractions of the end are dismissive of the recalcitrant and brusquely assembled individual features of nature. The final statement of revelation has a willed, constrained air; the repetitions are intended to quash opposition; and the 'midst' of the final line can be felt to be bombastic and pedantic. Even greater violence against nature is manifest in 'Nutting'. About halfway through the fragment one encounters the following lines: 'with my cheek on one of those green stones / That, fleeced with moss, under the shady trees, / Lay round me, scattered like a flock of sheep – / I heard the murmur and the murmuring sound'. Here the writing moves associatively from the reference to the 'fleece' on the moss to the likeness between the stones and sheep. The equivalence has some of the luminosity of one of Samuel Palmer's paintings. The important thing to notice, however, is the relationship between this imaginative transformation of inanimate stone into animate sheep and the later withdrawal of the projective empathy with nature. Wordsworth writes that in such surroundings the heart 'luxuriates upon indifferent things, / Wasting its kindliness on stocks and stones, / And on the vacant air'. This kindliness is the faculty of imagination, which uses metaphor to assimilate nature to human-kind: they become of one kind, as it were. But Wordsworth feels a sudden rage against the nature upon which he has 'wasted' his kindliness, and ravages the unsullied spot. This anger, however – like the image of nature fused with a projection – is itself self-mystified. It is anger at the absence of a fellow human being; specifically, of *woman*. Although woman is nowhere mentioned in the poem, the vocabulary is tinged with erotic sensation: 'Voluptuous, fearful of a rival', the speaker 'eyed / The banquet', which stood before him 'Tall and erect, with tempting clusters hung, / A virgin scene!' The height, the clusters, the voluptuousness and virginity: all suggest a nature conceived of as female. [4] Hence the appropriateness of the injunction to the Maiden at the end: it brings to the surface the sexuality which has wrought havoc within the poem's effort to suppress it. The destruction of nature, on the one hand, vents frustration at the absence or unattainability of the feminine; and, since Wordsworth utters a fear that he may be confusing past and present, one has to see this frustration as both present and past: longing for the unattainable mother; yearning for the forbidden sister. On the other hand, to destroy nature is of course 'to rape it'. The poet exults as he leaves 'the mutilated bower': his feelings are ones of mingled conquest and revenge.

Wordsworth's irritation with nature reflects his discomfort with movement. For him, the sleep of the body is the prelude to the moment of vision: in 'Tintern Abbey' he writes of how, when 'the motion of the blood' is 'Almost suspended, we are laid asleep / In body, and become a living soul'. This state of suspended animation renders *vision* (and visions) possible, as at the end of 'Strange fits of passion': the eye can 'see

into the life of things'. Wordsworth freezes or thins out reality to ease its
visual appropriation. His dislike of the city is partly a defence against the
unassimilable multitude of sensations with which it assails the
passer-by. His double negatives[5] create empty spaces around the object
and the poetic self: *breathing-spaces*, in which nothing is happening;
frames. Only when the teeming of reality has been arrested can the
faculty of vision come into play; only in silence is sublimity possible. In
Book IV of *The Prelude* Wordsworth encounters a discharged soldier by
the wayside, whom he describes as 'a man cut off / From all his kind, and
more than half detached / From his own nature'. This is a description of
Wordsworth himself as he projects the soldier onto the empty screen of
his own mind. His wonderment in the face of such figures as the soldier
or the leech-gatherer is the self's fascination at its own division and
continued existence – a marvelling over the power of the imagination
and its relationship with the body from which its projections issue – and
is rather like the wonderment of a soul staring down at its own body
before returning from closeness to death. (There are numerous anec-
dotes of such corporeal self-alienation.) Such self-alienation is surely the
primary source of 'the Sublime'. The figures he perceives are 'forms' or
'images' – to use two of his favourite terms. They materialise with the
mysteriousness of ghosts. Wordsworth does not question them in order
to obtain wisdom but so as to assure himself of their, and his own,
existence – to run a wondering finger over the tactile form of his half-
separated projection, rather as he once clutched a tree to confirm his
own being. He is interested in people asleep, near semblances of death,
more object than person. The more object-like they are, the less likely to
disturb his self-communing vision. Their sleep is the sleep of reason in
the reverie of his own blank verse. Spider-like, the sleep-walking poet
spins their images from his own entrails. Their agedness matches and
reinforces his youth. (This youth–age dichotomy dominates his work,
and it may be that it declined when his own aging rendered the
questioning youth an implausible persona.) They deserve to be looked at
more closely.

The relationship between Wordsworth and an aged or destitute figure
is central to much of his greatest work. Consider, for instance,
'Resolution and Independence'. The relationship here is not tainted with
the self-congratulation of the alms-giver, as in 'The Old Cumberland
Beggar', but is shot through with desperation and fear: fear of early
death, of the fate of Chatterton, 'the marvellous boy', and of 'despondency and madness', which are said to await the poet in his latter
days. Throughout Wordsworth's work the old are seen to outlive the

young, or to continue to live in places the young have abandoned; and in a sense this second alternative, continued life in the same place, is a variant on the first one: metaphorically, it expresses the fact of survival, departure being tantamount to death. Such is the case in 'Michael', 'The Thorn' or 'Lucy Gray': the old mourn their offspring. In a sense, Wordsworth himself is using his projections to mourn the inevitable youthful death of the poet. It is as if he intuits his own future poetic death. He seeks the company of the old to assure himself, as it were, that the imminent death will only be that of his Muse – of Lucy? – and not a real demise. The sight of the old provides consolation: they are conjured to provide signs of the possibility of living life to its end, even in conditions sufficient to induce 'despondency and madness' in most men. Wordsworth's identification with the old, with figures upon the verge of death, is also a magical act: he identifies with death in order to avoid dying. The identification is to inoculate him against the disease of mortality. But, because he himself is still young in actuality, he has his reservations. 'Animal Tranquillity and Decay', for instance, speaks of the 'peace so perfect' attained to by the old man and envied by the young, but adds that 'the old man hardly feels'. Riven by emotion and the fear of early death, Wordsworth aspires to and admires the stoicism of the old; at the same time, he fears that to be thus 'insensibly subdued / To settled quiet' may itself be a form of death. His verse equivocates between a Miltonic admiration of 'calm of mind, all passion spent', and terror of self-petrification.

In 'Michael' Wordsworth writes of 'having felt the power / Of Nature by the gentle agency / Of natural objects': the individual objects within nature point metonymically to a larger, overarching whole. The analysis of the Simplon Pass fragment of *The Prelude* presented earlier in this essay should indicate that the movement from natural objects to Nature is by no means unproblematic, and is arrived at through coercion as well as gentle agency. What I should like to concentrate on here, however, is Wordsworth's passion for *totalities*. Old men interest him because they are evident wholes, their lives almost rounded in completion. At the end of 'Michael', with the death of Michael himself and the disappearance of his son Luke, a cycle has ended, thus creating the totality Wordsworth loves to contemplate. The view of the totality is facilitated by the starkness of the Lakeland landscape, which simplifies the diversity of objects, paring away distractions and providing a concrete basis for philosophical abstraction. It eases the generalising movement from nature to Nature.

Another reason for Wordsworth's interest in the old is the immobility

common among them; thus the leech-gatherer can be likened to a stone.
For them, as for Wordsworth himself, motion and locomotion are often
problematic. The rhythm of Wordsworth's thought often seems to lead
to, and break off at, a reference to 'motion'. The thought paragraphs of
The Prelude frequently conclude with the word (for example, 'I heard
among the solitary hills / Low breathings coming after me, and
sounds / Of undistinguishable *motion*, steps / Almost as silent as the turf
they trod' – I. 329–32; 'with what *motion* moved the clouds' – I. 350; or
'huge and mighty forms, that do not live / Like living men, *moved*
slowly through my mind / By day, and were the trouble of my
dreams' – I. 425–7).The famous winter-skating passage concludes with
the boy stopping short as the 'solitary cliffs' continue to 'wheel by' him
(I. 480–9): again, the paragraph ends with the idea of movement. Stanza
XI in 'Resolution and Independence' – to draw an example from beyond
The Prelude – refers in its final line to cloud that 'moveth all together, if
it move at all'. (The suggestion that the cloud may not in fact move at all
is strikingly surreal: it recalls the magical suspended rocks of Magritte.)
If Wordsworth is fascinated by the fact that things move – whilst often
ignoring just what those things are (the 'forms' and 'images' he mentions
are deliberately vague) – it may well be because he himself feels unable
to do so: because the energy that generates movement has been
transferred by his projection to the objects of his visions. The
petrification of the self and its desires – the decision to spend most of
one's life in the same place, and to admire those whose entire life has
been bound to one spot ('Michael') – means that it is the objects around
or in front of the self that move instead: as happens at the end of 'Strange
fits of passion'. Motion is problematic because of its generally goal-
oriented nature. Wordsworth's world, however, is one from which goals
have vanished. This may have something to do with the experience of the
failure of the French Revolution. In any case, to yearn for one's
childhood is to pursue an impossible goal. The lack of goals is reflected
in the absence of a single overriding poetic theme. Much of the first book
of *The Prelude* is taken up with enumeration of a series of rejected poetic
themes; one may well feel that its postponement of choice of a theme is
inscribed already in the repetitions and paraphrases of Wordsworth's
blank verse. When he writes of 'a redundant energy / Vexing its own
creation' (I. 46–7), one may be right in sensing a description of the
mechanisms of his verse. Book I is aswarm with Miltonic echoes, for the
problem of how to locate one's own theme had, notoriously, been
Milton's as well: Arthurian subjects had been among the list of themes
rejected before the composition of *Paradise Lost*. Thus it is fitting that

Wordsworth should mention Milton before enumerating several of his own rejected projects (I. 179–80); Milton's own rejection of 'British' themes leads one to expect Wordsworth to do likewise. Wordsworth's verse circles round on itself, seeking a point of departure but unable to depart; it wishes to teach but lacks *a text to expound*: the Bible had already been appropriated by Milton. It senses the writer's loss of authority in the Romantic age, and yet wishes to make the authoritative gesture. Reversion to childhood memories can be seen as a flight from the impossible burden of responsibility of the 'where to go?' with which the poem begins: a child, after all, is no teacher. Thus *The Prelude* remains what its title says it will be: an antechamber to the great unwritten philosophical poem ('The Recluse'), the composition of which Wordsworth already disavows in lines 228–38. Historically, the poem is equidistant from the confident didactic generalisations and abstractions of a Milton, and the particularity of concrete rendition of Imagism and modernism: the semi-abstract Lakeland landscape can be seen as the counterpoint of this historical point of balance. The verse of Wordsworth is situated at, and baffled by, a moment of poetical transition.

SHELLEY: THE DISLOCATION OF THE SENSES

Synaesthesia

The presence of synaesthesia in Shelley's poetry has often been remarked on. Nevertheless, its function in his poetics seems to have passed unnoticed.[6] Broadly speaking, Shelley employs synaesthesia for its totalising effect: the separate senses are united as they are in the mind that decodes the data with which experience presents it. Its use serves to elevate the mind's deductions above the raw reality from which they derive. It is the mind that assembles the unity of the world process from the reports of the separate senses. Synaesthesia dislocates one sense into another: it can thus be related to Shelley's interest in and practice of translation. For the translation is to the original text as the leaves in the woods are to the clouds in 'Ode to the West Wind'.

Shelley's world is founded on simultaneity. Because of this it knows neither first cause nor God. All objects – and all senses – melt into one another. The inability to 'grasp' objects castigated in Shelley by Leavis[7] (Shelley himself would surely have stressed the less praiseworthy implications of an insistence that poetry be 'grasping') may be partly the effect of the poet's own myopia, which could have taught him to regard reality as a blur, a smear, a veil, and may have strengthened his penchant for metaphysical thinking. The resort to synaesthesia is as it were prompted by the inadequacy of one sense, which forces the observer to draw on others for additional information: visible objects become cloudy 'visions'. But the failure to hold fast the isolated object has as its corollary an unprecedented awareness of the connectedness of a scene. Its unity is structured by repetition and parallelism. In some respects, 'Ode to the West Wind' is a verbal equivalent of a painting by a Delacroix tutored by a Cézanne: it combines the tumultuous, deliquescent energy of the former with the sense of structure, of objects echoing each others' forms, found in the latter. But by describing reality as a (structured) totality Shelley placed himself outside it, outside the picture frame as it were, in the position of the exile. Perhaps that is why it is his Italian work that brings to a peak his ability to evoke a scene as an architecturally structured whole. An Englishman, he stands outside the local scene, possessed of no more substantiality than a ghost.

Perhaps I should give an example of what I have in mind. The simultaneity and sense of parallelism mentioned above are perhaps most evident in the following lines from 'Ode to the West Wind', which fuse height and depth by employing as metaphors for realities on high words that simultaneously serve to denote realities below ('stream', for instance):

> Thou on whose stream, mid the steep sky's commotion
> Loose clouds like earth's decaying leaves are shed,
> Shook from the tangled boughs of Heaven and Ocean,
>
> Angels of rain and lightning: there are spread
> On the bright surface of thy aëry surge . . . [8]

The combination of 'stream' and 'steep' here recalls the upwardly spiralling boat of *Alastor* and establishes the intercommunication of levels of reality: the tanglement of real boughs and the branches of the World Tree. The echoing sound patterns reinforce the sense of unity as the wind conveys sounds from one word to another, linking 'steep' with 'stream', 'clouds' with 'decaying' and 'boughs', 'leaves' with 'loose' and 'clouds', 'shed' with 'shook', and so on. This effect of phonetic reverberation is characteristically Shelleyan and renders his verse both self-involved and rhetorically declamatory. The lines evince the mixture of the solid and the ethereal Fogle rightly deems typical of Shelley. For

Shelley superimposes upon a solid scene a series of similes that both derive from it and divert the attention away from it: the scene is preserved within the simile whilst being masked at the same time by its exfoliations. Metonymy becomes the basis of metaphor (as Genette says it is in Proust): the scene provides the metaphor that comes to obscure it just as the branches of a tree sustain the leaves that shroud its skeleton. The force of kinetic energy is caught by a variety of multiple exposure that builds the image up into a palimpsest. Thus in *Prometheus Unbound* Ione can remark of a chariot,

> Its wheels are solid clouds, azure and gold,
> Such as the genii of the thunderstorm
> Pile on the floor of the illumined sea
> When the sun rushes under it.[9]

'Solid clouds' suggests a source for Fogle's excellent generalisation, but the passage is most intriguing in its fusion of levels: the movement from high clouds to sea floor to sun (from a height to a depth to a greater height, which is then situated 'under') welds all three planes into a single, swirling reality, and the reader feels himself somersaulting weightlessly and giddily. At the same time however the improbability of this vertiginous movement in and out of air pockets draws attention to the fact that the image has been *constructed*. As such, it is both a modest fantasy (like the marvellous *Witch of Atlas*) and an idealist statement that the only true reality is one constructed by the mind.

Shelley's eye swiftly crosses the world to perceive its unity in a blur. The speed with which he demands to be read is of course a conventional index of the presence of 'inspiration'. Nevertheless, it is also an embarrassed covering of tracks in which the sentence doubles back upon itself to undo the violence of its initial self-assertion. For his verse is both quickened by the urgency of self-flight[10] and mired in its own selfhood, the coils of its self-analysis. This ambiguity can be observed even in the narrowest crevices of the text: for instance, in the use he makes of the compound adjective.

The compound adjective favoured by Shelley may seem simply to enhance the speed of the verse and the pairing of words may even suggest the linguistic equivalent of Godwinian pan-eroticism. It also serves, however, to arrest the flow of words. The result is a dual rhythm that demands of the Shelleyan reader that he both hunt with the pack of racing words and linger upon the complexities compacted within the compound adjective. It may be that the presence of these two contradictory poetic strategies in his work – one that requires the reader to work, one that simply drags him along at speed – exiled Shelley from the potential audience on both sides: he strove to write both enlightening, fiery prophecy for the masses and finely honed lines for the 'five or six', as he said, who would read *Prometheus Unbound*. His work fell apart along the line separating the esoteric from the exoteric. *The Cenci* was written with a large audience in mind, *Prometheus Unbound* was directed only to the few. Suspended between writing as a secondary activity, the handmaiden of speech, and *écriture*, between the aesthetics of the eighteenth century and those of Symbolism, between rhetoric and musicality, Shelley's verse became a network of contradictions. But of course the contradictoriness of the poetry embodied an awareness of the contradictions of the social system he sought to see as a whole, first by entering an internal exile and then by actually departing the country. For Shelley, to be part of English society was to be of one party within it, subject to the consequences of an aristocratic background. In leaving that society he sought a unity beyond class divisions, a second – Utopian – self.

Self and Other: 'a treacherous likeness . . . '

I should now like to consider more closely the relation between Shelley and his second self. One can take *Alastor* as an example. According to Earl Wasserman, this poem 'develops a skilfully controlled ambiguity whereby confidence in the adequacy of nature and aspiration to perfect self-fulfilment in after-life undercut each other'.[11] This ambiguity, however, is such as to render questionable the terms of Wasserman's analysis. He argues for the existence of a clear-cut distinction – sustained throughout the poem – between two figures he terms the Narrator and the Visionary. (This terminology may lead one to suspect him of having rebaptised Shelley's own 'the Poet' in order to sharpen the contrast by suppressing the signs of a poetic function common to both Poet and Visionary.) For Wasserman, the Narrator is complacently content with his position at the heart of nature, whilst the Visionary is driven by a boundless desire to transcend nature: his love is love earth denies, quest for the ideal object withheld from the imperfect subject. Before indicating the falsity of this viewpoint I should add that the alternative position – the vulgarising view shared and repropagated by Leavis,[12] which deems *Alastor* no more than a narcissistic autobiography – is equally false. One juxtaposes the two views as examples of the most widespread misreadings of Shelley: whereas

Wasserman overestimates his objectivity, Leavis exaggerates his subjectivism. The former view dissociates Shelley from the Visionary (using the figure of the Narrator as a wedge to divide them); the latter collapses them into a mass of confusion. Both overlook the unresolved tension from which the poem derives: a tension generated by the Shelleyan self's habit of slipping in and out of its husk (the self-denying Shelley, for instance, is the one interested in translation). To use the terms of Wasserman's thesis, 'the Narrator' and 'the Visionary' overlap as representatives of the two possible reactions to the experience of the world as a unified whole. (The unity thematised in the poem's imagery of interdependent trees and sights and sounds interwoven by synaesthesia.) One view sees the unification of experience as a source of comforting oneness with the Earth who is the mother of all things;[13] the other believes that 'all is one' institutes a blank indifference akin to that of the moon in one of Shelley's most justly famous lyrics, which is 'ever changing, like a joyless eye, / That finds no object worth its constancy'.[14] (The lines about the moon are so fine because of the delicacy of their balance between criticism of and sympathy with the moon: they impart both the haughtiness and the desperate solitude of that luminary.) The earth thus becomes both Utopia and a place of exile. On the one hand, all earthly places simply present the Platonic Visionary with more obstacles to be traversed and forgotten in the course of his quest for the Ideal Form – which is identical with Death. On the other, earth enfolds the narrator in a warm interiority. The points in the text at which the vocabularies associated with these two viewpoints overlap are very numerous and indicate an intermittence of identity: one may even feel that the unsatisfactoriness of the poem is owing to its inability to crystallise these viewpoints into the separate personalities conjured by Wasserman. The fascination and frustration of the poem stem from the inadequacy of its mastery of its own material. Wasserman's identification of the Narrator with Nature ignores both the Narrator's own 'questionings' (l.26) and the 'love and wonder' the Visionary feels when confronted with 'the varying roof of heaven' (l.96): similarly, as the Narrator observes 'the darkness of Earth's steps' (l.21) his vocabulary anticipates that of the Visionary in pursuit of 'Nature's most secret steps' (l.81). The poem's shifts destabilise Wasserman's rigid distinction. The Visionary is associated with the realm of death, but the Narrator too has made his bed 'in charnels' (l.24); whilst the ideal maiden of the Visionary's dream, whose 'voice was like the voice of his own soul' (l.152), adopts the solemn tones previously used by the Narrator when speaking of his own song (cf. l.19). The true, and indeed somewhat Gothic, nature of the relationship between Narrator and Visionary is revealed in the following lines:

> as the human heart
> Gazing in dreams over the gloomy grave
> Sees its own treacherous likeness there.

(ll. 472 – 4)

One may feel that whilst staring at a grave the Narrator has projected himself into it: the rest of the poem being a flashback. At the outset 'he' (in a sense, 'Shelley', fearful of imminent death by tuberculosis, as Mary Shelley informs us) envisages a figure enclosed in a charnel; he then projects his own emotions onto a poet who lies interred (as Shelley himself will later do with Keats), a poet who is both a suffering *alter ego* and a scapegoat who perishes on his behalf. This movement from narcissism to projection is fundamental to the poem. It structures a passage such as the following:

> Hither the Poet came. His eyes beheld
> Their own wan light, through the reflected lines
> Of his thin hair, distinct in the dark depth
> Of that still fountain; as the human heart,
> Gazing in dreams over the gloomy grave,
> Sees its own treacherous likeness there. He heard
> The motion of the leaves, the grass that sprung
> Startled and glanced and trembled even to feel
> An unaccustomed presence, and the sound
> Of the sweet brook that from the secret springs
> Of that dark fountain rose. A Spirit seemed
> To stand beside him – clothed in no bright robes
> Of shadowy silver or enshrining light
> Borrowed from aught the visible world affords
> Of grace, of majesty, or mystery; –
> But, undulating woods, and silent well,
> And leaping rivulet, and evening gloom
> Now deepening the dark shades, for speech assuming,
> Held commune with him, as if he and it
> Were all that was, – only . . . when his regard
> Was raised by intense pensiveness, . . . two eyes,
> Two starry eyes hung in the gloom of thought,
> And seemed with their serene and azure smiles
> To beckon him.   (ll. 469–92)

I quote the whole passage in order to demonstrate the circularity of this movement. Even as the world seems to commune with the Poet, his primary engagement is with the image of the alienated self at which he continues to stare in his mind's eye. Initially the Poet regards his own eyes and their wan reflected light; by the close of the passage, he is staring at their after-image, the suspended starry eyes (again, height and depth become one in Shelley): the water and the sky are mirrors exchanging their contents: he has gazed at self so long it has been absorbed into the Other. The eyes secede from his image: they belong to the *Doppelgänger* Shelley was to swear approached him near the end of his life.

It is not only the Poet of *Alastor* who possesses a Double: so does the noun, in the form of the adjective. When used profusely, as it is in *Alastor*, the adjective can be termed the compulsive shadow of the noun. The adjectives here embody a desire to linger, a fear of what may come, a wish to obstruct the narrative whose teleology leads to death. Lyric ornamentation helps the story to drag its feet. The repeated adjectives invest the nouns with solemnity, add mystery (interiority) to their directness, infuse doubt into their reality. For the object upon which the adjective battens is an uncertain one, on the verge of vanishing, decomposing into its separate characteristics. Here, as in the *fin de siècle*, the period of the renaissance of the adjectival style, it represents a terror of the fading light, 'the gloom of thought' in which the poet's image secedes from himself. And in l. 689 the adjectives persist in grief and mourn the loss of the noun: 'the brave, the gentle, and the beautiful' are seen to have fled. Only the three adjectives persist in the absence of the people and objects they once adorned.

The insistent dogging of noun by adjective is part of the compulsion to repeat enacted in Shelley's poems. It stems from a Promethean failure to achieve an End, an Apocalypse that would give birth to a new world. As Wilson Knight notes, the repetitions assume the shape of cloudy spirals: 'Shelley is fond of moving in spirals and after one amazing journey gives you another just like it'.[15] One repeats words out of unwillingness finally to let them go: the esoteric visionary recalls them in fear of the fate that awaits them in the world (in fear of betraying the mystery); the exoteric writer does so in order to equip them the better for public efficacy.

Hillis Miller has mentioned the importance for Shelley's imagination of the 'parasite flower'.[16] The bloom, the bright efflorescence of the flower, is parasitical upon the plant and abandons it like a briefly visiting butterfly, but the word 'flower' also denotes both bloom and plant: 'the sensitive plant' is a flower that loses its bloom, the flowering otherness of its projected sister soul or epipsyche (the gardener). A 'parasite flower' is both a particular kind of flower and an image of each and every flower. Similarly, the adjective buds forth from and attaches itself to the noun. The Shelleyan reiteration marks time, for its temporal progression represents no growth: the apparently new developments were inherent in the original seed.

Such reiteration shapes *The Triumph of Life*. Rousseau's vision of the chariot is a modulation of the narrator's earlier vision, and the duplication hints at a transmigration – as if the narrator himself had once been 'Rousseau'. The nightmarishness of the poem stems from a fear that death might prove impossible (one recalls Shelley's fascination by Ahasuerus, the Wandering Jew), that death simply delivers one over to the renewed bondage of life: which is why the 'triumph' is a triumphal march of subjugation, with humanity chained in a shuffling circle like Rodin's burghers of Calais. In *The Triumph of Life* the second chariot is an alternative version of the first one, and the fact that neither vision is accorded primacy is underlined by the way the second chariot follows the first in poetic time but precedes it in real time (Rousseau's vision preceded that of the narrator, but is recounted after it). The otherness in which Shelley habitually places his hopes (for instance, the otherness of the female in *Alastor* or *Epipsychidion*) is forfeited as it is recuperated into an earlier event, as the refigurings of the figura (the chariot is welded of allusions to Ezekiel, Spenser and Southey) create a delerium of simultaneity, and as 'Rousseau' degenerates into merely a projection (the misinterpretation of an overgrown bank by the imagination): the reversed time-lapse film sucks the parasite flower back into the bulb. Whence the completeness in fact of what appears to be a fragment: there could only have been more of the same, endless recurrence. The progress of the text involves an attempt to reword itself, to cushion the violence that stamps the firm imprint of an origin. As it moves forward the poem retreats in time to blur the edges of its own separate being, its being as separation. (The persistent allusiveness of Shelley's poetry is one means whereby he strives to overcome this separation, to hint at the total nature of events.)

This thirst for oblivion (for the metaphor's extinction of the situation from which it arises, its original referent) runs through the following passage from a letter to Peacock: here too the quest for transcendence is frustrated.

The curse of this life is that whatever is once known, can never be unknown. You inhabit a spot, which before you inhabit it, is as indifferent to you as any spot on earth, and when, persuaded by some necessity, you think to leave it, you leave it not; it clings to you – and with memories of things, which, in your experience of them, gave no such promise, revenges your desertion. Time flows on, places are changed; friends who were with us, are no longer with us; yet what has been seems to be, but barren and stripped of life.[17]

The last sentence describes the triumph of life as the victory of meaningless displacement; Shelley's own 'desertions' in life appear part of a quest to find the truly Other. The feeling is restated in a later letter, again to Peacock: 'Rome is a city, as it were, of the dead, or rather of those who cannot die, and who survive the puny generations which inhabit and pass over the spot which they have made sacred to eternity'.[18] The sentence asserts a characteristic ambiguity: the Romans are cursed with a living death, but their accursed state has a magnificence which dwarfs the present. As often in his work, one half of the sentence seems to be barely connected with the other, and only an unconscious dialectic of reversal and self-revision binds them together.

I have remarked above that the Shelleyan text strives to reword itself, to erode the exposed particularity of its own outlines. This mechanism can be seen at work in the following lines from *The Triumph of Life*:

> And the Sun's image radiantly intense
>
> Burned on the waters of the well that glowed
> Like gold, and threaded all the forest maze
> With winding paths of emerald fire – . . . .
>
> (ll. 345–8)

'Burned' applies to the sun, but grammatically 'threaded' could refer either to the sun or to the waters (again, self becomes other: the fiery element migrates into its watery opposite). The grammatical possibility is of course semantically impossible, for although the waters might theoretically have threaded the forest they remain enclosed in the well (even as 'waters' suggests an outspread expanse of wetness). The result is a superimposition upon each other of the agencies of fire and water, the mingling of opposites presupposed by the term 'emerald fire'; thus grammar and semantics are played off against each other in the interests of a reiteration that both complicates and undoes the earlier formulation. The multiple waters are concentrated in a single well: as often in Shelley, singularity is understood to be a concentrate of multiplicity, and plurality occupies a single place (the site of the totality). Shelley equates

origin with falsity – he always rewrites – and this may be a consequence
of his atheism; however, it also reflects the laboriousness of his own
poetic development (on which Milton Wilson has remarked[19]). Shelley
was no master of unpremeditated art, no 'blithe spirit', but perpetually
self-schooling, self-revising, as is evident from the chaotic look of his
manuscripts: the scrawled revisions render them near-indecipherable.

The effect is one of self-erasure (echoed in the almost suicidal gesture
of entering a boat in a storm though unable to swim?). It is repeated in
the following lines, which carry on from the ones I have already quoted
from *The Triumph of Life*:

> there stood
> Amid the sun, as he amid the blaze
> Of his own glory, on the vibrating
> Floor of the fountain, paved with flashing rays,
>
> A Shape all light, which with one hand did fling
> Dew on the earth, as if she were the Dawn . . . .
>   (ll. 348–53)

'A Shape all light' stands 'amid the sun', 'as if she were the Dawn': the
'she' is embedded in the sun, which according to convention is male and
represents her opposite; the 'he' melts into 'she', and the dissolution of
sexual difference drags the other back into the location of the self. Man
as sun, woman as dawn: each sex can be transposed into the key of the
other. This androgyny is fundamental to Shelley's conception of the self
as self-and-other: it is thanks to this dual conception, for instance, that
in l. 528 people can be said to *send forth* shadows rather than to cast
them. Otherness, of which the shadow is classically a cipher, inheres
within selfhood. Proceeding with the same sequence of lines one
encounters the words,

> And still before her on the dusky grass
> Iris her many-coloured scarf had drawn. –
>
> In her right hand she bore a crystal glass . . . .
>   (ll. 356–8)

Apart from the Shelleyan fusion of high and low (grass and rainbow)
one notes here that the juxtaposition of the sentences renders 'her'
ambiguous, permitting the pronoun to suggest an identity (the hint is
reinforced by the parallelism of the lines) between 'her' and 'Iris', then

only to suppress 'Iris', who nevertheless remains present as an after-image absorbed into the train of 'her' identity. (The pronoun as shifter!) This Shelleyan strategy simultaneously over- and under-determines the image. Here, as in 'To a Skylark', he surrounds the poem's subject with a series of similes each of which is then cancelled, apprehended as inadequate. The strategy is typical of him, but he begins to systematise its use after encountering it in his reading of Calderón. Thus the object becomes akin to all other objects whilst remaining sequestered in a mysterious, indefinable realm apart (the realm of the Platonic Form). In this way Shelley exploits language to suggest the extralinguistic. Just as synaesthesia stretches one sense organ until it snaps or throws one back on the resources of another, so this excess of definition directs one to the heart of silence at which the object is beyond definition. This will to go beyond is a recurrent feature of Shelley's mode of apprehension. He remarks to Peacock, 'You know I always seek in what I see the manifestation of something beyond the tangible and present object'.[20]

One consequence of this method is that the poem becomes part of an associative trance of overlaps and dissolves. Their rhythm is awkward. The woman evoked in the lines of *The Triumph of Life* quoted above is described as bending her head 'under the dark boughs, till like a willow / Her fair hair swept the bosom of the stream' (ll. 364–5). One can see how the willow simile is generated by the conjunction of hair and dark boughs (though its midwife is the *terza rima*). The procedure is reminiscent of Eisenstein's theory of cinematic montage: out of the juxtaposition of two images arises a third, which partakes of a certain abstraction and balances between image and concept.[21] When one bears this in mind one realises the nature of Paul de Man's error when he describes each event in the poem as 'a positional act, which relates to nothing that comes before or after'.[22] For all these acts are impacted in a single complex, so the poem is not – *pace* de Man – a 'sequential narrative'[23] but the shattering of a single moment, the effulgence in which the initial image of the sun engenders a constellation of associated images, such as dust, insects, bedazzlement and the chariot. The sense of the fertility of associative logic is augmented in this poem, as in 'Ode to the West Wind', by the use of *terza rima*, which creates effects of tangles of echoes, overlapping, dissolving, erasing the contours both of beginnings and of ends. Symonds has admirably characterised the use of *terza rima* in Shelley:

It is not without perplexity that an ear unaccustomed to the windings of the *terza rima*, feels its way among them. Entangled and impeded by the labyrinthine sounds, the reader might be compared to one who, swimming in his dreams, is carried down the course of a swift river clogged with clinging and retarding water-weeds. He moves, but not without labour: yet after a while the very obstracles add fascination to his movement.[24]

The form of *terza rima* thus corresponds to the double nature of the Shelleyan progression, both accelerating and retarding at one and the same time, which I have mentioned above when discussing the compound adjective. The dual effect of 'swiftness' and 'clinging' Symonds mentions surely has something to do with the fact that *terza rima* composition in English is considerably more arduous than it is in Italian.

The legato, the continuousness, of *terza rima* reflects Shelley's belief in the power of a vision to exfoliate, growing with the sun that opens *The Triumph of Life* from a small blazing speck to an engulfing brightness; it delicately echoes the involutions of his subordinate clauses. In the earlier poems the use of subordinate clauses had expressed an apocalyptic desire to say everything, to exhaust both self and speech and arrive at their frontiers; in *The Triumph of Life*, however, the *terza rima* reconciles this apocalyptic passion with a sense of continuity: each triple-rhyme unit embraces a small eschatology – but each fades out gradually as it overlaps with the next. *Terza rima* is an unfolding image of the intertwining network that obsesses Shelley from *Alastor* onwards. Because *terza rima* is so much harder to sustain in English than in Italian, its usage evokes something of the painful obsessiveness and magicality of a vision: obsessiveness, for the repetition of the rhyme transports it beyond its normal limits; and magicality, because the sheer technical virtuosity that achieves such a longevity of rhyme seems almost to suspend normal poetic reality. Much of Shelley's work appears to be a quest for the right metre. It is surely no accident that the two works most commonly conceded to have been his most successful (*The Triumph of Life* and 'Ode to the West Wind') should possess the same metre.

In English the third rhyme of the *terza rima* has the status of a phantom or an after-image: its persistence was unlooked for. This quality of overlap is part of the poet's concern with the undying and the undead: part of his identity with the cloud which says, 'I change but I cannot die'. The streaming dead–live crowds of *The Triumph of Life* are of a piece with the rippling rhymes. The mixture of movement and stasis, progress and tableau, appears particularly clearly when one brings together the Iris fragments quoted piecemeal above:

> In her right hand she bore a crystal glass
> Mantling with bright Nepenthe; – the fierce splendour
> Fell from her as she moved under the mass
>
> Of the deep cavern, and with palms so tender
> Their tread broke not the mirror of the billow,
> Glided along the river, and did bend her
>
> Head under the dark boughs, till like a willow
> Her fair hair swept the bosom of the stream
> That whispered with delight to be their pillow.
>
> (ll. 358–66)

This passage contains superb effects of quickening and retardation: the interpolation of l. 362, delaying the arrival of the verb 'glided', induces a palpitation and delicate suspension of breath; the enjambement 'did bend her // Head' ought to be as famously effective as the instance in Keats's 'To Autumn' singled out for praise by Leavis (the poem's initial apparent surrender to the demands of the rhyme scheme is triumphantly vindicated); and the internal assonance rhyme 'her fair hair' springs the rhythm of the following 'swept'. The meaning is also that of a stillness shot through with movement. There is a tread, but it leaves no trace, the billow remaining as tranquil as a mirror; the hair sweeps the stream that is also its place of repose (the use of palms for the soles of the feet emphasises the delicacy with which the billow is trodden); the whispering delight with which the stream welcomes the hair to its bosom invokes the more erotic connotations of pillows. As often in Shelley, there is a vertiginous fusion of height and depth in the 'deep cavern' *under* whose 'mass' the girl moves. The effect achieved by the recurrent overlaps is summed up in the following lines:

> And still her feet, no less than the sweet tune
> To which they moved, seemed as they moved, to blot
> The thoughts of him who gazed on them, and soon
>
> All that was seemed as if it had been not – . . . .
>
> (ll. 382–5)

The observer's thoughts are absorbed into the tune of the metrical feet as words sink into blotting-paper: one becomes what one sees.

Shelley belonged to the second generation of the Romantics and was thus among those who experienced the rotting of the fruits of the French Revolution. The Revolution is one of the main themes of *The Triumph of Life*, which documents – among other things – how the wheel of progress revolved into its opposite, the Napoleonic dictatorship. In examining this failure Shelley is responding to the bankruptcy of his own earlier Englightenment ideals. The fondled words of his private vocabulary are a guerrilla army of silence, hiding out in the hills after the defeat of the main batallions of Enlightenment: the conventionality of language, the encoded weight of the past, had betrayed the individual's and the period's attempts to break through into a new reality. In Shelley's situation, the authentic aspects of the Romantic rebellion could be preserved only through despecification and generalisation; liberty and fraternity could no longer fire aspiration, since the quest for them had culminated in the victory of unfreedom. Hence his opposition to tyrants is nebulous, whilst his positive proposals are private dreams. 'The Mask of Anarchy' thus seems to me to have been overpraised: an explicitly political poem ought to be more realistic: it naïvely translates the tyrant's mental self-destruction into a physical fact. Hard-edged at the outset, it evaporates in dreamy platitudes.

The Triumph of Life aligns various versions of the same 'shapes' or configurations. Its self-rewording can be correlated with the Romantic tendency to write alternative versions of poems: Keats's two versions of *Hyperion* or Wordsworth's revised *Prelude*. The Romantic rejection of authority had come to entail rejection of the authoritative gesture of the single fixed text. The separate versions criticise and parody one another, as do the visions experienced by the Rousseau and the poet figure of *The Triumph of Life*. Parodying himself, the poet rattles the bars of the individualism of the modern age. The accumulated versions strive to assuage the guilt of individualism, to mitigate the violence of solitary statement: they are negative imprints of the absent community the poet would like to address. In the case of Shelley, this is an eminently Platonising procedure: the one unwritten text remains, the many versions fade and die. The various versions of texts found in Keats, Wordsworth and Shelley or Hölderlin and Goethe prefigure the modern aesthetics of permutation, The different versions are akin to alternative *translations*.

Translation

Shelley may appear to have held translation in low esteem:

the language of poets has ever affected a sort of uniform and harmonious recurrence of sound, without which it were not poetry, and which is scarcely less indispensible to the communication of its influence, than the words themselves, without reference to that particular order. Hence the vanity of translation; it were as wise to cast a violet into a crucible that you might discover the formal principle of its colour and odour, as seek to transfuse from one language into another the creations of a poet.[25]

Yet for all that Shelley himself translated extensively. His belief in the universality of poetry demanded that it be transmissable to all humanity, and was underpinned by a conviction that 'the grammatical forms which express the moods of time, and the difference of persons, and the distinction of place, are convertible with respect to the highest poetry without injuring it as poetry'.[26] Shelley's own translations can be seen as attempts to undo the curse of Babel. In his Oxford days he translated Buffon, Aristotle and Pliny in order to disseminate their ideas; later he was to seek to bring languages closer together by permitting English a partial appropriation of the sound patterns of another tongue. When, in the quotation given above, Shelley questions the importance of the particularity of grammatical forms, the conception may harbour an anticipation of Nietzsche: the atheist may have realised that to depose God one must first abolish grammar. In any case, the attempt to revoke the divisions of Babel itself defies the divinity.

The two quotations from *A Defence of Poetry* juxtaposed above indicate the existence of a contradiction at the heart of Shelley's theory of translation. In the end it led him to a practice of dual translation in which two versions are placed side by side: one literal, the other an independent poem in itself. For on the one hand he believes in the universality of the ideas poetry 'contains' (the metaphor of the receptacle implies an easy transfer of contents to another linguistic bottle); on the other, he declares the sound patterns of a particular poem specific to the language in which it is written. The unresolved contradiction is reflected in the manner in which he presents his versions of the introductory poem of Goethe's *Faust*: one, cast in rhyme, enjoys a hectically independent Shelleyan life that inevitably obscures the original; the other is an unrhymed, painstaking transposition. The two versions correspond to the two aspects of Shelley's character: impatient idealism deems all verse instantly convertible, and leads him at times to translate without an adequate knowledge of the language of the primary text (if meaning is believed to inhere in sound, to reproduce phonetic patterns is to adequate that meaning); conversely, there is his almost feminine wish to be led, which enables him to learn a multitude of foreign tongues, passionately to admire a series of authors, and uncomplainingly to wear the yoke of Godwin's economic graspingness. This second trait is the submissiveness that grants him the patience to recognise the otherness of the other and to seek to acquire its virtues: his work bristles with images of the mind becoming what it contemplates.

The contrast between the two types of version is not, however, absolute; otherwise its implications would have impressed themselves far more forcibly upon Shelley: in fact, his decision to print alternative versions of Goethe's 'Zueignung' (Dedication) marked a moment of exceptional self-awareness. Even so, Shelley is one of the very few translators to concede that an inevitable bad faith infects his enterprise. More frequently, the two practices are so intertwined as to render it hard to discern whether he is misreading the text or reconceiving it – a problem noted by Timothy Webb in *The Violet in the Crucible*, his fine study of Shelley's translations. But even within these confused versions the duality I have mentioned is still present. Thus the expansion of the original may serve either to introduce some of its sense or some of its sounds. He renders Goethe's line 'Hier leuchtet Glut aus Dunst und Flor' as 'Here the light burns soft as enkindled air, / Or the illumined dust of golden flowers'. The first line rivals the poetry of the original, whilst the second takes its cue from the sound patterns of Goethe's German ('Dunst' suggests 'dust'; 'Glut', 'golden'; and 'Flor' becomes 'flowers'. The *u* of 'Glut' is preserved in 'illumined'.) Something similar occurs in the version of Goethe's 'die unvollkommne Scheibe / Des blanken Mondes', which Shelley reads as 'the blank unwelcome round of the red moon'. As Webb has noted,[27] 'unwelcome' is an alchemical transformation of 'unvollkommne' (imperfect). But is it a misreading? Such translation may well follow the word associations laid down in the collective unconscious of the language. The imperfect is unwelcome, as it were.

The dual translation implicitly recognises that once the process of translation has been initiated it can proceed *ad infinitum*: once one has admitted the principle of the convertibility of meaning, there can be no end of its exchange. The dual translation refuses to masquerade as an original text: its deliberate display of the signs of its own intertextuality goads the reader's conscience, attacks his complacency, by showing that Babel's scar is only partly healed. Translation can pour scar tissue into the place of the wound, but it cannot restore the original flesh. One can mitigate the effects of the curse – one can learn languages, or fondle their sounds – but one cannot undo it. The translator is thus revealed to be a tragic idealist.

Shelley's practice as a translator undoubtedly reinforced his existing propensity – documented earlier in my remarks on *The Triumph of Life* – to reword and unword his works. Each rewording is an attempt to blow new life into the 'fading coal' of the inspiration. Nevertheless, in the end inspiration gutters and the poet is faced with the problem of how usefully to occupy the interval between the now-exhausted poem and the advent of a 'new' one. Translation fills these gaps. Webb has interpreted Shelley's translations as private exercises, undertaken to tide him over difficult periods.[28] Even so, the translations themselves flow naturally into the poems that succeed them, a continuity which erodes the hallowed distinction between primary and secondary texts: Shelley's work is an object lesson in intertextuality (which should not be understood in the trivial sense of plagiarism in which Leavis construes it, writing of *The Cenci*). 'To Wordsworth', for instance, translates into a modern context Shelley's own version of Cavalcanti's sonnet to Dante; and the magnificence with which the new age is celebrated in the chorus to *Hellas* borrows some of its light from his version of Goethe's 'Zueignung'. The influence of Calderón increases the confidence of the alternative metaphors with which the absent bird is surrounded in 'To a Skylark'.

In all three cases, however, the sole spin-offs from the process of translation are isolated lyrics. Not until the very end of his life is Shelley prepared to construct extended poems with the aid of techniques acquired through translation. The poems in question are, of course, *Epipsychidion* and *The Triumph of Life*, both deeply indebted to Dante. Webb remarks that ' "Epipsychidion" is, in fact, an extraordinary example of the way in which translation can interlock with original composition. More than any of Shelley's other poems it might be described as bilingual in conception.'[29] Indeed, Trelawny was convinced that the poem had first been formulated in Italian, and only afterwards Englished. The decision to found poems of such scope upon imitation suggests that at this point Shelley begins to employ translation as a means of systematic self-transformation (and self-effacement) rather than as an occasional prop to a faltering voice. The death wish that underlies this willingness to discard his own voice tallies with the sense of overall failure that attended his later days, as well as with the manner of his death: just as he tempted annihilation by sailing whilst unable to swim, so he induced his own obliteration magically by submitting to the power of Dante's assumed voice. The attempt to step in Dante's footmarks may in any case have been doomed: the Italian poet could have been his Virgil, but who could have served as Beatrice? Could Shelley ever have devoted himself entirely to a single female figure?

There is another factor at work in the symbiosis between *Epipsychidion* and *The Triumph of Life* and the versions of Dante which serves to distinguish them from his earlier translations of, say, Moschus, Goethe or Calderón. Translations carried out at some distance from the native countries of the translated writers do not require the translator to interrogate the tongue of his own daily use, the prime agent of his communication with his immediate environment. Shelley could translate German, Spanish and Greek authors with blithe eclecticism. But when he begins to translate from a tongue he himself is forced to employ in everyday life – when he translates Dante whilst living in Italy – he weakens the barriers between his own language and the language he is translating. (Moreover, he rendered several of his own poems into Italian for Emilia Viviani, including three excerpts from *Prometheus Unbound*, ll. 1–13 of the 'Ode to Liberty', and stanzas i–iii and part of stanza iv of *Laon and Cyntha*, canto ii.) As soon as the barriers between languages had been removed, the Spirit of Dante entered into him, lifting his awareness and his verse to a level of intensity that perhaps destroyed him.

Nevertheless, this near-mediumistic relationship with Dante is simply the dazzling culmination of a form of relationship with foreign texts that seems to have begun with his move to Italy in 1818. It is as if he aligned himself with the poets he translated because their works, like his, had been either maligned or misunderstood by their contemporaries. The imitation of their verse structures embodied an awareness that the advent of Romanticism had rendered structure a thing of the past, the rejected sign of convention. The Romantic writer considers traditional structure at best a necessary evil: by imitating the works of various different poets from diverse ages and languages he emphasises the exterior nature of their traditions. Negatively capable, he moves through them and then discards them, like Keats's chameleon poet. And in this respect Shelley is akin to Eliot, his great future enemy. *The Triumph of Life* is to Shelley's earlier work as *Little Gidding*, ii, is to Eliot's previous poetry: in both cases, the reverential submission to Dante is the new beginning understood as an end, a summary on the threshold of poetic silence.

FORM AND FORMLESSNESS IN THE POETRY OF
HÖLDERLIN: THE IMPLICATIONS OF HIS THEORY OF
WECHSEL DER TÖNE

Introductory Note

The literature on Hölderlin's theory of the *Wechsel der Töne* is an
extensive and difficult one. Its key texts – those of Ryan, Walter Hof
and Beissner – deal first and foremost with the mechanisms regulating
the transitions between the tones and with the problems criticism faces
when attempting unequivocal identification of the precise tonality of a
particular strophe. The problem of deciding whether or not a particular
verse is in the heroic, the naïve or the idyllic mode is further complicated
by the combinatory tables Hölderlin devised to demonstrate that
different tones are present simultaneously, whilst nevertheless one is
dominant on each occasion. Given the persistence of critical polemic in
this field, the problems of identification appear enormous and nearly
insuperable. That is why the following discussion shifts the debate to
another plane, one which I hope may yield greater critical consensus.
Instead of attempting to identify particular tones at particular textual
moments, I propose to study the functions of the tonal theory in
Hölderlinian aesthetics, its correspondences in the poet's psychology
and social and religious aims, and the effect upon the reader of the poetic
forms – or formlessness – it dictates.

(NB. The reference numbers in parentheses that follow the quotations
from Hölderlin relate to the Grosse Stuttgarter Ausgabe of his works,
edited in 1946 by Friedrich Beissner.)

Wechsel der Töne: self-creation and self-destruction

Hölderlin's remarks on the modulation of tones in his poetry have long
been a problematical keystone in the discussion of his work: ignored by
those who present him as a rapt mystic, one-sidedly deployed by others
to manoeuvre round the question of the links between his poetry and his
madness, despite the possibility of arguing that the alternation of tones
was devised to lend a freezing reality the semblance of change.
Antitheses between the precision with which he applies his theory,
shifting from ideal to heroic or naïve tones, and his leanings towards
mysterious, musical modes of apprehension remain superficial – the two

are dialectically entangled. That he should have gone insane and yet have been a great poet is of primary importance: all the more so, since his poetry is centrally concerned with what poetry should be and with the proper state of mind of the poet. Tempting though it would be to rest content with a merely metrical analysis of his verse, which reveals its piercing beauty most often in the minutiae of transition, of pause and suspension, there are larger issues arising out of the verse's propensity to disclose its greatest beauty at the edge of silence. (Hölderlin is perhaps the supreme master of lineation.) Kafka's sentence 'niemand singt so rein als die, welche in der tiefsten Hölle sind' (none sing so purely as those in the most profound Hell) [30] strikes to the heart of the problem.

Hölderlin originally devised the theory of the modulation of tones during his Frankfurt period and probably did so with the aim of overcoming his 'Scheue vor dem Stoff' (shying away from subject matter–vi. i, 249) and of limiting the 'Weitschweifigkeit' (long-windedness) of the Tübingen hymns, against which Schiller had warned him (vii. i, 46). The compulsion to alternate tones would restrict the danger of overlengthy dwelling on a single note. The theory would thus enable him to acquire the exemplary wholeness and balance that would fit him to rebuke the Germans for their insufficiencies whilst demonstrating through his own person how they might be rectified. In *Hyperion* he had written,

> Ich kann kein Volk mir denken, dass zerissner wäre, wie die Deutschen. Handwerker siehst du da, aber keine Menschen, Denker, aber keine Menschen, Priester, aber keine Menschen, Herrn und Knechte, Jungen und gesetzte Leute, aber keine Menschen – ist das nicht, wie ein Schlachtfeld, wo Hände und Arme und alle Glieder zerstückelt untereinander liegen . . . ?

> (I cannot imagine a people more riven than the Germans. You see craftsmen there, but no men, thinkers, but no men, priests, but no men, masters and servants, young men and established ones, but no men – is it not like a battlefield upon which amputated hands, arms and all other limbs lie intermingled . . . ? iii, 153)

By eliminating the private fault of one-sidedness, he hoped to play a part in the imminent German awakening he expected to flow from the French Revolution. In the Frankfurt odes, where he first applies the method of modulation of tones, each strophe usually expresses a single tone (which sometimes extends across two strophes), and this leads one to think that he began with a series of short phrases which he then expanded within the boundaries of the strophe in order both to preserve the identity of strophe and tone and to avoid a merely bald logicality. The repetition of the original idea within the strophe reflects the demands of the versification, but it probably also stems from the disinclination to change the tone (the 'Weitschweifigkeit') he is at the same time attempting to counteract. This is a residue of the time when he deemed himself 'wortreicher und leerer' (wordier and emptier – I. i, 250). It is as if the precipitate ebb and flow of the emotions made the moment of change painful – the proximity of contrary emotions arouses doubts about the coherence of the self – prompting him to vary the original statement in order to buffer the shock of transition. (Though repetition also fosters the blindness to the future for which change is a shock.) Language wavers in the presence of the divine, which it cannot grasp: the true statement exists somewhere in the negative space between the first statement and its modulated repetition. Hölderlin's theory also appears to attempt to bring into his poems the contradictory moods of his own daily life, personalising them whilst at the same time disciplining the personal by subordinating it to a predetermined schema of alternation. The upshot will be a poetry in which disintegration takes place as it were spectrally, independently of the personality that is disintegrating.

Every theory undergoes dialectical modification in the course of its application. The tables in which Hölderlin defines each tone as also containing the other two in subordinate form are too complicated to have provided guidelines to actual composition – unlike the simple three-tone distinction – and probably represented his attempt to convince himself that the alternation would not threaten the unity of the work, since each tone would be implicitly present in all the others. The tables are his response to doubts arising from the poems created using the simple triple-tone theory: albeit controlled, the odes appear formless, their sentences in a state of perpetual dissolution. This ghostliness is unnerving: the verse almost stream-of-consciousness (one notes that in 'Brot und Wein' [Bread and Wine] Hölderlin praises 'das strömende Wort' [the gushing word] – II. i, 91). The abrupt changes of tone lead the reader to clutch at any recurrent feature that offers an apparent point of reference. The simplicity of Hölderlin's vocabulary, which renders repetition inevitable, and his habit of carrying a single metaphor through a poem (very often the metaphor of a river – 'das strömende Wort'), help to draw parts magnetically towards each other and allow one to perceive or ignore any of a multiplicity of possible connections. (Adorno considers this recapitulation 'musical',[31] but it appears to be at least partly unconscious, since all the themes recapitulate each other simultaneously!) The dynamism of the poem's rhythm drives from line to line in the form of enjambements, melting them into each other, and yet there is always a slight shudder before the metrical foot dips into the water of the new line: it is the fear of the courted change. Tone shifts are emotional enjambements.

The reader's desire to secure a place for himself on the unstable sands of the modulations has created the prevalent form of Hölderlin criticism, which traces the genealogies of motifs and extrapolates philosophy from them. The distortion preserves the critic's safety: for in actuality the poems are the solvents of Hölderlin's private philosophy. The poems are disturbing partly because they move in two directions simultaneously (such a line as 'Dorther kommt und zurück deutet der kommende Gott' [Whence comes, and towards which points, the God who will come] in 'Brot und Wein' evinces this clearly, both in its position and in its content – II. i, 91). In the odes the bias is centrifugal: trap doors open and plunge the reader into other poems. Thus the beginning of 'Ermunterung' (Exhortation – II. i, 35) is a variation on the ending of 'Wie wenn am Feiertage' (As, when on a holiday – II. i, 120): both term the poet an outcast, akin to Tantalus, and share the mythical dimension inherent in the word 'ewig' (eternal). Hölderlin seeks to separate opposed feelings by their duplication. In the Pindaric fragment, for instance, punishment is just; in the ode, it is unmerited. Such partial transvaluation of terms is apparent in the references to the 'armer Seher' (poor seer) of 'An die Deutschen' (To the Germans – II. i, 10) and of 'Rousseau' (II. i, 12). In the elegies and hymns, the larger compass causes a centripetal bias: the poem includes the interdependent oppositions previously relegated to separate poems. 'Brot und Wein' (II. i, 90–5) and 'Der Rhein' (The Rhine – II. i, 142–8) provide good examples.

'Brot und Wein' is a prismatically reflexive poem. The physical night of the first strophe is the metaphysical one of the seventh; the fourth strophe's lament juts up unexpectedly in the middle of the sixth; the multiplicity of the manifestations of the Divine (Father Ether, the Highest, the Torchbearer, the silent Genius, the Heavenly Choir) suffuses the poem with transformations of its own images; the wreaths and chalices of the second strophe point to the arrival of the Wine God in the eighth; wine is itself divine but it is also a consolation for the absence of God; the Heavenly Choir may or may not be connected with the poets who are said to give praise. The poem moves awesomely on multifarious levels of time and space.

'Der Rhein' is equally hallucinatory and fluid. The opening lines of

the sixth strophe recall the theme of the second; the end of the eighth
resembles the 'Denn eher muss die Wohnung vergehen' (For sooner
must the home perish) of the seventh; the opening of the ninth is similar
to the whole of the sixth; and the beginning of the eleventh recalls the end
of the third. It is as if everything is subject to transformation and
metamorphosis: which is why the Rhine passes unmentioned during two
thirds of the poem; both it and the hero are each other's metaphorical
personifications. The poem is suspended between them. Implicitly,
Hölderlin cancels everything he writes as he writes it, and the writing
represents an attempt to remove an obsession from consciousness. Each
sentence is a new beginning. The lack of an audience leads Hölderlin on
the one hand insistently to reiterate his ideas, lest in losing them he lose
himself, and on the other perpetually to reshape them, owing to doubts
regarding their adequacy. As the reformulations interact with one
another one gains the unsettling impression that the poem has never
really begun, that it is continually deflected by something inexpressible.
'Der Einzige' (The Only One – II. i, 153–64) thematises this absence as
the absence of a central figure, a God. The machinery of modulation
operates as it were independently of the poet's presence, as if he were
relying on it to sustain his flagging spirit. Because the odes reiterate all
their pleas, one experiences them as an ongoing lack of response: every
line has the silence of the other as its background. As he speaks in a void,
the poet feels his personality evaporate. Something analogous occurs at
the start of the hymns, which extinguish the poet's personality and carry
him away like a medieval dream poet. The notion of *Begeisterung*
(inspiration) symbolises the poet's inability to understand why he is
writing: words appear without tangible reason. 'Der Menschen Worte
verstand ich nie' (Human words I never understood – I. i, 266) Hölderlin
writes: he thus withdraws from the writing that is a substitute for speech
to writing that exists in and for itself alone, mutely unwilling to speak a
false tongue. In him the rhetoric of a Klopstock abandons the Christian
tradition that gave it a social function and becomes self-referential (the
'jetzt' [now] of the hymns is thinking out loud in the process of
composition). Hölderlin's tragedy is his inability to reconcile himself to
the loss of the vocative rhetorical dimension: in dedicating poems to
friends he clutches at the phantom, fading possibility of an addressee.
The transitional status of his poetry renders it both modern and
classical: a modern sense of instability coincides with a traditional desire
to subordinate the fragmentary to an overall design. Thus the modulation of tones enables him both to write spasmodically and to create a
whole. The incomplete stanzas in the middle of many of his poems

suggest that work on the poems was not continuous: problematic stanzas could be left for later revision.

The hymns provide perhaps the best examples of how the impulse to fragment is both given its head and ordered. Sentences are infiltrated by counter-sentences which cloud clear statement to protect him from the overweeningness of assertion: his desire to be 'allumfassend' (all-embracing) is one for security on all sides. Even so short a sentence as the famous opening of 'Patmos' is self-interrupting: 'Nah ist / Und schwer zu fassen der Gott' (Near / And hard to grasp is God – II. i, 165). 'Nah ist' resembles an indisputable assertion, but the copula awakens his unease, since nothing owns a clearly defined sphere of being. Uncertainty causes him to truncate the line and add the counter-thesis 'Und schwer zu fassen'. The variable line length in the hymns is a response to the doubt that may overtake one's words at any point: and the frequent copulas and pseudo-logical conjunctives emphasise the weakness of the links between the parts. The lines break off when the links collapse. The associative, dialectically self-denying movement of thought in the first lines of 'Patmos' can be seen at work again in the fourth strophe of 'Friedensfeier' (Celebration of Peace – III, 533–7), which begins by mentioning the shadow of the mountains and then adds, 'Und die lieben Freunde, das treue Gewölk, / Umschatteten dich auch' (And the dear friends, the faithful cloud, / Shadowed you round too). It proceeds, 'Ach! aber dunkler umschattete, mitten im Wort, dich / Furchtbarentscheidend ein tödlich Verhängnis' (More darkly, alas, you were shadowed around in mid word / By a terribly decisive, lethal destiny). The shadow appears here in three forms: as a real object (as usual in Hölderlin, nature is initially empty), as a positive principle, and then as a negative one. 'Umschatten' is a focus of several ideas. The undertones of 'Schatten', which he at first represses through rationalis-ation (its presence ensures that 'der heiligkühne / Durch Wildnis mild dein Strahl zu Menschen kam' [the holy-daring ray / Came mildly down to men through wilderness]), assert themselves as language turns against him and he too is interrupted 'mitten im Wort' and his momentary idyll breaks down. Language glides beyond his direction: the pun that turns 'Volk' (people) into 'Gewölk' (a cloud) suggests to him the complex relating to storms and lightning (expressed most fully in 'Wie wenn am Feiertage') which cause the destruction of the Christ, the poet, in short: the mediator figure. That the associative logic of language is responsible for the catastrophe is further evident from 'Furchtbarentscheidend': the word is a thunderclap accompanied by lightning. Like the copulas and the pseudo-logical connectives ('Denn', 'Also' and so on), the pun is a treacherous bridge between the parts of the poem. Stable itself, its multiple reference generates instability. Hölderlin's habit of self-interruption gives the poems their scrupulous, open, intimate tone. In the elegies he builds the reader into the text (each poem has an addressee among his friends) to overcome his fear of the real vacuum in which he is writing: only if there is someone to receive one's thought is there any reason for objectifying it. It is perhaps significant that the majority of the hymns that were completed bear dedications. The modulation of tones had prepared the way for a polyphonic writing, so when he writes, 'Seit ein Gespräch wir sind' (Since we have been a conversation – III, 536), he is – on one level – referring to his own multiple personality. Language as it were speaks through him, irrationally. The interruptions, for their part, are models of introjected others engaged in dialogue. For Hölderlin internalised the voices of others and, taking them all seriously, attempted to unite polytheism, pantheism, Christianity and the tenets of the Enlightenment under the banner of Idealism. If compound words quite often appear just before the end of his sentences ('Furchtbarentscheidend' here; 'heilignüchtern' [holy–sober] in 'Hälfte des Lebens' [The Half of Life]), the strenuousness of their attempted synthesis is surely a harbinger of imminent silence. Hölderlin's philosophical synthesis appears similarly doomed.

I have remarked above that one of the lubricants of Hölderlin's poetry is the etymological pun. Its effect is to evoke a timeless reality in which no thing preceded any other. For did 'Schicksal' (fate) precede 'geschickt' (sent/gifted)? Did 'Denken' (thought) pre-exist 'Danken' (to thank)? Was there 'Güte' (goodness) before 'Gott' (God)? Did 'Andenken' precede 'Gedächtnis' (remembrance and memory) – or was it the other way round? Unable to decide, he places them next to each other, the paratactic juxtaposition a sign of helplessness. Thus in 'An Eduard' (To Eduard) one has 'dich *birgt* / Der ernste Wald, es hält das *Gebirge* dich' (the sober forest covers you, the mountains enwrap you – II, i, 42); and in 'Blödigkeit' (Faltering), 'Gut auch sind und *geschickt* einem zu etwas wir. . . . Doch selber/Bringen *schickliche* Hände wir' (We are good and sent for a purpose . . . and ourselves bring fitting hands – II. i, 68, emphases added). Such etymological associations seem to stem from the requirement that the poet be childlike in order to hand the divine revelation to the people without himself suffering harm: with childlike trust he derives ideas from language's acoustic echoes. Thought becomes dependent on the external characteristics of the word, and meaning hovers between these words. The poet has to write endlessly to suggest the reality between the lines. Endless writing asserts his identity as universal mediator ('Wie wenn am Feiertage', Holderlin's most prolonged meditation on the function of the poet as mediator, is rich in 'All-' compounds), but the universality becomes a concealed curse: only in writing, and not in reality, is reality meaningful. Etymological poetry is childlike, for it treats its own language as an absolute. Eventually, language displaces reality, which becomes akin to the system of opaque signs depicted by Hawthorne in *The Scarlet Letter*: one may seek to read nature allegorically, but it will never confirm or disconfirm one's reading. As he stands 'ahnend' (divining: a key word in Hölderlin) before reality, he can never be sure he is not just hallucinating.

Etymological verse isolates the word within the sentence. In the hymnic sentence, the distance between the words increases, and as the single word is granted the special status of a magical talisman it becomes a harbinger of the dissolution of the sentence. As his poem 'Lebenslauf' (The Course of Life – II. i, 22) shows, Hölderlin was concerned to unite the beginning and the end of his work, so there is a deadly irony in the fact that many of the lines in the hymns are so fragmented that they resemble (and perhaps even *are*) the lists of key words he generally drew up before composition. His use of oxymoron and paradox represents a counter-attack on the principle of disintegration, for they constitute moments of fully conscious synthesis, but in so far as this synthesis is violent and momentary it leaves the rest of the poem outside the sanctuary of meaning. Moreover, such tropes destroy the specificity of language by making it refer to everything at once: the mirage of totalisation furthers disintegration. Thus one could interpret the despairing second stanza of 'Hälfte des Lebens' as a reaction to the shotgun wedding of opposites celebrated in the juxtaposition of 'trunken' and 'heilignüchtern'. As in 'Der Rhein', in this short poem reconciliation occurs momentarily at the evening of time 'Bevor das freundliche Licht / Hinuntergeht' (Before the friendly light / Goes down – II. i, 148): it is perhaps the generalised regret of any departure, when one forgives everyone because no one in the vanishing world will ever wound one again.

For Hölderlin the primary reconciliation is between culture and nature. Nature is 'allgegenwärtig' (omnipresent – II. i, 118): the poet must achieve a similar status, encompassing all reality through the modulation of the tones. In 'Wie wenn am Feiertage' poet and nature are one: the poets 'scheinen allein zu sein, doch ahnen sie immer, / Denn ahnend ruhet sie selbst auch' (They appear alone, yet always anticipate, / For she too rests in anticipation – II. i, 118). The present participle and the duality of 'ahnend', which refers to the future but also to the 'Ahnen' (forefathers), distends the poem's scope to cover all temporality. But the self-identification with nature by the poet exiles him from the human community. And, if the poet is at one with nature, then language (culture) can assume an existence independent of his directive will: the subject–object division that first appeared in the form poet–nature acquires the form poet–culture. This separation from his own language may be the source of the poignant impersonal purity of Hölderlin's verse. In 'Der Abschied' (The Farewell – II. i, 24–7) 'ein Gespräch' (a conversation) is said to lead the lovers up and down. Language becomes independent of the person. In the historical night without gods there are only voices, no visible presences. As Hölderlin loses Diotima and fails to achieve poetic recognition he has to people the void with his own disembodied, projected voice. In the later work he ceases to speak of his poetic mission (the poets of 'Brot und Wein' are 'sie' [they]) and uses the principle of the modulation of tones to sustain the poem's existence when there is no external reason for it to come into being. The opening lines of 'Mnemosyne', in the second draft, relate what has happened: 'Ein Zeichen sind wir, deutungslos, / Schmerzlos sind wir und haben fast / Die Sprache in der Fremde verloren' (We are a sign, uninterpreted, / Painless we are and have almost lost / Our language in a strange land – II. i, 195). There is pathos in the first person plural, for the disappearance of language would remove the possibility of community; there is unnerving pathos too in the suggestion that language only exists to register pain. The 'we' is the voice that speaks in three tones. These lines suggest it may have been the imminent collapse of his own language that drove Hölderlin to translation in his final phase: he needs another tongue to support his own, whence the literalism of syntax and semantics in his versions: he can only cling to the original, his own hopes as a poetic mediator to the Germans having been blasted. There is virtually no idiom left to translate back into. Supporting his language in this fashion, he drifts ever deeper into incomprehensibility, near-silence. One recalls the laughter with which Goethe and Schiller greeted his version of 'Antigone'. The 'Gott im Menschenwort' (the god in human speech – II. i, 35) is 'schwer zu fassen' (hard to grasp): he speaks in a foreign tongue. The towering sentences in the middle of the revisions of 'Der Einzige' show a writer almost overwhelmed by language. To read them is to be reminded of Waiblinger's words after visiting Hölderlin during the period of his madness: he discerned 'an unhappy conflict that destroys his thoughts at the moment of their conception'.[32] Hölderlin wrote of his own fear of brute subject matter, and that is why his poems effect an abstraction from a German to a Greek landscape. In 'Buonaparte' he voiced a fear that representation of the immediate might shatter his verse (I. i, 239). Total abstraction from immediacy, however, propels the verse towards silence. In his later verse, the image of nature becomes an allegory of the subject buried alive within it. The modulation of tones varies the oppression of form by accommodating formlessness. The tones express the dead poet as the seasons express nature.

Negative mythology

Hölderlin's theories dictate the form of his poems, as well as their concessions to formlessness, and this was the reason why he wished to found a literary periodical in which poems and essays would appear together and justify each other. The theoretical disquisitions would reveal the form underlying the apparent formlessness. His inability to launch such a periodical means that when one wishes to understand, say, the meaning of the term 'God' in his thought one is forced to revert to 'Über Religion' (On Religion – IV. i, 275–81) or his correspondence. In a letter to his brother he talks of 'the divinity that exists between us' (VI. i, 293): relationship is the category of the divine. Or, as Walser puts it, God is 'whatever still takes account of him'.[33] This view of relationships explains the awe and fear he felt in company: 'every relationship with other people and things engrosses me completely and I have difficulty leaving them behind for anything else' (VI. i, 388). The difficulties in understanding Hölderlin's use of such a term as 'God' can be illustrated by the following stanza in 'Ermunterung', in which he speaks of the future time of revelation:

> Und er, der sprachlos waltet und unbekannt
> Zukünftiges bereitet, der Gott, der Geist
> Im Menschenwort, am schönen Tage
> Kommenden Jahren, wie einst, sich ausspricht.

(And he who rules without speech and unbeknown / Prepares the future, the god, the spirit / Within human words, upon a bright day / Shall once more address the ages to come – II. i, 36)

One could interpret the stanza as follows: God is latent in human speech and will reveal himself in some indefinable future. But, if this God is inherent in human speech, how is it that his reign is 'sprachlos'? Would it perhaps not be more consistent to speak of a language which has become inexpressive but will, at some future date, radiate divinity – to speak of a passage from the 'sprachlos' to a plenitude of language? This is not the meaning of Hölderlin's lines, however. The relationship between God's silence and his presence within human words remains problematic. It is as if Hölderlin wished to place God above language – humbly conceding the inferiority of his own verse – and within it – proudly asserting the poet's status as mediator of the divine. The result is an incoherence, a disparity between intention and achievement. The poem is meant as an 'Ermunterung' to lift the self by referring it to something outside itself, but the multitude of reflexive forms in the poem as a whole shows that its primary relationship is in fact with itself. 'Es fehlen heilige Namen' (Holy names are lacking – II. i, 99), for the objects that would sustain them do not yet exist, are muffled in the historical night that comes between the cycles of day: they are Platonic Forms yearning for embodiment. The world does not yet exist, so it becomes impossible to speak of it, and speech turns reflexively back on itself. The poem without a subject (the 'Scheue vor dem Stoff'), which denies the present in the name of abstract futures and pasts, must eventually become its own subject and thereby dissolve the fictive hope of a better reality that has underpinned it. The disparity between intention and result in 'Ermunterung' is apparent again at a crucial point in 'Wie wenn am Feiertage', at the end of the long sentence that spans the fifth and sixth stanzas (II. i, 119). Hölderlin writes, 'Der Gesang, damit er beiden zeuge, glückt' (The song, so it can give witness to both, succeeds). The grammatical uncertainty in the German here functions like a parapraxis to reveal the underlying hubris that is not manifested in full until the end of the poem: Hölderlin writes 'zeuge' (witness/create) and omits the dative 'von' required to resolve the ambiguity and make the word mean 'witness to', as he intends; unconsciously, he abjures his willed role of passive witness. The slip reveals the poem to be a purely hypothetical vision whose despairing pathos is rooted in his knowledge that it is only a personal creation, no true revelation of the divine.

In 'Ermunterung', the latent meanings of the word 'God' and Hölderlin's own conception of the historical unfolding of the divine principle diverge from each other. There is a similar discrepancy between the immanent direction of his Greek motifs and the significances he accords them. In 'An die Parzen' (To the Fates – I. i, 241), for instance, the Fates are termed, in accordance with convention, 'die Gewaltigen' (the powerful ones), the forces that determine mundane events and to which even Zeus must submit. But Hölderlin goes on to

speak of his own 'göttlich Recht' (godly right) and this republican note
explodes the mythical framework. Unanswerable questions arise: is this
a threat to the Fates? how does the stated holiness of the poem relate to
theirs? and, if the poem is holy, why do they not protect the poet
themselves? This use of the Fates is an attempt to create figures to whom
to pray, but their abstraction and the internal inconsistencies testify to
their objective absence.

There are, however, good psychological grounds for this use of
obsolete mythical forms. They can be freely shaped, and the safety of
this transvaluation provides (albeit chimerical) proof of one's liberty.
Hölderlin employs mythological figures from an alien tradition because
'der *freie* Gebrauch des *Eigenen* das schwerste ist' (*freely* to direct *our
native powers* is the hardest thing of all –vi. i, 246). Nevertheless, the
foreign material displays the lineaments of the traumatic and repressed
present: the inhabitants of the Greek pantheon are levered out of place
by the pressure of the Christianity he found so problematical and whose
problems he sought to escape. And so the mediating role he attributes to
the demi-gods attracts the image of Christ into the poem: moreover,
the historical succession of mediators culminates in Him. When
Hölderlin wrote in the drafts to 'Friedensfeier' 'Und schöner, wie
sonst, o sei, / Versöhnender, nun versöhnt' (Be more fully than
otherwise, / Reconciler, reconciled – ii. i, 131) he both doubted and
affirmed Christ and speech in their unity as Logos. The Saviour has yet
to earn His name: prayer is combined with a challenge. The name of the
true mediator is unknown, for He has not yet emerged. Chronologically,
Hölderlin lives after Christ, but the persistence of the contradictions of
reality in the world AD demonstrates that the name of 'mediator' still
awaits embodiment. Hölderlin's hymnic statement is possible because of
the traditional Christian belief (though his remark is not Christian) that
Christ appears twice, a difficult duality of being and temporality that
explains the fusion and impacting of time scales in his work. This
absence combines with a fear of rendering the future impossible by
attempting to pre-empt it – of inviting destruction through one's
hubris – to effect the disappearance of names. Hence 'der Fürst des
Festes' (the Prince of the Feast) in 'Friedensfeier' is neither Christ nor
Napoleon nor any other concrete figure, not even the allegorical
incarnation of Peace (if it were that it would lack the pathos of
Hölderlin's yearning for the incarnation of the abstract, the absolute).
The return of the gods envisaged by him mirrors the Christian's hope of
a Second Coming and does so all the more effectively because the poet's
isolation reflects the alienation in the world the Christian ought to feel

but, because of the institutionalisation of Christianity, is no longer capable of feeling. Hölderlin takes the strait gate. The typological teachings of Hamann and of the Higher Criticism entail a fusion of mythologies, but this is easy to execute on an abstract philosophical level, for it is tantamount to their destruction, to the self-aggrandisement of philosophy through absorption of the poetic. Hölderlin, however, fuses mythologies in order to become a heretic to all faiths, including rationalism, and undergoes the danger of becoming a 'falscher Priester' (false priest – II. i, 120), though such a position is essential if the Christian imperative of allowing all men to come to Christ is to be realised. (It is interesting that Trakl, whose poetry alludes extensively to that of Hölderlin, should have shared this suicidally tolerant faith.[34]) It must be possible, for instance, to perceive in Greece not merely a prefiguration but an incarnation of the divine. (Even so, Hölderlin's philosophy fosters a dangerous synthesis whereby a Christian eschatological framework is preserved only through removal from a Christian context. This synthesis permits him to abstract qualities from Christ – Reconciler [II. i, 130], Prince [III, 533], The Only One [II. i, 153], the warrior who inaugurates the Millennium [III, 533–4] – to form new beings, probably on the model of the Greek pantheon.)

One's difficulty in comprehending Hölderlin derives in part from the dual status of the poems, which are both exoteric and esoteric. The two-level poem is a trap, a means of ascertaining the degree to which communication is possible. It is in part a protection against hostile and unwanted understanding; partly the product of a nostalgia for the true, all-embracing relationship in which the other is able to read one's mind. (This feature is even more pronounced in Celan, whose poems are genuinely both hermetic and open.) Poems are addressed both to friends and to the German people and postulate a language that will unite individual and community.

The strict delimitation of Hölderlin's vocabulary is simiarly ambiguous. It permits an extreme simplicity, but the over-determination of words creates an air of recurrent self-quotation, of slippage of meaning, and calls forth extra texts in an effort to stop up the gaps. But the repetition becomes obsessive: in repeating the word the poet magically identifies himself with it, refuses to part with it, lest in doing so he forfeit a portion of his self irrevocably. Self-quotations become talismans in a battle between the poet and the situation about which he writes: they are introduced into new contexts to defuse their danger. Information theory has shown that not everything in a text can count; if it does, there will be no communication. Paradoxically, the text in which everything *is*

significant – and Hölderlin's are the prototypes of such texts – will have
the effect of an hermetic, incomprehensible chant. The magical element
may become explicit in the lists of exotic names in the hymns, but it is
latent in the earlier verse also.

Hölderlin's syncretic anti-myths revoke the boundaries between
systems of thought and so increase the likelihood of non-
communication. In 'Brot und Wein', for instance, one cannot determine
whether the subject is Christ or Dionysos, whilst the final lines combine
motifs from Christ's Harrowing of Hell with the Greek god's journey
through Hades (II. i, 95). To say, as Ryan does, that it would be 'an
absurd undertaking to try to distil any abstract religious teachings from
Hölderlin's poetry, for basically he understands by religion the 'native
realm' of poetry itself'[35] is both to state the truth and to fail to observe
the effects exerted upon the poems themselves by this belief. Ryan treats
Hölderlin as if he were a modernist, rather than a problematic precursor
of modernism: he sees the ideas as indifferent. In fact, Hölderlin seeks to
expound his ideas in verse, the immanent force of which erodes those
very ideas. For Lawrence Ryan, philosophy and poetry are separate in
Hölderlin; in actuality, they are mutually supportive and mutually
destructive. Hölderlin turns to the iconography of demi-gods and heroes
because of his concern with the problem of mediation. But as he
combines and parallels them with each other he unwittingly reveals the
abstraction and uncertainty that underlie their apparently concrete
status: they suffer the irresolution of the intermediate figure. To cherish
several heroes is to stalemate oneself: there is no 'Einzige' to carve out a
reliably singular path. The multitude of mediators betrays uncertainty
concerning the relationship between men and God or gods. When, later,
he stands Christ's teaching on its head and states 'Nun erkennen wir ihn,
/ Nun, da wir kennen den Vater' (Now we recognise him, / Now that we
know the Father – III, 535), he suggests a possible explanation of his own
powerlessness. Without the father the son as it were does not exist.
Hölderlin only knew his *step*-father.

For Hölderlin, who appears to have been drawn to Orphic beliefs, all
religion is poetic by nature ('so wäre alle Religion ihrem Wesen nach
poetisch' – IV. i, 281). The poet mediates between the people and its god.
Even if this had ever been the case, however, it was no longer so by the
end of the eighteenth century: society no longer ascribed such a function
to the poet. Thus the problem arises of whether it is legitimate or
possible for a single individual to arrogate to himself such a communal
role. In the second version of *Der Tod des Empedokles* (The Death of
Empedocles) Hermokrates utters the curse, 'Hinweg mit ihm, der seine

Seele bloss / Und ihre Götter gibt' (Away with him who lays his soul bare / And its gods – IV. i, 97). Empedokles has offended, he states, by framing in words 'Unauszusprechendes' (what should not be spoken). Empedokles has betrayed the unreal reality of his private gods by transposing them into the public medium of language: 'Hinweg mit ihm' is a call for a straitjacket. The lost unity that precedes the drama is a condition anterior to the differentiation of the community into characters, the creation of language. God lies outside and before speech, for He is ineffable: speech about Him destroys itself, is of necessity blasphemy. The persistence of a silence at the heart of the play, between all the separate statements, is the basis of the hope of its return: Empedokles is a hero because he consents to the renewed advent of silence. Hölderlin's declaration that Empedokles dissolved his own personal synthesis so as to permit others to be reconciled is both a sophistry (if the hero's action is so similar to that of Christ, why suppress all mention of Christ as the primary model?) and a camouflaged truth: for with this work Hölderlin renounces the notion of the poet as mediator, because of the remnants of elitism it contains and because of the danger to which it exposes the poet, whose heart may be split by the lightning of the divine anger or crushed by the failure to reach the entire nation. (The notion of 'the divine anger' may of course be simply a personification of the sense of desolation following the departure of the gods – that is, the dissolution in the poet's heart of the belief that the word 'god' has an objective correlative.) In his later works he retreats from the position of the prophet to that of the viewer: in the hymns he merely watches, playing no part, and even his words lack fecundating power.

In 'Friedensfeier' Hölderlin writes of the Prince of the Feast, 'Nur Eines weiss ich, Sterbliches bist du nicht' (I know one thing only: you are not mortal) – III, 535). God is defined by negation. This theme is the problematical core of the first draft of 'Der Einzige' (II. i, pp. 153–6). There is a central ambivalence inasmuch as 'Der Einzige' has been both been withheld by the gods ('Wo ihr den letzten eures Geschlechts / . . . verberget [Where you conceal the last of your line]) *and* has himself chosen to withdraw ('warum bleibest du aus?' [why do you stay away?]). The hymn resists bondage to any single deity: it says 'zu sehr / O Christus! häng ich an dir' (O Christ, I cling to you too much). Hölderlin seeks a nameless figure above the variegated divisions of belief, beyond the separate religions of Greece and Christendom. The negative theology of pietism provided him with a convention that permitted him to express despair at God's absence whilst retaining hope. It enabled him to justify God's ways in the hope that He existed whilst rebelling against Him by refusing to address Him as God. The blasphemous local power of 'sein Licht war / Tod' (His light was / Death) or the depiction of Christ's shadow as 'wie eine Seuche' (like a plague) (both phrases come from the later stages of 'Patmos' – II. i, 182–3) express his frustration; but it was not something he could consciously vent, and only the belief that he was interpreting 'der feste Buchstab' (the fixed letter – II. i, 172) permitted him this relaxation of self-censorship. Derivations of the word 'God' appear with such frequency in his poetry because the divine absence devolves quasi-divine qualities onto a multitude of lesser beings. Negative theology allowed an indeterminate and hypothetical discourse that hovered between blasphemy and praise. As the certainty of absence established itself, the poems dissolved into silence.

Synthesis and disintegration

In some respects Hölderlin's poems are 'impossible objects', respecting which Gombrich states that the viewer's discomfort lies in 'the difficulty of matching successive fixations'.[36] The same difficulty arises through the modulation of the tones. Sentences stem from one another whilst denying their connection. Perhaps the most succinct and best-known example is 'Hälfte des Lebens':

> Mit gelben Birnen hänget
> Und voll mit wilden Rosen
> Das Land in den See,
> Ihr holden Schwäne,
> Und trunken von Küssen
> Tunkt ihr das Haupt
> Ins heilignüchterne Wasser.
>
> Weh mir, wo nehm ich, wenn
> Es Winter ist, die Blumen, und wo
> Den Sonnenschein
> Und Schatten der Erde?
> Die Mauren stehn
> Sprachlos und kalt, im Winde
> Klirren die Fahnen.

(With yellow pears hangs down / And full of roses wild / The land into

the lake, / You gracious swans, / And drunk on kisses / You dip your
heads / Into holy-sober water.

Alas, where shall I find, when / The winter comes, the flowers, and
where / The sunshine / And shadow of earth? / The walls stand /
Languageless, cold, in the wind / Weathercocks clang.)

That the two strophes require each other like the positive and negative of
a photograph has often been remarked; but the mechanism that
connects them is not, as usually assumed, one of simple reversal or
complementarity. The first strophe appears to be a description or
idealised image of an external Utopia, yet certain tremors betray the
presence of the suppressed poet and are precursors of the explosion in
the second strophe. These tremors include the unusual 'das Land in *den*
See' (emphasis added), the vocative, and the paradox of the close, a
schematic fulfilment of the poet's dream of a synthesis of the demonic
and the holy–sober. The first strophe is apparently idyllic –
nevertheless, its jerky breathlessness; the undertones of apocalypse in
'das Land in *den* See' (the swans too dip their heads: everything sinks out
of sight into the mirror world of the water); the undeveloped vocative
(cf. Trakl); the self-reflecting, self-interacting, nature of a landscape that
has no need of the human subject; the hint of mechanisation of thought
in the final paradox; the fact that reconciliation occurs in an eerily
depopulated landscape (as in the 'helle Nacht' [bright night – ii.i, 96]
and 'kühlende Blitze' [cooling lightning – ii. i, p. 118] of other Hölderlin
poems, the paradoxes are positive so long as they are located in nature
and are not referred back to the self that perceives them, a process which
would reveal them to be projections); and the prevalence of yellow,
which Kandinsky likens to a madman 'who disperses his force in all
directions, aimlessly, until it is completely gone'[37] – all these features
are unnerving. The landscape of the first strophe is trembling even
before it breaks down. The second strophe openly declares the implicit
despair of the first strophe and is, for all its jaggedness of sound patterns
and enjambement, strangely reassuring: here the tone is at least no
longer self-undermining, overheated with the pangs of giving birth to
another strophe. In a sense, the air clears, revealing a passive courage:
the last three lines have a strange majesty, as the poet himself becomes
languageless. Bravely, he contemplates a final destitution.

'Hälfte des Lebens' proclaims a revelation which it proceeds to
unmask. The same self-unmasking structure shapes 'Wie wenn am
Feiertage' (ii. i, 118–20). In this poem the synthesis is presented at length

and in ramified form: yet its essential momentariness, the precariousness of its balance, is intimated by the large number of present participles. As in 'Hälfte des Lebens', the poem collapses the moment an attempt is made to refer the synthesis back to the observing self. The central theme is appearance and reality: the gods, for instance, are seemingly absent but actually present. Many things appear twice and are comprehended only in their second incarnation. The morning breaks twice, in the first and third strophes; the phrase 'in Knechtgestalt' (in the guise of labourers) in the fourth strophe recalls the 'Landsmann' (countryman) of the opening lines; the poets seem to be alone but are united in expectation with the totality of nature. But this tendency to repeat and unveil leads to the poem's eventual unmasking of itself, as the vision fades, to be followed by its preconditions, which render it purely hypothetical: as the mediating cloud of 'Dichter', the other poets, evaporates to reveal that there is only one poet: Hölderlin, stricken by 'der andere Pfeil' (the other ray/arrow). Like demons' script, the poem is written backwards. The passion for revelation of the secret seeds of future time causes the fiction that is the poem itself to dissolve. Why did the poem collapse? (Hölderlin left it untitled, evincing his dissatisfaction with it, a monitory and magnificent ruin at the end of a particular line of poetic development.) The reason may be that poet who conceives of Utopia as poetically mediated places unbearable, unfulfillable demands on himself, as he strives with despairing hubris to re-enact God's creation of the world through speech utterance. 'Wie wenn am Feiertage' has rightly been deemed to represent a transitional stage between the odes and the hymns, between the odic hope of poetic mediation and the hymnic declarations of helplessness. The insistence that child-like passivity is the prerequisite of the poet's mediating role drives the poem into an impasse, for Hölderlin's age does not ascribe any priestly function to the poet, who can only acquire it through the self-assertion he castigates. Perhaps the 'Wie' (as) of the very first line is a sign that the poem is to be constructed on the sands of hypothesis. In the hymns, poetic mediation passes without mention and the reconciliation between gods and men is described from a ghostly distance from which the poet has no hope of participating: reconciliation resembles the exhaustion that no longer perceives the difference between opposites that have fought themselves to a standstill. Its occurrence before 'das freundliche Licht / Hinuntergeht' (the friendly light / Goes down – 'Der Rhein', ii. i, 148) is a chilling hint of Hölderlin's foreknowledge of his own 'Umnachtung' ('enfolding in night': the word employed throughout Hölderlin scholarship to describe, and aestheticise, his breakdown).

'Wie wenn am Feiertage' is the focal point of the transition from odes to hymns: consequently, it is destroyed by it. 'Brot und Wein' (II. i, 90–5), produced during the same period but at a greater remove from the catastrophe, is scarred by it but survives. Hölderlin marked the transition by using experimental poetic forms to which he never returned, the Pindaric hymn and the elegy, the latter being a form he considered of secondary importance (VI. i, 338–41). (One might also add the dramatic experiment of the Empedocles tragedy.) Experiment is both a means of responding to a fear that one has reached an impasse and a refusal to admit that one is lost: for the form one employs is an alien one, implicitly held at arm's length by a self which as yet tentatively withholds commitment from it. I shall now look at 'Brot und Wein' in some more detail.

Perhaps the most striking feature of the poem is that in it logic becomes pseudo-logic – the apparently logical connection functions more as an emotional 'Steigerung' (enhancement, intensification) than as a logical articulation. The very points at which such words as 'weil', 'denn' and 'darum' (because, for, therefore) appear are those at which the logical connections are most unclear. Thus in the second section of the first triad Hölderlin writes of the night,

> So bewegt sie die Welt und die hoffende Seele der Menschen,
>   Selbst kein Weiser versteht, was sie bereitet, denn so
> Will es der oberste Gott, der sehr dich liebet, und darum
>   Ist noch lieber, wie sie, dir der besonnene Tag.

(So she impels the world and the hopeful souls of all mortals, / Even the wise do not know all her conceptions, for this / Is how the Highest would have it, who loves you dearly, and therefore / Dearer to you than she is the reason of day.)

The preference of Heinse (the addressee) for the sober day is attributable either to his knowledge of God's will or to a normal human inability to comprehend the night. The logical link words appear at the ends of the lines: they are buffers against the experience of ending, of disconnection (serving to maintain the singing sweetness of the rhythmic continuity). Hölderlin asserts the reasonableness of the world to shield himself (from divine anger?) during the vulnerable moment of transition. The praise of obscurantism in 'Selbst kein Weiser versteht' produces a floatingly ambiguous sentence: Hölderlin here adopts a confusing dual perspective, professing to understand ('denn so') whilst withdrawing from the pride of knowledge: divine and human viewpoints are superimposed, but the result is not mediation but obfuscation. Shortly thereafter he writes,

> Ja, es ziemet sich, ihr Kränze zu weihn und Gesang,
> Weil den Irrenden sie geheiligt ist und den Toten,
> Selber aber besteht, ewig, im freiesten Geist.

(Yes, it is fitting to dedicate garlands to her and songs, / For she is hallowed by the wanderer and the dead, / Though persisting herself with spirit eternally free.)

One cannot determine whether or not the night should be revered because it is consecrated to the insane or because, despite this fact, it remains 'im freiesten Geist'. Madness may represent either a positive or a negative principle. At such points the poem is over-determined, though the hopeful mood that awaits the inspiration of night holds the oppositions together. Later, in the third triad, this unity will vanish. Remaining for the moment in the first triad, one notices in the third strophe the obsessive use of the copula. The abstraction of this strophe summons up the concretion of the next strophe as its necessary complement. Thus the first three strophes, the first triad, can be described as concrete, abstract–concrete and abstract, successively: the abstraction corresponds to the access of 'das Offene' (the open), to the removal of constraint that sloughs off the present and takes flight for Greece. The whole poem passes through the same sequence: from the concrete initial triad in a German town, to the use of Greece in the second triad to fuse the abstract types and motive laws of history with reality, and then finally the abstraction and rationalisation of the third triad.

The second triad, because it is both concrete and abstract, occupies a time scale that embraces and transcends the whole poem and anticipates the disappearance of time in the abstract final triad, which enunciates the laws governing the intersection of archetype and existence. The use of the present tense transforms this triad into the reality that underlies the ostensibly present opening. The magic of the present tense endows the past with immediacy. Nevertheless, the nature of Hölderlin's conception is such that the traffic between times is two-way: if the past can invade the present, so the present can subvert the claim to presence (to persistence, continuance) made on behalf of the past. This occurs when sections of lament jut up into the account of the advent of the gods, disturbing the historical narrative sequence. The overwhelming sadness of the present dissolves the imaginative projection of the past and only abstract consolation remains. By casting the past in the present tense Hölderlin sought to avoid the self-imprisonment in nostalgia that would separate him from the immediate world, but in so doing he admitted the destructive forces of the present into the idyll.

Thus the following triad, the one with the purpose of rational explanation and consolation, is the most deeply riven. Hence these lines in the seventh strophe:

Aber Freund, wir kommen zu spät! Zwar leben die Götter,
  Aber über dem Haupt, droben in anderer Welt.
Endlos wirken sie da und scheinens wenig zu achten
  Ob wir leben, so sehr schonen die Himmlischen uns.
Denn nicht immer vermag ein schwaches Gefäss sie zu fassen,
  Nur zu Zeiten erträgt göttliche Fülle der Mensch.

(But my friend we have come too late! The gods truly live still, / But far above our heads, up in a different world. / There they are endlessly active and seem to care little / If we are living, so sparing towards us the Heavenly are. / For feeble vessels are not always able to hold them, / Only sometimes can men bear the divine plenitude.)

Here the couplets no longer even belong together, except as means of compensating for and erasing each other. The second is in itself bitterly ironic, with the irony stressed by the caesura, yet the poem continues with confusingly limpid piety, as if the previous line had never been, frantically covering the tracks of its blasphemous irony. A few lines later it stumbles frighteningly towards incoherence, in the lines, 'und was zu tun indes und zu sagen / Weiss ich nicht, und wozu Dichter in dürftiger Zeit' (And what to do or say in the meantime / I do not know, nor why there are poets in barren times). The repeated 'und' threatens abandonment to the lack of connection between things, a harbinger of the helpless, paratactic style of the hymns. The line again slopes away alarmingly after the caesura in the final strophe: 'aber so vieles geschient, / Keines wirket, denn wir sind herzlos' (But so much happens, / Nothing works, for we are heartless). The sheer effort needed to hold everything together is apparent from the towering sentence that dominates the eighth strophe, where 'nämlich' (namely) – as in the hymns – attempts to steady the self, to impose order. Hölderlin's inconsolability leads him to attribute the encouraging ideas at the end of the seventh strophe to Heinse (he is alienated from his own ideas): 'Aber sie sind, sagst du, wie des Weingotts heilige Priester' (Ah, but they are, you say, like the holy priests of the wine-god). 'They' are the poets. 'They', not 'I' or 'we'. The 'like' distances the idea even further: it is only an inefficacious analogy, a failed consolation.

The modulation of tones, which obeys the dictates of theoretical reason, dethrones that reason, for the 'ideal' (theoretical) sections become simply fleeting moments in the unfolding of the whole. Ryan rightly criticises Hof's thesis that the three tones enact a dialectic in which the ideal tone provides a privileged synthesis. One could argue more convincingly for a pre-eminence of the heroic tone as a stoical mid point between the naïve world of the sons of the earth and the divine realm of ideas and refined essence. It may be that this middle tone reels the other two tones in and out (their movement as the movement of this tone stretching its legs). The introduction of philosophy into poetry had been part of a search for synthesis, but their alliance had been dictated by a mutual sense of weakness and they come apart in the hymnic alternation between bleak abstractions and unmastered, overwhelming experiences. Once night has started to fall, as it does in 'Brot und Wein', words become fluid, for the events they would have celebrated and drawn strength from have been soaked up by the darkness. At night there is only the separate dreaming self, no surrounding world in which to act. With the pathos of repeated beginning, Hölderlin's poetry seeks to restore the sunken world, the Atlantis that is Greece. Repetition serves as a variety of self-hypnosis that renders the poem a continuum in which every line echoes every other one. The three tones anticipate the split nature of the self in Freud's writings (Ego, Id and Super Ego: the beleagured Ego might correspond to the heroic tone). The poems are planned as accumulations of fragments radiating from a silent centre, and all their lines are related by their common absence and are perhaps interchangeable. (Kirchner's quarrel with Beissner over the order of the strophes in 'Der Frieden' might suggest this.[38]) How is one to read such poetry? The poetic repetitions justify the search for parallel passages that might throw light on an obscure formulation. But all the passages are obscure *in context*. Only quotations from the poems are comprehensible (which is why so much criticism has dealt with themes and ignored their transforming contexts): as wholes, they are incomprehensible: the whole is a stream washing over the individual statements to erode them into the silence they have violated. The network of contradictory cross-references upon which the oeuvre rests adds up to a silence. One may read the poems continuously, with a hypnotised submissiveness, held by the plastic beauty of the verse, which is what Kafka would have termed the beauty of the condemned. Or one may juxtapose lines here and there to reveal the personal philosophy the poems feed on and destroy, like flames dancing on logs. One may read Hölderlin in the former 'temporal' manner or the latter 'spatial' one. If neither mode of reading is adequate, it is because of the impossibility of harmony on which the poems are founded. The Romantic upheaval lit a brief hope that through the crack in society known as art the underground fire of religion would manifest itself. Hölderlin seized the opportunity and committed himself to poetry on these terms: his concern with intermediate states was part of this sense of possibility. But the intermediate state was only momentary. When it resolved itself he was trapped.

THE GHOSTLY MEANINGS OF EMILY DICKINSON'S POEMS

One need not be a Chamber – to be Haunted –

(670)[39]

Emily Dickinson's poetry is haunted. Ghosts, after-images or prefigurations of events, wash over a scene, which one views as if looking through water at the sea bed; then the tide of the haunting recedes and events are separate again. The gravestone stands for the absolute nature of this separation. If the charnel is the dominant image in Emily Dickinson's verse, this is not simply the result of her Puritan proclivity to meditate on her own demise, nor because of the nineteenth-century obsession with catalepsy and spiritualism, or because of her own living death as the Amherst recluse – though all these factors, and other ones I have left unnamed, play their part. It is rather because the unbridgeable divide between the living and the dead stands for all forms of separation: 'A Clock stopped – / Not the Mantel's – / Geneva's farthest skill / Can't put the puppet bowing – / That just now dangled still' (287). And it is also because of the link between the unfettered imagination and the image of death. Because death initiates a state of which we have no concrete knowledge, it is the only theme capable of energising the imagination to white heat. Because it is known to us only through the agency of our imaginative projections, to write of it is to proclaim the supremacy of imagination. The imagined blankness of death writes a blank cheque for the imagination. This world of death is the scene of surrealism: like Dickinson, its greatest precursor, it juggles the bones of a dead creation. Sartre has stressed that only the absent person or object (actually absent, or in fact non-existent) are imaginable. Thus non-existence – death – and imagination go hand in hand. Whence the enormous power of Dickinson's verse.

As I have said, Emily Dickinson is obsessed by the impossibility of crossing various divides. They can be linked however by imagination: 'The Brain – is wider than the Sky –' (632). It even bridges the gaps between poem and poem: each line is accompanied by a ghost, a variant phrase, that hovers above or below it; 'the same poem' becomes a different one in letters to different correspondents. The precondition of the triumph of imagination seems to have been non-publication: it granted her writing a licence refused to the male poets of the period, whose words grew rigid and stilted in the straitjacket of expected edification. Her isolation distilled a poetry purer even than Rilke's, which is tainted by the felt masculine imperative to philosophise and explain. The power with which the experience of negativity is rendered in her work is surely – like that of Charlotte Brontë – in part a response to society's dismissal of the spinster. To be one, as Charlotte Brontë also notes, is to be no one: 'I'm Nobody! Who are you?' (288). Interestingly enough, both Brontë and Dickinson needed to interpose screens between themselves and the public, behind which to write. Charlotte Brontë's screen, however – the pseudonym of 'Currer Bell' – was a porous one; society penetrated it and found out her true identity. Dickinson's screen – so much more hermetic – was non-publication. Its greater density and strength correspond to the greater radicalism of the work done behind it.

Emily Dickinson's non-publication is also a mocking image of the silence prescribed to nineteenth-century woman as seemly. It is also pride: she writes, of the 'Brave Black Berry', that, whereas other people 'tell a Hurt – to cool it – / This mourner – to the Sky / A little further reaches – instead' (554). The sky, however – God – gave no indication that it had perceived that berry's aspiration towards it. Her poems are steeped in a longing for the burden of mystery to be lifted. That is why her imagination seeks to go beyond death and self in moments of ecstasy: to find out the Other. When she realised that no explanation was forthcoming – that the berry was reaching in vain for the sky – she drifted towards silence. Her poetic life is haunted by the after-life of her own questioning voice of the years of 1862–5: by the mocking echo of a cry that failed to provoke God into answering.

In one of her poems Emily Dickinson writes of children 'Who weary of the Day – / Themself – the noisy Plaything / They cannot put away'

(423). Her poems about death are an attempt to put the self away, and see what remains. The famous 'It was not Death' (510) goes even further:

> It was not Death, for I stood up,
> And all the Dead, lie down –
> It was not Night, for all the Bells
> Put out their Tongues, for Noon.
>
> It was not Frost, for on my Flesh
> I felt Siroccos – crawl –
> Nor Fire – for just my Marble Feet
> Could keep a Chancel, cool –
>
> And yet, it tasted, like them all,
> The Figures I have seen
> Set orderly, for Burial,
> Reminded me, of mine –
>
> As if my life were shaven,
> And fitted to a frame,
> And could not breathe without a key,
> And 'twas like Midnight, some –
>
> When everything that ticked – has stopped –
> And Space stares all around –
> Or Grisly frosts – first Autumn morns,
> Repeal the Beating Ground –
>
> But, most, like Chaos – Stopless – cool –
> Without a Chance, or Spar –
> Or even a Report of Land –
> To justify – Despair.

'It was not Death' is one of Emily Dickinson's most compelling evocations of negativity: of the terrible isolation in which one tries, and fails, to find words for one's individual experience, the very uniqueness of which renders it impossible to frame in language, that product of convention. The poem proceeds with great deliberation, rejecting alternatives one by one. Every feature compels one to enunciate the verse slowly, intensely: the deliberate monosyllabics of the first verse set the tone, which is maintained in the alliterations ('Frost' – 'Flesh';

'Fire' – 'Feet'; 'Siroccos' – 'crawl'), liberal commas and frequent capitals of the later lines, all of which serve to isolate and weigh each individual word. The deliberation is that of death-bed speech – last utterance. The experience is defined by a double negation. Death is negativity, but 'It was not Death': that is, it was death, and something more (the whole poem, as we shall see, is about the excessiveness of experience over the metaphorical forms that attempt its petrification). The alliterations and assonances of the poem work at times with great complexity towards the definition of this experience. 'Repeal the Beating Ground', for instance, is a key line. The repeated 'ea' sound is the throb of the beating, which also echoes the death knell of the bells in the opening stanza (bells that grotesquely put out their tongues in mockery of the imagination's feeble attempts to define experience). The line suggests a beating that occurs underground: the beating of the tell-tale heart, buried alive. 'Repeal' and 'beat' mingle to generate 'repeat'. Alliteration is used equally effectively in the first line of the last stanza: instead of the deadlocking of two alliterations previously found in the poem ('Fire' and 'Feet', for instance), one has a movement of deadlock ('Chaos – Stop-') and release ('-less – cool'). The final liquid *l*s are instinct with expansiveness. It is the sense of freedom that accompanies successful definition of experience. This definition is however an anti-definition, achieved through abandonment of the defining effort: 'it' (that key word in Emily Dickinson's work) is not like anything; it is a 'Chaos' that is said to be 'Stopless' because of the possible infinite multiplication of failed metaphors. (And if a new one begins immediately after the Chaos – which becomes the waves of a sea that tosses the self – this simply emphasises the inadequacy of even the most apt metaphor.)

At the end of 'It was not Death' Emily Dickinson writes of a report of land as justification for despair. What does this mean? It means that a landing would induce despair, for it would bring to an end the endless ocean-borne journey of the self. Dickinson's work projects a world without a final goal – without a purpose or after-life. The endless motion recurs at the end of 'Because I could not stop for Death' (712) (again, the inability to stop – to die – is stated in the very first line): the horses' heads are pointed *towards* eternity; they never arrive. The satisfaction of meaning is continually postponed. Dickinson's poems head towards a meaning that never crystallises. Neither do their forms: it has been cogently argued that no final form for her poems can be said to exist.[40] They shift like shot silk, emitting a variable light. This renders them akin to *Vexierbilde* (puzzle pictures) which frustrate the reader.

An obvious parallel to this aesthetic of postponed meaning can be found in the novels of Hawthorne; indeed, many critics have compared the two writers, though usually in terms of a shared Puritan self-scrutiny and concern with the signs of election and damnation. Less obvious, but equally important, is the congruence between the kaleidoscopic effects Dickinson achieves by incorporating all variants into the poem (non-publication permits her to do this) and the Hawthornean formula of multiple possibility: Donatello in *The Marble Faun* may have had a faun's ears, or he may not. The issue is left unresolved. Both writers insist that reality is a place of possibility where all that is could have been different; they insist on the fundamental arbitrariness of expression. This insistence reflects the author's loss of a defined audience in the mid nineteenth century.

'It was not Death' concludes by fusing the images of infinity and sea. Their interconnection is also the basis of the following resonant short poem (695):

> As if the Sea should part
> And show a further Sea –
> And that – a further – and the Three
> But a presumption be –
>
> Of Periods of Seas –
> Unvisited of Shores –
> Themselves the Verge of Seas to be –
> Eternity – is Those –

'Further' is a key word here, as often in Dickinson's work. The poem as it were drops a stone in the pool of consciousness and watches its reverie ripple away without end. Its aspiration and yearning are as poignant as those of Blake's 'The Sunflower'. Again, as in 'It was not Death', the last line is a definition that is no definition: a germ of pure possibility beyond incarnation. The infinite aspiration of this poem is that of captives 'who tight in Dungeons are' (661). The endless reverberation of the event helps us realise why Dickinson can say elsewhere that 'Time never did assuage – / An actual suffering strengthens / As Sinews do, with age' (686). It is the experience of permanent, unmitigated isolation: time only assuages when it brings new sensations to blot out the wound of an earlier one; but no new things can impinge upon the individual who remains imprisoned inside his or her own individuality, and the word from the past echoes on forever in the mind, as in an infinite well. Time brings the moment in which a door swings open to reveal a sight of 'Wealth – and Company', but then it shuts again, leaving the self 'lost doubly' (953). And yet company is also feared: poem 421 states that the charm of a veiled face may vanish the moment the veil is lifted. And so the lady keeps her veil on, fearing rejection when others see her true face. The veil is preferred by Dickinson because it defines the face by negation, and provokes imagination.

Emily Dickinson's verse can be said to negate itself at birth: 'Ended, before it began' (1088) could apply to it. Her famous description of herself as having eyes 'like the sherry the guest leaves in the glass' catches the pride and the desolation of her negation. The eyes are wine, but they are left as if they had been unpalatable dregs, and their very existence is dependent upon the absent elsewhere from which the guest comes: for had he not been a guest he would have drained the glass. This guest has the aura of a god – as do so many of the male figures in Emily Dickinson's verse – through whose disinterestedness and indifference she seems to be. Her very being, as it were, arises from being passed over. She treats her poems with the same indifference. Thomas Johnson comments on the difficulty of determining a presentable final draft of her work:

> In one instance I thought she herself had provided a solution. One of the poems which she copied into a packet had several suggested readings for eight different words in the course of the five stanzas, but with no indication of her choice. . . . Then I found the same poem included in a letter to Higginson with choices made in every instance. Here, then, seemed proof that she had established her final version. But in another letter to another correspondent written at substantially the same time, she has included the same poem – also evidently a final version – wherein she adopted six of the choices made in the Higginson letter, but selected two from among her variants in the remaining instances. If any conclusion is to be drawn from this citation, it would seem to be that there are no *final* versions of the poems for which she allowed alternate readings to stand in the packets.[41]

This permutative use of variants echoes Keats's practice in 'La Belle Dame sans Merci'[42] and foreshadows the permutational aesthetics of Trakl. It challenges the notion of authoritative statement. The accumulation of variants also mediates between the unique occasion of the poem's gestation and the more terrestrial brightness of Emily

Dickinson's everyday speech: they defuse and diffuse the aura of the poem, which she is in the process of disavowing even as she writes it. (Another reason for non-publication, which thus becomes akin to self-censorship.)

Emily Dickinson's poetry is concerned to identify the unidentifiable – to discover experience where none was suspected. 'I dwell in possibility', she writes (657). This is the possibility, among other things, of an event's transformation by poetic alchemy into something of symbolic import: the discovery of landscapes and values hidden, not known to exist, because they lie within the self. Poem 700, for instance, begins trivially enough, as a description of a balloon rising. By the fourth stanza, however, great intensity has been generated:

> The Gilded Creature strains – and spins –
> Trips frantic in a Tree –
> Tears open her imperial Veins –
> And tumbles in the Sea –

The power of the vocabulary here indicates that more than a balloon is at stake. Thus, when, in the final line 'Clerks in Counting Rooms / Observe – "Twas only a Balloon" – ', they are patently wrong: the balloon has risen from being 'only a balloon' to the height of tragedy. In criticising the clerks, the poem also criticises its own point of departure, celebrating the process whereby poetry imaginatively translates a trivial event into one of great moment. In fact, many of Dickinson's most trivial poems can be seen to have originated in the hope that as the writing proceeded the mechanism of transformation would begin to work and everyday language and notions become incandescent. Thus many of her poems are wagers with the Muse. Yet it is possible that another explanation exists for the large amount of trivia she left behind her in her verse packets. The intensity of her few great productive years must have annihilated her later work in her own eyes. Once her poetry had fulfilled its purpose in that brief luminous period – the purpose of discovering value at the heart of nothingness – she put it aside as no longer necessary. The earlier poems must have seemed to be the work of a different person. For in the later poems her Shakespearean daring of conceit is trivialised by its deprivation of material adequate to its own negative capabilities. It is possible that she later buried the poems of her great years beneath billowing trivia out of a wish to unwrite them and undo the terror of fear and ecstasy they record: a wish that nevertheless dialectically contains a contrary desire to carry on writing to earn favour with the poetic incubus by showing willing, in the hope that it might feel flattered, come again and impregnate her words with meaning. She must have doubted the purposefulness of continued writing: 'Rime by Rime, the steady Frost / Upon Her Bosom piled' (804) could well be a punning portrait of the poet frozen underneath her rhymes – shunning real human love for a departed demon lover.

Much has been made of the irregularity of the procedures of Dickinson's verse: irregularities of metre, punctuation, capitalisation and rhyme, among other things. They were indeed a powerful impediment to publication in her own age. Her imperfect rhymes are images of the insistent disjunctions of experience, which combine conformity to the past (to the original rhyme word) with a crucial divergence from it. Her God rhymes with the God of her fathers – but only imperfectly. The dashes she employs as punctuation render the brokenness of unattended speech. The sheer force of will power required for the maintenance of such speech may explain the relative brevity of her great productive period. But these breaks are also dramatic pauses in a spine-chilling narrative: her imagery is very close to that of Poe, whose fear of burial alive and living death achieve infinitely greater significance in her work. (This fear may have been native to the writer using English in America before the establishment of a local American tradition. Could burial alive be an image of the effects of distance from what was then the language centre?) The deliberation and ritualistic intensity distilled by the dashes are augmented by the capricious capitalisation: both help to emphasise the weight of each word, casting upon it a light that reveals behind it the shadow word of a Platonic Form of language. The fact that not all nouns are capitalised whilst capitals are sometimes bestowed upon adjectives as well lends the text an added dimension of mystery, as we strive to decipher the mechanisms that govern the distribution of the capital letter. As we do so, language drifts away from us towards the unspoken speech of the Other.

3 The Word Unheard

INWARD ECHOES: THE SYMBOLISM OF RILKE AND TRAKL

The success and failure of Rilke

If Adorno is right and 'the greatest works of art are those which succeed even at their most dubious points',[1] then in the case of Rilke this means that the very vagueness of his metaphysical apparatus – the Angels, unrequited lovers, young dead and animals among others (why not the insane or the old dead?, one is tempted to ask), all of whom are strangely interchangeable – serves to validate his expression of his confusion. When he writes in the First Duino Elegy that we are not at home 'in der gedeuteten Welt' (in the interpreted world) he is as it were admitting his own dissatisfaction with his own private metaphysics, his own *Deutung der Welt* (interpretation of the world). He realises that each time he arrests his questioning arias with an indicative – as in 'Das alles war Auftrag' (All that was commission) – he is grasping impatiently after a chimerical certainty. He immediately concedes that he is 'von Erwartung zerstreut' (distracted by expectation), by a feeling 'als kündigte alles / eine Geliebte dir an' (As if all things were announcing / a lover to you). 'Das alles war Auftrag' is bad not simply because the word 'Auftrag' belongs to what Adorno terms the *Jargon der Eigentlichkeit* (jargon of authenticity), but because it distorts the meaning of a series of separate epiphanic experiences by bundling them together. And, if the moments are conspiring to announce *a* lover, and not *the* lover, their enumeration can seem to be a fuss about nothing, and the solemn air of anticipation specious. The same pattern of evocative moments and their strained and unsuccessful interpretation is repeated later in the same elegy. After writing 'Aber das Wehende höre, / die ununterbrochene Nachricht, die aus Stille sich bildet' (But attend to that blowing, / the uninterrupted news given out by the silence), the private exegesis of 'Es rauscht von jenen jungen Toten zu dir' (Its murmurs reach you from those youthfully dead) has a ghastly predictability: once again the *Deutung* is pitifully inadequate to its concrete occasion. The gap

73

separating these moments from their often wilful or whimsical interpretations is the yawning divide within Rilke himself between the precision of the eye and the confusion of the deductive mind: between the *Neue Gedichte* (New Poems) and the *Duineser Elegien* (Duino Elegies), to use the terms of traditional Rilke criticism. The disparity is the result of the inductive crisis in modern verse described in Hofmannsthal's 'Chandos letter'.

For Rilke, all things are in transition, poised between positivity and negativity. The questioning sweep of his rhythms relativises individual statements so that each one exists only as a record of the passage through it of that rhythm. This rhythm is seductive, seducing individual phrases into being and then casting them aside: as Kierkegaard observed, the speech of Don Juan is closer to music than to words. Had Schnitzler recorded the interior monologue of a poet too fixated upon the rhythms of Hölderlin to realise their inappropriateness to desacralised modern experience, the result might well have resembled the *Duineser Elegien*. Pretentious in quotation, Rilke's verse is convincing as a melting, provisional means of recording a rhythm, which becomes all the more apparent the more grotesque the linguistic deformations required for its notation. His verse, as it were, sings a hymn of transcendence whose words have been forgotten – so one now pretends to mouth them. Dubious as Rilke's abstractions are, they are fruitful because they indicate the difficulty of comprehending objects and events caught off-balance and on the point of vanishing into the whirlpool of modern technological change: the repeated use, in his poetry, of the hypothetical expressions 'wie' and 'als ob' assert ruffled subjectivity's power to interpret events whilst at the same time conceding the possible inadequacy of the interpretation, which is purely speculative. His use of negative forms, his obsession with the object that does not exist or is not perceived, register the fact that the object has as it were been whipped away from under the nose of the would-be leisured observer. The way the negative forms catch the object in the moment of its impending dissolution or transformation is similar to the strategies used by Cubism to place itself between realistic and abstract painting – photographing the self in the moment of its explosion, before it had dispersed so far as to lose all resemblance to its primary shape. The Cubist movement lasted so long and was so influential precisely because it set up a graduated scale upon which the artist could hover between the real and the abstract before deciding which way to turn. Cubism fractured the lines of division between the object and that which was not the object, for the lines that represent distortions and alternative views of the object shade off into those that have nothing to do with it, ripples sent out by the object after its fall into the pool of the canvas. The ambiguity of the moment of Cubism permitted the rapid spread of borrowings from it, which transformed its tropes into decorative *parti pris* (the post-war Picasso was to be one of the prime revisionists of Cubism, but even Juan Gris is only problematically 'a Cubist'). Cubism was first dissipated and then repressed, for the tension between figurative and abstract painting within the Cubist canvas recalled a painfully insoluble stylistic dilemma.

I have included this excursus on Cubism because it seems to me that its project is very similar to that of the Rilke of the *Neue Gedichte*, and that both have been repressed for similar reasons (the *Neue Gedichte* have never enjoyed the popularity of the *Stundenbuch* [Book of Hours] or the later *Elegien* among German Rilke exegetes). When Rilke took to heart Rodin's injunction to record his observations of objects, he submitted himself to a discipline but could not fully shed his solipsism. What is more, the vanishing of the object created a fatal blank space to be filled out with speculation, whimsy, 'wie' and 'als ob'. This empty space is however an interesting margin round the edge of the object, a frame within which we observe it; it is far less compromised than Rilke's earlier use of the bouncing blank cheque of 'God', or his later use of the Angels. As the object disappears it leaves Rilke describing not its properties but the structural laws he intuits behind it. The result is an empirical physics whose formulation as a law brings it to the verge of metaphysics. Thus in the famous 'Römische Fontäne' (Roman Fountain) he traces the circular movement of the water through the object: its movement is the disembodied intention of the earlier work playing round an object to which it is bound by the enclosing magic circle of the act of phenomeno-logical isolation. The fusion of physics and metaphysics can be seen in the best moments of the *Elegien* also: when he talks of how his cry repels the other, one can imagine a picture of sound-waves coming between them. The mechanism, the law, is deduced in the absence of the object, which both vanishes of its own accord and is wished away by an imagination seeking room for manoeuvre. Moreover, the generalised nature of language is such as to transform the would-be precise description of the single object into an exemplification of the class to which it belongs. Rilke's attempt to redeem the whimsical remark – which at its worst coyly solemnises it – is also an attempt to maintain contact with the childhood that is its native element and parallels Freud's ability to discern in the parapraxis a significant pointer of inner events. Rilke attempts to relate his emotional projections onto objects and people to their reality *an sich*, to separate out the elements confused in

Romantic anthropomorphism: he so often selects man-made objects as a basis for meditation because the fact that they already belong to the human sphere rules out the temptation of anthropomorphism. The stiltedness and unexpectedness of whimsy dissolve the conventional Romantic image of nature, whilst preserving another feature of the Romantic tradition: the privileging of the child's speech. The *Neue Gedichte* represent an uneven compromise between the modernist quest for hard line, its consciousness of the machinery of the body, and traditionally nineteenth–century poetical subjects (Classical myths, biblical stories, and images of nature). The concise sonnets are more interesting than is the mannerism of 'Orpheus. Eurydike. Hermes', whose form and subject are in the mainstream of decadent Romanticism. One of the volume's main problems is that of the relationship between the poem and its title, the presence of which can trivialise the work it precedes by reducing it to a variation on a theme. This too is a problem Rilke shares with the Cubists. Like them, he is using new methods to rejuvenate old themes (for the Cubists these were the still life and the portrait), so his project is constantly in danger of mere formal decorativeness. Like the Cubist painting, the poem accumulates multiple viewpoints of the object to render its three-dimensionality (a reflex of Rilke's interest in statuary, in the many-sided). But the title disrupts the temporal unfolding, the 'hide-and-seek', by calling out from in front of the curtain, 'Here I am', at the very outset. The title may reassure the reader that the writer knows what he is doing, but it also plays down the seriousness of his examination of the process of perception. Thus such a poem as 'Der Turm' presents the tower not as an object but as a process, and hesitantly evokes the winding experience of the tower from within in a long sentence the continuousness of which marvellously enacts the unsatisfied desire of the eye to reach the tower's roof and stare out into the landscape. As in so many of the poems of the *Neue Gedichte*, its lengthy saying embodies a negativity of seeing. This focus on the object ties in with the declared nominalism of the *Elegien*, but the stubborn resistance and *haeccitas* of the object have not yet been quashed by the process of internalisation that dominates the later poems (when in Spain, Rilke described his aim as to go blind round the images stored within him). The problem of the relation between the title and the poem is further compounded by the ambiguity of the term *Dinggedichte* (thing poems), which is often used to describe these works. It is hard to know whether the 'thing' is the poem or the object it takes as its occasion, perhaps because Rilke had in mind the fusion of subject and object through a magical mimesis. Nor is it easy to ascertain the degree of symbolic import ascribed by Rilke to the various objects.

Rilke was acutely aware of the fragmentation of his own nature, of his lack of control over his work, but unfortunately he mystified his helplessness by ascribing it to the unpredictability of a quasi-divine 'inspiration'. The sense of fragmentation generates a concern with the moments of transition between the fragments, with the spaces between separate images. He is fascinated by the wobbling of the drum before it tips over (*Malte Laurids Brigge*) or with the way the panther walks in ever-decreasing circles until it collapses into the torpor in which only images interest it. 'Uns aber, wo wir eines meinen, ganz, / ist schon des anderen Aufwand fühlbar' (We, however, where we fully mean one thing, / already feel the display of another), he writes in the *Elegien*. This sense of the threat to the equipoise of a single feeling is the source of his mixed metaphors, which reflect the degree to which the changeability of self and world render grotesque the premisses of commitment to any moment: the object one speaks of vanishes as one is speaking. The strange conjunctions that result – a girl is said to stand on the hills of her breasts, for instance – are proto-Surrealist, the cocoons out of which Surrealism was to arise. Within several lines in the Third Elegy Rilke passes from a sentimentalised and almost Victorian view of the Mother to an abrasive, pseudo avant-garde description of the jungle that grows within one. The tremolando of the sub-hymnic style in the *Elegien* attempts to mediate between the internalised extremes of the old sentimentality and the new ruthlessness. The rapid changes of mood can even evoke bathos. Thus in the Tenth Elegy Rilke writes at one point, 'O, wie spurlos zerträte ein Engel ihnen den Trostmarkt, / den die Kirche begrenzt, ihre fertig gekaufte: / reinlich und zu und enttäuscht wie ein Postamt am Sonntag' (O how an angel would stamp out their market of consolations so no trace remained, / the one with the church beside it, bought ready for use: / neat, shut and disconsolate like the post office on Sunday). The lightness and pathos of the post office reveals the petulance of the lines that precede it: the pseudo-medieval invective appears overblown. Very occasionally, these effects of near-bathos – these movements from a grand style into preciosity – are engaging and amusing, as in these lines: 'Aber er lasst sie, kehrt um, / wendet sich, winkt. . . . Was solls? Sie ist eine Klage' (But he leaves her, turns round, / looks back and waves. . . . What's the use? She is a Lament). This has the appealing silliness of philosophical *Heimatkunst*, in which Hans the leather-shorted poet waves farewell to the phantom of Gretel. The stylistic lability finally leads to a fragmentation of the speaking voice and the emergence of another self out of the narcissist's mirror. The first lines of the *Elegien* depict the emergence of this other self: 'Wer, wenn ich schriee, hörte mich denn aus der Engel / Ordnungen? und gesetzt selbst, es nähme / einer mich plötzlich ans Herz: ich verginge von seinem / stärkeren Dasein' (Who, if I cried, would hear me from among the Angels' / orders? and even if one of them pressed me / suddenly to his heart: I should perish through / the greater strength of his being). Normally a scream bursts forth without the kind of forethought manifested in this passage. The desire to repress the cry is part of a double bind that both seeks and shuns expression. The power of the shout is transferred to the Angel as the speaker fears his own aggression may return to extinguish him. The Angel is the estranged mirror image that cannot hear him (like Munch's, this is a *silent* scream), and that does not need to hear him – for it is 'himself'. These lines are almost a *locus classicus* for Freud's account of the formation of the Super Ego. The repressed aggression of the self is transferred to the Super Ego, which employs it to keep the Ego in check: a sure sign of the presence of the Super Ego (of the *conscience*) is the flood of self-recrimination unleashed by these opening lines. The line has the violence of the cry it withholds.

The look into the mirror encounters time in the form of the difference between one's real self and one's self-image. Narcissus is an image of the self that relates to itself through memory: the water contains the self time has washed away. Self-reflexivity renders it possible to avoid the interaction with external objects that destroys those objects and that infuses the self with guilt: 'Die Dinge, die wir hatten . . . nie erholen sie sich ganz' (The things we had . . . never quite recover – 'Vor Weihnachten 1914' [Before Christmas 1914]). The reference in the same poem to 'Mein Handeln . . . mein Missverstehn' equates action and misunderstanding. The misunderstandings of action, of adulthood, evoke an aggression in the object: the myth of the creation of Frankenstein can be seen to underlie Rilke's *Dingkult*. The object known in childhood did not 'contradict' the self ('Noch war es nicht das Ding, das widerspricht'). It was not yet 'das bange, fast gemeine / Ding, das Besitzen heisst' (the anxious, almost base / thing one calls ownership). Rilke criticises the urge to possess, and in so doing justifies his own elusiveness as well. If things contradict the self through a stubborn otherness that denies the self's sufficiency, the self can revenge itself on the object by dematerialising and internalising it – by removing it to the absent space of language and the imagination – and can then put in its place its own mirror image. Rilke's scruples about possession are the guilty afterthoughts of the nineteenth century, and dignify its future decline with the aura of moral renunciation.

The period of the *Neue Gedichte* overlaps with that of *Die Aufzeichnungen des Malte Laurids Brigge* (The Notebooks of Malte Laurids Brigge), which probably represent the key to Rilke's work, embodying as they do the experiences that gave birth to his idiosyncratic philosophy of negation and renunciation. It indicates why Rilke can only achieve affirmative statements through devious by-ways, through wrapping up indicative statements in subjunctive formulations:[2] it is because the fundamental negativity of the experience can only be transformed by a sophistic negation of the negation, by darkening the revealing mirror with the devices of fiction. At the centre of the book lies the three-headed figure of the artist–hero, the vampire and the Double,[3] a constellation whose meaning is that self-worship is its own punishment, as the worshipped image swells to overshadow the worshipper. This knot of themes identifies Rilke as a writer firmly rooted in the problematic of the nineteenth century, whose concern with the dual nature of selfhood (*Faust*, Dostoyevsky's *Dvoynik* [The Double], *Frankenstein*, among others) reflected its knowledge of its own hypocrisy, of the contradictions of Id and Super Ego. (As Kierkegaard was to observe, *soi-disant* Christianity had been replaced by its tyrannous double, 'Christendom'.) The key moment in *Malte* that reveals the identity of the three images is the scene in which the child dons a mask and then discovers that it has expunged the self: 'ich war der Spiegel' (I was the mirror), it realises. The passage from dressing-up as enjoyable titillation to the donning of a mask that adheres to the face and so obliterates identity recapitulates the movement within the nineteenth century from harmless exoticism to self-doubt in the face of the obstinate otherness of the exotic, which one cannot understand and feels compelled to destroy. The mirror is described in parenthesis as 'schläfrig wie er war' (sleepy as it was), for the mirror seizes hold of the self when it has grown weary, borne down by a Decadent fatigue: Rilke can later write a sonnet to Orpheus on the identity of existence and the pulsing of the breath because to breathe at all is an effort in the claustrophobia of a culture that places itself in the place of the other and renders the world increasingly uniform. In *Malte* another self is perpetually disengaging itself from the ostensibly dominant one: when Malte acts out the part of Sophie, whom he correctly deems still alive, for she embodies a disavowed part of the self (its latent bisexuality); in the moment in the underworld under the table when a strange hand unexpectedly draws near to his own; in the descriptions of 'der Dichter' (the poet), who, because he is unidentifiable, becomes both Rilke and not-Rilke; in the statement that fame is a misunderstanding, which implies a need to cast off the names by which others know one; in the ease with which 'das Lachen' (laughter), 'der Tod' (death) or 'die Krankheit' (illness) become separate demons in possession of the person who experiences them, transforming that person into an allegorical figure; or in the possibility of 'seeing without seeing'. *Malte* is deeply concerned with the relationship between imagination and memory, which, like the Angels of the *Elegien*, declines to distinguish between the living and the dead. Thus Malte himself writes of his grandfather, 'Personen, die er einmal in seine Erinnerung aufgenommen hatte, existierten, und daran konnte ihr Absterben nicht das geringste ändern' (people, once they had been admitted to his memory, existed, and their dying could not change that in the least). 'Erinnerung' is, literally, 'internalisation': Rilke's later belief in the interiorisation of objects as a means of preserving them – which is also, dialectically, tantamount to their destruction – is anticipated. This belief is akin to a metaphysics of the photograph: the images secured on the film persist in a time and space outside that of the original event, in a meta-space. This continual displacement in time is a seeing of the non-existent, the result of a trauma, which obsesses the self as the branded eye everywhere sees sunspots. The spiritualism of the nineteenth century compensates the trauma of death by hallucinating the lost person, by viewing that person's image in the photograph's daydream. Thus the bed-ridden Christine seems one day to be invisibly present and the face of Fräulein Brache is said to have all the features of Malte's mother's face. The bodily fragmentation that permits the hand to exist independently of the will reflects the discontinuity of a self strewn through different times and rooms. Writing arrests time to enable memory to assemble the jigsaw shards of experience, but the splitting-off of the hand from the body simultaneously disclaims responsibility for the products of the writing, which are deemed unconscious and symptomatic. Sculpture gives Rilke's ideal of the gathered experience: a unity of the diversity of viewpoints from which it may be considered.

At one point in *Malte Laurids Brigge* Malte attempts to run but feels himself frozen, as only the crowd moves. Part of the book's obsessive claustrophobia stems from this sense of motionlessness: one cannot even walk up and down a hospital waiting-room. One cannot move because it is impossible to know what one may encounter: none of the expectations enshrined in generalisations are valid. Thus: 'ist es möglich, dass man "die Frauen" sagt und nicht ahnt (bei aller Bildung nicht ahnt) das diese Worte längst keine Mehrzahl mehr haben, sondern nur unzählige Einzahlen?' (is it possible that one says 'women' without guessing (for all one's culture, failing to realise) that these words have long since lost their plural forms and constitute an endless series of singulars?). This is what drives Rilke from description to metaphysics: no name is specific enough to render the particular object or experience. And so in the *Elegien* Rilke proceeds to eliminate the objects that cause language this embarrassment: once they have disappeared, so will the embarrassment. The absurdity of the name is the point of a passage that on first reading can seem pretentious: the passage depicting a man with a stick in whose body a 'Hüpfen' (hopping) is said to migrate from leg to neck. Because this 'Hüpfen' first appears in the leg, the twitching continues to bear the name of the hop when it appears elsewhere in the body, thus demonstrating the absurdity of using the same name for a feature one ought to name differently at each of its stages. Rilke never states that the man is about to undergo an epileptic fit, for to do so would falsify the (crippled) form of perception that prevented one foreseeing the imminent event. The man is unknown, and, being a stranger, resists all nomenclature: Rilke's novel encompasses a sociological perspective in relating the unintelligibility of the person casually seen to the inadequacy of language and the impersonality of the city: 'Paris n'appartient à personne' (Péguy). In giving the genesis of his own idiosyncratic language, Rilke here preserves it from appearing mannered. It registers an experience of horror and individual fragmentation that is veiled by a mist of generalisation in the later work.

In the *Elegien* that mist covers everything: the envoy of otherness – the Angel, the Hero, the Child – changes apparel in an endless masquerade of displacement, hide-and-seek. In choosing to conduct arguments with himself in public Rilke forfeits both the intensity and intimacy of the private tone and the rhetorical certainty of the elevated manner: such a line as 'Beginn / immer von neuem die nie zu erreichende Preisung' (Ever again begin the unattainable praise) is hamstrung between a hymnic rhetoric of praise and its perpetual collapse, its unattainability. The confession of limitation in 'nie zu erreichende' has the appearance of false modesty in public. 'We' sentences soaked in personal regret are specious; usually, when Rilke says 'uns' (we), one senses a sickly clinging that knows strength is in numbers. Only in the Ninth Elegy does he attain the truly impersonal confidence required to have the right to speak on behalf of others.

Mixed metaphor is metaphor in its death-throes. As society becomes increasingly centralised, everything becomes linked with everything else (the notion of universal guilt is a very modern one), and the notion of System arises to describe this condition. Mixed metaphor registers the fact that *a* connection is no longer *the* connection, for the metaphor is arbitrary and others would be equally valid: when objects start to move, the background behind them (once seen as their necessary shadow) shifts, new juxtapositions emerge. Mixed, metaphor becomes meta-metaphor: its own critique: outliving the coded tropes of metaphor and the unified public. In mixed metaphor, the over-sharpened blade snaps. Rilke is the greatest master of the mixed metaphor. Perhaps the most fruitful period in his work is that of the *Neue Gedichte*, when the interchangeable metaphors of the *Stundenbuch* are superimposed upon each other to indicate the absurdity of the attempt to interpret them. Pellucid as the *Sonetten an Orpheus* are, they are also very safe, all the more so because Goethe's final poems had set a precedent for poetry's pensioning off in old age to a temple of Orphic proverbs. In the *Sonetten* the whimsy that had turned the would-be prophetic utterance of the *Elegien* into bathos works its way free of the tragic pose. Myth becomes an admittedly alien object, a thing to be played with, and though this can lead to insubstantiality, it does generate a pleasing and surprising coherence. Yet Orpheus is not, as some critics have said, the outgoing counterpart of the Angel, for both are narcissistic, caught in the vortex of self and reflection that spirals down into silence. The mixture of subjunctive and indicative forms in Rilke testifies to the etherealisation of the solid world by its doubling in the mirror. His addiction to question forms posits an absent other (at its worst, the Princess Marie von Thurn und Taxis-Hohenlohe – and all her avatars), just as the rising intonation at the end of a question[4] reflects a sense of triumph at having shifted onto another the burden of making sense. The mirror provides an exit from claustrophobic self-enclosure ('so quillst du aus dir hinaus' [so you flow out of yourself]) and yet augments it by peopling the world with echoes of oneself. The mirrors are his poems; 'niemandes Schlaf . . . unter soviel Lidern' (no one's sleep under so many eyelids / songs), he is dispersed among his many songs, scattered like the limbs of Orpheus, printed on the eyes of those who read him and so temporarily lift his body from its grave. The closed eyelids are the sheeted mirrors in the house of the dead.

Georg Trakl: permutation and poetic roulette

Having spoken of Rilke, one cannot pass over Trakl. Not simply because both received the financial support of Wittgenstein, but because they are complementary. In Rilke, events are dynamic and melting, passing endlessly through a fountain in motion; in Trakl, the advent of winter has frozen its water. If the former talked of transforming the world by internalising it, the latter actually did so to such an extent that in his poetry nature becomes a taciturn allegory for which no interpretation exists. This poetry operates a self-denying ordinance whereby each statement cancels itself in an attempt to become the thing it cannot be: silence. The poems are constructed of fragments, each one an attempt to embody ambiguity definitively and so have done with it: each line has the sinking stillness of an arm solemnly waving farewell. Walter Killy has shown how a long poem such as 'Helian' grew up out of fragments as Trakl shuffled individual lines from poem to poem in search of the right fit. The ambiguity in Trakl is the result of a collision of description and metaphor, image and allegory, and it brings about a strange hovering of tone. Nature fuses with allegory – its significance as the graveyard in which all generations lie until the Resurrection can only be arrived at through the brooding of the allegorical mentality. As one broods on the ambivalences of Trakl's lines, an infinite regress of opening doors presents itself with mysterious quietude.

The degree to which Trakl's poetry steps through a door of dream through which it never returns is evident even in a poem as passionate as 'Klage' (Lament):

> Schlaf und Tod, die düstern Adler
> Umrauschen nachtlang dieses Haupt:
> Des Menschen goldnes Bildnis
> Verschlänge die eisige Woge
> Der Ewigkeit. An schaurigen Riffen
> Zerschellt der purpurne Leib.
> Und es klagt die dunkle Stimme
> Über dem Meer.
> Schwester stürmischer Schwermut
> Sieh ein ängstlicher Kahn versinkt
> Unter Sternen,
> Dem schweigenden Antlitz der Nacht.

(Sleep and Death, the dusky eagles / Circle nightlong round this head: / Man's golden image / May be devoured by eternity's / Icy wave. On terrible reefs / The purple body breaks up. / And the dark voice laments / Across the sea. / Sister of stormy sorrow / See a tremulous bark goes down / Under stars, / The silent face of the night.)

The first line suggests the opening of a Renaissance poem, whilst the later suggestion of the metaphor of life as a boat tossed by dark seas reproduces a common Baroque trope. There is a strange fusion of a public manner, with its solemnity of address and rhetorically coded imagery, with a private mode, for the sorrow it speaks of is personal and the images' referents have dissolved. (Whose, for instance, is the dark voice? The definite article can make it seem like a stage direction referring to a background noise.) The poem reads like a fragment of a Latin epic. The poem's lament is echoed in the lament of the dark voice, as if it were the dissociated and endlessly magnified voice of the poet himself. The colour symbolism of purple is enigmatic, suggesting both a wave-battered and -bruised and a regal body. The nightmarishness of the poem is apparent in the helplessness of its speaker: no sooner does he envisage a possibility (the golden image may be devoured) than it comes to pass. The sense of powerlessness is enhanced by the injunction to the sister: if one's own consciousness cannot make sense of events, perhaps another one can. Yet the sister is somehow implicated in the disaster of the boat: her sorrow is said to be 'stormy', and the 'silent face of the night' may in fact be hers, the stars a conventional trope for her eyes. The poem moves from a subjunctive fear for man's image into an area where thought is omnipotent and yet impotent in the face of the translation into reality of all its minor fears and stirrings. In retrospect, the allegory of the first line becomes surrealistic (since dream becomes reality quasi-automatically, there can be no return to the relative intelligibility of this opening): it is as if real eagles are whirling around the room. The last line has a Spenserian resplendence.

Throughout Trakl's poetry, the large numbers of generic nouns and intransitive verbs (*dämmern, tönen, sinken, fallen,* for instance [to shed twilight, to sound, to sink, to fall]) create a sense of objects existing at isolated intervals and rotting inwards: images implode in a slow motion like separate apples spaced out on the ground underneath an autumn tree. Whence the subsumation of change, and events, under stasis: no object affects any other one. There are no future tenses and few past ones: instead, there is the perpetual present of a flow of mystified images. The frequency of the *er-* prefix in Trakl (it denotes the fulfilment of an action or the attaining of an end) demonstrates his sympathy with closure. His ambiguous sympathy with *Verwesung* – the word means putrefaction, but also suggests an unbeing – is the result of his suspicion that the vital force of his work is released through a process of self-undermining: his later works, which are also his greatest, are riddled with self-parody, self-quotation and echoes of Hölderlin. Often he places the adverb/adjective (in German, they have the same form: Trakl exploits this as a means of subsuming the adverb under the adjective) at the start of a line, before we can know what it refers to: 'erschütternd ist der Untergang des Geschlechts' (shattering is the decline of the race), for instance. Together the adjective and the copula suck everything that follows them back into stasis: presenting the effects of an event before the event itself, they absolutise those effects and seem to reverse time and causality, throwing a veil of mourning over the later event. 'Erschütternd ist' suggests an hieratic ontology, and the biblical syntax lends tautness to the simplified vocabulary. The state of *Erschütterung* becomes more important than its cause: the subject is trapped at the bottom of a pit that is caving in on him. The dense sound patterns of Trakl's poetry render language visibly present as a tainted, tinted glass in front of reality (thus one could interpret the assonances and alliterations of Swinburne, for instance, as not simply Decadent and trashy, but also as anticipating the modernist self-consciousness about language). Trakl reshuffles his motifs and sounds kaleidoscopically. Consequently, the astonishing beauty of his lines is never precious, for the effects are partly accidental and casual: it is one aspect of Trakl's mimesis of nature that he achieves quasi-fortuitous effects by permutating basic types in the same way as nature does. In 'reworking' his 'old' ideas, he ascribes the same status to both old and new versions. His aesthetics of montage and permutation, however, do not simply mimic genetic combinations. They also represent a response to the inherent homelessness of the original statement, which suffers exile from its first context.

Trakl's poems are notoriously lacking in any dynamism or linear thrust. They unfold in an autumnal world of stifling decay. The lack of dynamism can be correlated with his statement that 'man kann sich überhaupt nicht mitteilen' (one cannot communicate at all). It can also, I think, be correlated with his incestuous tendencies (and here it is not ultimately important whether or not Trakl slept with his sister; merely that his imagination entertained the notion and so incurred guilt). His frequent uncompleted vocatives can be seen as reflections of a desire to affect the environment that is suddenly broken off: a breaking-off with a dual significance, both arrest of the guilty motion and failure to breach the charmed circle of the family and enter the outside world. Incestuous desires are perhaps the result of shyness and humble abrogation of the prerogative of choice: one takes the person placed closest to one by nature, for others are inaccessible. One privileges nature over the cultural codes. The incestuous relationship is fostered and preserved by walls, occurs in private rooms, and cannot be openly acknowledged: the

combination of the room and the return to nature engenders the
claustrophobic image of nature as a leaden-ceilinged chamber. The
brilliant ending of 'Untergang' (Decline) can be interpreted as over-
determined by the experience of incestuous desire: 'O mein
Bruder / Klimmen wir blinde Zeiger gen Mitternacht' (O my
brother / We climb, a clock's blind hands, towards midnight). The three
is of the second line are the midnight chimes. The sister's voice is adopted
by the poet; and midnight is the moment of symbolic incest when the two
hands, so long kept apart, melt into one, at the witching-hour, outside
the order of normal time. The blindness is the blindness of Oedipus, of
the libido, and of the fear that the partner one fails to see in the dark
could be anyone – and one could be violating taboos. All this may seem
very much like stretching an analogy, but in Trakl's case it is essential to
do so: his entire work is a process of stretching analogies, condensing
images, to render them maximally absorbent. The closed circuit of a
strictly limited vocabulary is endogamous, the logical conclusion of
Symbolism, to which Trakl is affiliated by multiple threads (cf.
Rimbaud). Incest is in a sense the ultimate expression of life in a mirror.
But there is a crucial difference: whereas for the French Symbolists it is
the world of artifice that encloses, in Trakl it is nature that is
claustrophobic, stifling one's breath. For Romantic anthropomorphism
transforms nature into man's extension, his mirror. It ceases to be other
and becomes a projected aspect of the self. Nature points beyond itself
allegorically, but because its allegorical reference is to the perceiving self
it is experienced as a prison.

This nature is inhabited by the neuter abstract. 'Ein Totes' (a dead
thing) or 'ein Krankes' (a sick thing) are terms that provoke one's
unease: one does not know the character of the referent, whether it is a
person, a thing or – and this is the primary source of our unease – a
person in the process of becoming a thing. The concern with borders is
apparent in the repeated evocations of dusk's encroachment or the
decay of autumn; as it is also in the use of contrast rather than similarity
as a means of association of images. The sudden contrasts are the shocks
of modern urban life projected onto the images of the countryside: it is
normally only after leaving an oppressive environment that one breaks
down – and here the jagged contrasts are after-images of the metropolis.
As objects decompose, adjectives detach themselves from them and
begin to lead a disembodied life, finally becoming independent in the
form of the neuter abstracts. In such a poem as 'Passion', the boy, the
bride, the sister and the blind man melt into one as people do in the
evening gloaming in which their outlines become blurred. Trakl dreams

of dusk as the time of reconciliation, when others become like himself, when the world's harsh tools are laid aside, and when he and his sister can leave their room and walk abroad unseen. The day transgresses when it turns into night.

HOFMANNSTHAL AND ELIOT: PERSONA AND QUOTATION

At first sight the lyrical poems of Hugo von Hofmannsthal appear to be very much of a piece, glued together by a pervasive luxuriance of diction. They are often treated as if they were unproblematic lyric coagulations – a suckling's lisping in numbers. Considered more closely, they prove much more complicated: their hollows are full of Goethean echoes and they wrinkle as they stretch themselves out between self-expression and five-finger-exercise dramatisation. Take the following poem, for instance:

> Manche freilich müssen drunten sterben
> Wo die schweren Ruder der Schiffe streifen
> Andre wohnen bei dem Steuer droben,
> Kennen Vogelflug und die Länder der Sterne.
>
> Manche liegen immer mit schweren Gliedern
> Bei den Wurzeln des verworrenen Lebens,
> Andern sind die Stühle gerichtete
> Bei den Sybillen, den Königinnen,
> Und da sitzen sie wie zu Hause,
> Leichten Hauptes und leichter Hände.
>
> Doch ein Schatten fällt von jenen Leben
> In die anderen Leben hinüber,
> Und die leichten sind an die schweren
> Wie an Luft und Erde gebunden:
>
> Ganz vergessner Völker Müdigkeiten
> Kann ich nicht abtun von meinen Lidern,
> Noch weghalten von der erschrockenen Seele
> Stummes Niederfallen ferner Sterne.
>
> Viele Geschicke weben neben den meinen,
> Durcheinander spielt sie alle das Dasein,

Und mein Teil ist mehr als dieses Lebens
Schlanke Flamme oder schmale Leier.

(Truly, many have to die down under / Where the heavy rudders of ships glide, / Others live above beside the rudder, / Know the birds' flights and the countries of stars.

Many always lie with their limbs heavy, / Beside the roots of entangled existence, / And the chairs are all prepared for others, / With the Sibyls, the Queens, / Where they sit as at home, / Light of head and with light hands.

But a shadow falls from the one existence / Over to the other existences, / And the light are bound to the heavy / As they are to earth and air:

Weariness of whole forgotten peoples / I can never remove from my eyelids / Nor withhold from my terrified soul / The taciturn downfall of distant stars.

Many fates are weaving away beside my fate, / Being interplays them all with each other, / And my part is more than the small flicker / Of this life or of my slender lyre.)

Here the 'freilich' of the first line fulfils a dramatising function: the casualness with which it alludes to the deaths of the underlings (their demise is merely a tiny malfunction in a well-oiled social order) identifies the speaker as 'aristocratic'. But the tone of voice also has a simplicity that suggests the pearly egotism of a child. The way that physical postures express social position in the second stanza is part of the hieratic simplicity of a fable about 'die leichten' and 'die schweren': a fable that is both child-like and a generalising strategy to render the fact of oppression comfortingly perennial. The tone is, 'This is how it has always been.' The speaker however, although 'youthful' and 'aristocratic', should not be identified with Hofmannsthal himself. (Especially since when the first person begins to be used in the second half of the poem a shift occurs from the language of vertical contrast to that of horizontal complicity and interaction.)

If one examines the poem's temporal progress one notes that the first stanza intimates a quasi-Classical reality (seen from a distance, class-differences are more clear-cut than they are admitted to be in one's own society): for the Greeks, drowning was the worst possible form of death, for the wet element would extinguish the soul's vital spark; the importance ascribed to the knowledge of the patterns of bird flight suggests a society that practises divination; whilst the mention of stellar patterns suggests primitive navigation. (Though 'Länder der Sterne' also emits a certain provocative Symbolist vagueness: those who know the lands of the stars are identified, as it were, with the birds whose wings beat the absent interplanetary air, whilst the ocean at the bottom of which the dead lie is also the earth's atmosphere. At this level of the poem's semantic possibilities, it is less about social systems than about a general earthly inferiority to an extraterrestrial They.) The Greek coloration of the first stanza is reinforced by the reference to the Sibyl in the second stanza, which casts a sidelong glance at Iphigenia's song 'Es fürchte die Götter / Das Menschengeschlecht' (Let humankind / Fear the gods) in Goethe's *Iphigenia auf Tauris*. As often, Hofmannsthal sleepwalks into something akin to a Goethean cadence and mode of thought: this involvement with another poet cements the general sense of human implication (the opposites of the beginning – dialectically – become complements). Interdependence is further proclaimed in the phrase 'Doch ein Schatten fällt von jenen Leben / In die anderen Leben hinüber'. This is ambiguous. The shadow falls, and thus leads one to assume that it comes from above, but it is nevertheless said to fall 'hinüber': across. The vocabulary of verticality becomes horizontal. Moreover, there is also a sense in which the shadow falls *upward*: it is the lower plane that is conventionally termed the *Schattenreich* (the realm of the shades). The 'leicht' and the 'schwer' are revealed to be inter-dependent as well as contrasted. At this point the self appears. And, although it is a Symbolist self, burdened with 'wearinesses' it would be too much effort to specify, it is also locked into the genetic chain in a manner reminiscent of its contemporary opposite movement, Naturalism. This conjunction of artistic movements in this poem can be seen as part of the duality of Hofmannsthal's voice. (I shall later be returning to the question of eclecticism in his works, which at first is midwife to this voice and then smothers it.) In this poem, meanwhile, the self experiences the accumulated weariness of the past and the horror of a present that is always already past (the 'ferne Sterne' have long since fallen by the time one comes to see them): the present evaporates. 'Viele Geschicke weben neben den meinen'; it is as if the surrounding tumult distracts the self from its own being. The weaving *nearby* and the rhyme 'weben neben' suggest an identity and a difference between self and others: the others, the Fates, circle the self as if casting a petrifying spell. The way 'weben' catches at 'neben' evokes an envious longing to grasp the real fate or destiny possessed by the others, to acquire a reason for being. The last two lines pinpoint the poem's fine equivocation: the poet is identified with the 'schmale Leier' and the Pater-like 'schlanke

Flamme', for he too feels a Decadent weariness and thinness of resource, but because that weariness belongs to the past generations that linger on in a spectral half-being it is typical neither of the poet nor of the present. Whence the sense of *freshness* with which Hofmannsthal presents the idea of exhaustion. The feminine line-endings may reinforce the air of ghostly survival, for the lines do not end but dissolve, echo; but their lack of final firmness, a sign of tiredness, is also a generator of continuity – the continuity of the generations – as the lilt eases one into the next line. Hofmannsthal designates the fact of human interdependence with a word that has an undertone of disdain: a 'Durcheinander' is a chaos. This is in compensation for his envy of those who feel they belong. And yet of course he too is part of a tradition: past voices speak through him. The whole poem emerges out of the contradictions experienced by the Decadent poet who is not content merely to let his predecessors do his living for him.

The self-dramatising lyric, the lyric in which the poet dons a persona, is a halfway house between the pure lyric and the drama. Drama becomes possible when the self has slipped irrevocably away from itself. Again and again in Hofmannsthal one finds him using repetitions to rein in a self that is drifting away. The drifting is dramatised in 'Erlebnis' (Experience):

> Ein namenloses Heimweh weinte lautlos
> In meiner Seele nach dem Leben, weinte,
> Wie einer weint, wenn er auf, grossem Seeschiff
> Mit gelben Riesensegeln gegen Abend
> Auf dunkelblauem Wasser an der Stadt,
> Der Vaterstadt, vorüberfährt. Da sieht er
> Die Gassen, hört die Brunnen rauschen, riecht
> Den Duft der Fliederbüsche, sieht sich selber,
> Ein Kind, am Ufer stehn, mit Kindesaugen
> Die ängstlich sind und weinen wollen, sieht
> Durchs offne Fenster Licht in seinem Zimmer –
> Das grosse Seeschiff aber trägt ihn weiter
> Auf dunkelblauem Wasser lautlos gleitend
> Mit gelben fremdgeformten Riesensegeln.

(A nameless homesickness for life was weeping / Within my soul, and it wept soundlessly, / As a man weeps, when, on board a great sailing-ship / With massive yellow sails, towards the evening, / Upon a dark blue water, he sails past / The town, his father town. And there he sees / The streets, hears all the fountains playing, smells / The fragrant lilac bushes, sees himself, / A child, stand on the shore, with a child's eyes, / Which fill with fear and want to cry, and sees / Through the wide-open window, light in his room – / But the great sea-ship bears him ever onward, / Gliding upon dark waters soundlessly / With massive yellow sails, of strange design.)

The 'Vaterstadt' that is being left behind here is the site of tradition, from which the child drifts away, but towards which it also mysteriously returns (again, the subterranean force of naturalism, of genetic predetermination in Hofmannsthal), just as the passage itself circles round from that which is 'lautlos' within the self to the ship, the objectified and alienated form of selfhood, which is 'lautlos' at the end. The homesickness cries because it is 'namenlos': the long simile that follows is the form whereby the poet grants it a name. The transformation of the self is enacted in the structure that turns a simile into an extended metaphor, a contrary world from which there can be no return to this one. One begins to realise that Hofmannsthal's reservations about Symbolism stem from a fear that its reliance on the associative powers of imagination may lead one, step by seductively small step, away from oneself and into an irrevocable self-exile. Here the self stands on the boat looking but also remains rooted to the wharf from which it stares: for the phrase 'mit Kindesaugen / Die ängstlich sind und weinen wollen' applies both to the forlorn child on the wharf and to the adult bound inexorably for the feared maturity in which he will perish, in the evening, falling from the tree of life. As elsewhere in Hofmannsthal, the repetitions reflect a desire to cherish the security of the past, but they also recognise the split nature of the self: the same remark is reiterated because the discontinuity of personality renders one unconscious of having already uttered it. An exit from one place is – simultaneously, eerily – an entrance elsewhere. Repetitions seek to cheat death but in fact enact it: they measure the distance covered since the first utterance.

The fear of death that runs through Hofmannsthal's inspired early poems is also a fear of life, of the adolescent's awakening into an adulthood, a sexual maturity (one may think of the sultry, guilt-laden atmosphere of 'Vor Tag' [Before Day]), that will alienate him from himself. The fear is particularly acute in Hofmannsthal, who is a Romantic poet before ceasing to be a child, for the youth idealised by Romantic ideology is about to slip away from him and this may cut the ground from under his poetic feet. Perhaps he feels a premonition of the expiry of his poetic gift. The inevitable step into adulthood would break the enchantment of enclosing familial protection, which gives one the sense of security one needs in order to lower oneself into mental depths: there is a parent above holding the rope. The fear of adulthood is also fear of responsibility for one's own words. The early Hofmannsthal uses pseudonyms as an actor's mask, the most striking of which is that of Loris, the last irresponsibly incandescent flower of a moribund Romantic tradition that calls for fundamental renovation. Romanticism begins and ends with boy poets who are parodists, the parabola stretching from Chatterton to Hofmannsthal. Because he is an authentic poet, Hofmannsthal will approach the required renewal, but will prove incapable of carrying it out. He is too at home in the Viennese tradition to muster the saving barbarism of an Eliot or a Joyce. His poems thematically link childhood and depth (the deep eyes of the children in 'Ballade des äusseren Lebens' [Ballad of External Life], the deep well into which the child stares in 'Weltgeheimnis' [World-Mystery]). The famous 'Und' opening of several poems privileges this sense of childhood: the child is one whose discourse always commences with 'And', for he is as yet able only to decorate, or parody, a world that is already essentially given. The idealisation of the child becomes a concomitant of conservatism: his poems begin with 'Und' too. He is a self-confessed latecomer in the 'Abend' of time.

The copula with which the poem opens is, however, also an image of the disconnectedness of things: atomistically, it lays one thing beside another. This is the vision of Lord Chandos. As Hofmannsthal became older, as his reading multiplied, the effects of his allusive pliancy began to be debilitating. The early poems arise through the parodic, mediumistic appropriation of another voice, usually Goethe's. Later, however, the outlines of the works were to be blurred by the multitudes of ghostly parallels flitting through them. The idealisation of the actor reflects admiration of the man able to subordinate his separate selves, retain them in the position of satellites revolving round a point of unity. A work such as *Der Turm* [The Tower] subsides beneath its allusions to *Robert Guiskard, Kejser og Galiler* [Emperor and Galilean], *La Vida es Sueño* [Life is a Dream] itself, and the medieval pageant. Only in *Der Schwierige* (The Difficult One) does he recover the assured tone of his early works. For its protagonist, a phantom from pre-war Vienna, all speech is 'indezent', a belief that tells us several things about Hofmannsthal's own development. The indecency of speech was first revealed to the young Loris by the obscure shamefulness of receiving adoration from men older than himself: it violates the necessity of nature by depriving him of reasons for growing up. This embarrassment –

betrayed by the adoption of pseudonyms – was later reinforced by the withdrawal of the inspirational warrant for his poetry, which infused a further tinge of indecency into his speech. Moreover, for the conservative, all speech without external validation is indecent, and the speaking silence of the tradition is to be preferred. To continue writing once inspiration – the Romantic lodestone – had evaporated was shamefully to woo a departed Muse. The lack of inevitability (of *immanent* authority) of this continued composition made him willing to submit to others' suggestions (for instance, Reinhardt's editorial suggestions). To write for the theatre was to write for the others who expected one to continue writing: writing for others, rather than for the self whose silence one traduces, as the final consequence of conservatism, unwillingness to contemplate a change of role: the fixed hierarchy holds all men in position.

Hofmannsthal's passage from poetic truth to a somnambulistic self, though self-dramatisation, arriving finally at a compromised theatrical speech, was later to be repeated by a poet for whom the question of the relationship with tradition was also crucial: T. S. Eliot. In his work, however, the overturning of the earlier self was a long revolution the complication of which is mirrored in the mixture of authenticity and other-directed and self-delusion in *Four Quartets*. When one compares *The Waste Land* with *Four Quartets* one realises that Eliot's career is as broken as Hofmannsthal's. *Four Quartets* is an almost-success tinged with bad faith, which one could judge as Pauline Kael's judges Bergman's *Cries and Whispers*: 'it feels like a nineteenth-century European masterwork in a twentieth-century form'.[5]

If the 'Und' with which some of Hofmannsthal's poems and many of his individual lines open is an admission that the poem is an embarrassed latecomer on the scene of existence, then the epigraph as used by Eliot is both that and more. The epigraph privileges the past, the withheld origin, and presents the self as already disintegrated: it is a limb that has dropped off the poem that follows it, a drifting remnant of a previous verse. The loss of one part threatens the beginning of a process that will explode the entire self, the entire text, into a whirl of fractured atoms. Eliot's first two collections, however, evince a fear of this imminent explosion of the self. The martinet exercises after Laforgue and Corbière seek to reassert control by substituting stylistic changes for psychic ones.[6] But, although the epigraph is a sign of the partial dissolution of the self, it also halts that dissolution: it keeps the quotation – the voice of the past that menaces the coherence of the present – outside the poem. It asserts a difference between Eliot-as-poet and Eliot-as-critic: it is a signpost to the poem's meaning that also diverts one from that meaning. Placed outside the poem, the quotation establishes a dichotomy between the critic, a man of taste sticking an orienting-label on the poem for the consumer, and the demonic poet. In the early poems 'tradition' is subject to manipulation, a safe kitty to be raided – part of the arsenal of criticism deployed against Sweeney, Burbank and Bleistein. But the moment the quotation is let loose within the poem it undermines the fixity of the self and sends all pronominal relations spinning, for one can no longer determine who is speaking: the language, as it were, manifests itself through the invisible poet, speaks on his behalf. This is what happens in *The Waste Land*.

The opening of *The Waste Land* shares the terror of the self's impending disintegration that is characteristic of the early poems: 'Winter kept us warm'. Spring is feared: 'In the juvescence of the year / Came Christ the tiger'. (Although these two lines stem from 'Gerontion', one recalls Eliot's intention of publishing this poem as a prologue to *The Waste Land*, before Pound dissuaded him.) The self is apparently safely absorbed into the 'we' of tradition. But the absorption is only partial: 'April is the cruellest month' may recall Chaucer's Prologue to *The Canterbury Tales*, but the implications are diametrically opposite. 'The Chair she sat in' summons up *Anthony and Cleopatra*, but only to demonstrate the absence of the colossal grandeur of Shakespeare's play. And 'at my back from time to time I hear' – not Marvell's chariot, but a taxi bearing Sweeney. These ironic contrasts are a commonplace of Eliot criticism, but I list them here in illustration of the extent to which the self that seemed protectively absorbed into tradition (using it as a stick wherewith to beat the present, as the critical cliché has it) is in actuality becoming aware of a disparity between that tradition and experiences whose bitterness distorts the quotations, wreaks vengeance upon them for their inefficacy as charms (*carmina*) against the present. The distorted quotations betray the inappositeness of tradition. As the poem progresses, they will appear with decreasing frequency (an evolution towards the manner of *The Hollow Men*) and the newly distilled 'we' will emerge with a multi-voice that speaks across times, transcending the inadequacies of the Western tradition, in the tremendous sustained aria of 'What the Thunder Said'.

The Waste Land sets up a dialectical interplay between its more dream-like parts and those that are flatter and more rhetorical: the dream-work of the poem shuttles back and forth between these two poles of selfhood. The consequence is an uneven texture which mesmerises one, ringing the changes with such speed one barely has time to pronounce one section more or less successful than another. The constant resort to quotation destroys the reader's attempt to establish an intratextual context – a norm to determine why the poem should be so and not other (Coleridge). The unremitting intertextuality expresses a yearning for the Other. The poem can be seen to move from a largely dream-like (evocative, polysemic and polymorphous–perverse) first section ('The Burial of the Dead') – which shifts into a more conscious and deliberately virtuoso idiom from the séance with Madame Sosostris onwards – into a more rhetorical one, which touches the ground-bass of dream at the beginning of 'The Fire Sermon' before entering the rhetorical mechanical ballet of the typist's seduction, after which it triumphantly reestablishes the links with dream-discourse at the close, in the final two sections. The passages referring to the Grail myth and to the workings of the Tarot are perhaps the weakest in the poem, for they represent a unifying principle engineered onto it by a level of the mind far more superficial than that from which the majority of the first and all the final section float up into awareness. Here one can perceive the seeds of a certain dishonesty towards experience, which foreshadows the dubieties of *Four Quartets* and the disaster of the plays. Thus one cannot maintain a dichotomy between *The Waste Land* as an ore-laden masterpiece and *Four Quartets* sadly diluted by the prosaic business of doctrinal exposition: quite apart from the fact that the Christianity of the *Quartets* is exploratory (and its slides between Anglo-Catholicism and Buddhism are achieved through a technique that owes something to legerdemain), the earlier poem anticipates the lumpiness of the later one. It too juxtaposes deeply personal lines, whose pain and depth stem from their resistance to integration within any system of ideas, with a pseudo-anthropological apparatus whose spinsterly fraudulence invites all the parodies lavished upon it. For in the end there is little to choose between Madame Sosostris and Myra Buttle.

The final section of *The Waste Land* differs from the preceding ones in that its dream-like quality is less a matter of the workings of montage, condensation and displacement, the Freudian principles found in the first three sections, than of the archetypical conceptual landscape of the waste land itself. The poem sheds all the metaphorical meanings that cling to its title to arrive at the immediate unvarnished fact: the land is dry and waste. Paradoxically, this simplicity renders the sequence even more subjectively evocative than the others, which approximate far more closely to the opinion of Western civilisation consciously entertained by Thomas Stearns Eliot. The continual rhythmic repetitions of this section enact both the weariness of the self and the patience with which it is prepared to search. 'In my beginning is my end' could be its motto: for the final section is the poetic awakening repressed by the poem's own middle section, which had smothered the new life (and so lent it time to mature and emerge full-blown) at the behest of the original fear of spring, which had been a fear of movement: of movement away from the European tradition. It is surely significant that Eliot composed this concluding section in a continuous burst whilst recuperating at Lake Leman. A glance at the facsimile of the manuscript shows that it and the first section were the parts of the poem least doctored by Pound, which would lend weight to my thesis that the poem involves a dialectical movement from self into an anti-self, which is then followed by an *Aufhebung*, a transcendence, of the two initial alternatives. The work begins in fear of, and longing for, emotion; graduates into the angular ideal of 'escape from emotion'; and finally reverts to the 'turning loose of emotion' castigated in 'Tradition and the Individual Talent'. Are these perhaps the three voices of poetry isolated by Eliot in a later essay? May they not be Ego, Super Ego and finally Id?

The Waste Land begins and ends with quotations, as do many of its sub-sections (four out of five close with a modified citation). Throughout the poem, quotation is used both as a means of speaking when one's own voice is silent, and as a method for ending the potentially endless series of associations generated by the isolated mind (thus Eliot resolves the problem of how to control associations, to which Hofmannsthal could find no solution). The garrulous solipsism of the bottled Sibyl or of Gerontion is curtailed by the dissolution of the individual into the collectivity that silences his speech. Thus a reference to Baudelaire concludes the first section, a remark by Ophelia in her madness ends the second, and the collocation of St Augustine and Buddha closes the third. The quotations are brief associative bridges spread by the mind across the abysses of trauma, talismans against a private darkness. They are more or less absent from the final section, for at this point the self feels sufficiently robust to proceed without them. Up to the final section a two-way interrogation of context by quotation and quotation by context is at work: the citation either has to be altered to reflect its textual environment or it condemns that environment. The author feels pain as his experience edges him out of the security of the quotation, relief as he slides into its cover at the end of a section. The dense mass of quotations in the final ten lines of the poem however is not so much a gliding into the harbour of tradition as the transcendence of tradition. Tradition is revealed to be the cocoon from which the individual finally emerges: the last lines stretch out helpless arms to him as he vanishes among the stars like Chaucer's Troilus. All the quotations could have spoken on the poet's behalf, but the fragments he has shored against his ruin prove superfluous. They are not used, are not transformed by the absorbent individual, but quoted correctly. They are discarded. Eliot rejoices not to have needed to don these unnecessary masks.

The problem of who it is that is speaking, of the nature of the authorial 'voice' (and the additional problem of what happens to a 'voice' when it becomes a series of black marks on paper that are no longer read out loud) is a fundamental one in late-nineteenth- and early-twentieth-century poetics and comes to a head in the dramatic monologue. Who are Bishop Blougram, Prufrock and Crazy Jane? One asks because the poems in which they appear are repeatedly fractured by the way an authoritative and far more memorable (authorial?) voice upsets the smooth flow of the characterisation. This uneven texture is symptomatic of the growing tension in the period between verse (discursive and produced to order) and 'poetry' (the absolute image or Symbol) – a tension that finally undermined the illusory Victorian consensus and made a laughing-stock of the institution of Poet Laureate. The breaks in tone prompt one to ask, does a particular set of words come from the 'author' or from the 'character'? The question may seem naïve, and in drama proper would indeed be so: it is obvious that Shakespeare is not 'Hamlet'. But a dramatic monologue forgoes the explicit interpersonal interplay that disperses a dramatist's ideas and prevents us from 'identifying' him with any one of his characters. Instead, the addressee is absorbed into the text (dramatic monologue as a model of poetry without an audience, in the Symbolist ivory tower) – thus Bishop Blougram rhetorically propounds objections on behalf of his dumb interlocutor and then gives his pat answer. The questions have been planted by the Absolute Ego. The problem is compounded by the force of Nietzsche's influence: Nietzsche both dons masks, treating style itself as a persona, *and* reintroduces into philosophy the argument *ad hominem*. At one and the same time he supports and denies the substantial unity of self and language, the possibility of *expressivity*.

The late Victorians and early modernists, feeling the accumulated weight of past styles and fearing their own possible inability to find a way from them to the new, relieved themselves of some of the weight of responsibility for their own words by carefully sheathing them in the inverted commas of the dramatic monologue. Should their works, for instance, happen to lack conviction of tone, then this failing could be explained as a means of characterising the deliverer of the monologue: the defective poem could drop into the safety net of the novelistic. (It is also possible that writers incorporated novelistic elements into poems in order to recapture a poetic readership that was beginning to vanish.) The works of this period hung suspended between an exploded drama (for Romanticism had internalised drama), the sole remnant of which was the isolated voice, and Imagism, in which objects invade the vacuum caused by the erosion of the self in the modern city. The adoption of the dramatic monologue generally inclines the reader to interpret any passages of unexpected intensity as originating in the poet. Thus the passage beginning 'Our interest's on the dangerous edge of things' is 'Browning' rather than Blougram; that beginning 'The fog that rubs its back', 'Eliot' rather than Prufrock. These passages affect one as akin to Arnoldian touchstones. They beg to be quoted, and usually are. And so the personality the poet appears to have sacrificed through mimicry reasserts itself in the exhibitionism of the quotable line, the conceit. This corresponds to the basic paradox of exhibitionism: by exhibiting a part of oneself as if it could stand for the whole, as if it enjoyed metonymic status, one in fact amputates it, so it ceases to represent one at all. The poem acquires a split personality. The gap between the poetic and 'the real', which had loomed large in the *fin de siècle* disputes between Symbolism and Naturalism, and which poets had sought to overcome by replacing the diction of Pre-Raphaelite Princesses with the speech of real men, reiterates itself in the disparity between the long-windedness of the characterisation (its *prosaic* quality) and the forcefulness of occasional passages. In 'Prufrock', for instance, one can establish a general distinction between the deliberately trivial remarks about drawing-rooms, which are in the 'Prufrock' voice, and the murderously intent ones, which belong to 'Eliot'. The poem hits alternate 'Prufrock' and 'Eliot' notes. Faced with the sort of divided self found in 'Prufrock', Hofmannsthal adopted the facile, ready-made solution and turned to drama. Eliot, however, achieves a genuine solution, though it did not arrive until *The Waste Land*. For *The Waste Land* retains monologue whilst dispensing with characterisation, for its primary 'character', Tiresias, is disembodied, multi-voiced, a bisexual anti-character: his monologue is also polylogue, to adopt Kristeva's term. The waste land is coursed by the sands of the eroded subject, worn down by modern city conditions, industrialisation and a generally growing impersonality. It seems somehow appropriate that Eliot should have worked at this time as a clerk with city feet tramping incessantly close above his head.

4 Nature's Double Name: the Poetry of Bolesław Leśmian

> Property was thus appall'd,
> That the self was not the same;
> Single nature's double name,
> Neither two nor one was call'd.
>
> (Shakespeare, 'The Phoenix and the Turtle')
>
> Annihilating all that's made
> To a green thought in a green shade.
>
> (Marvell, 'The Garden')

INTRODUCTORY NOTE

The title of this chapter may appear to be as enigmatic and obscure as the poem from which it is drawn. Nevertheless, it gnomically indicates the cardinal features of the poetry of Bolesław Leśmian, the greatest of twentieth-century Polish poets, and one of the greatest of modern European ones. It encapsulates the *Leitmotiv* of his verse: the relationship between nature and mankind. For Leśmian, mankind, which constituted itself through secession from nature, is perpetually on the verge of being seduced back into it. The song of the 'demon of Green' weans man away from culture – though so long as he uses language, so long as he remains a poet, he refuses to abandon culture. Observed by Nature, man is self-consciously exhibitionist even when most apparently alone: in his moments of greatest solitude, moreover, he begins to make over parts of his being to Nature in the form of anthropomorphic projections. Nature employs these projections as *fata morgana* to draw

99

humanity back into original chaos. Leśmian's poems acknowledge the charm of the spell and the ruinousness of succumbing to it: he is an Odysseus, roped tightly to the mast of poetry, driven to the verge of madness by the seductive cadences of Nature's incantations. The basic tension in his work is between nature and the name. Between nature and the *double name*: for his own name, Leśmian, contains the Polish words for 'forest' (*las*) and 'the name' (*miano*), so designating the point of departure of his work, and is in any case in part a pseudonym.

'Bolesław Leśmian' was born in Warsaw about 1878, named Bolesław *Lesman*. He attended school and university in Kiev, where he participated enthusiastically in the beleaguered cultural life of the local Polish community: during a public recital of Mickiewicz's patriotic and Faustian 'Great Improvisation', he allowed that enthusiasm to spill over into a personal improvisation that earned him a prison sentence from the Tsarist authorities, though this was commuted shortly thereafter. The richness of the surrounding Ukrainian landscape impressed upon him the hypnotic, stupefying quality of Green, which was later to provide the background for the free play of his private mythology. At the turn of the century he moved to Warsaw and then travelled abroad, spending some time in Paris, where he married. An anecdote from this period of his life reveals the extent of his legendary impracticality: unable to wash his own linen, he was in the habit of disposing of it discreetly by wrapping it in brown paper and depositing it on park benches. As he scuttled away, he was often dogged by solicitous strangers anxious to remind him that he had forgotten his parcel. When he made his literary debut in the Young Poland (Secessionist) periodical *Chimera* he was unfortunate to be linked forever in the public mind with the programme of that magazine by a violent attack on its aestheticism delivered by Stanisław Brzozowski (a key figure in the Polish socialist movement whose views are ably summarised in Kołakowski's *Main Currents of Marxism*), who referred to Leśmian by name. His first volume of poems more or less reflects the *Chimera* programme, but his second – 'Łąka' (The Meadow) – evinced an imagistic compression and a neologistic vitality that are clearly alien to the pallid landscapes of Young Poland, the ideas of which it 'quoted' in order to alienate them. Although his distinction was recognised by the finest of the Polish inter-war intellectuals, such as the critic and novelist Karol Irzykowski, the subtle dialectics of his relations with an outmoded tradition were widely misconstrued and interpreted as a sign that he was a spent force. The successful cabaret poets of 'Skamander' simply diluted his techniques: their leader Tuwim would kiss Leśmian's hand, but did little to dispel the misconceptions surrounding his work. Thus, when a plebiscite was held among intellectuals in 1931 to determine who should be elected to the Polish Academy of Literature, Leśmian occupied the forty-sixth place – barely ahead of that well-known man of letters Józef Piłsudski. In 1933 matters improved when some friends managed to engineer his nomination to a new Academy, but this was offset by his catastrophic obligation to repay vast sums embezzled by one of his subordinates. His friends – Dr Dora Lebenthal, his devoted mistress, pre-eminent among them – made great sacrifices to help him, but the shock damaged his health, whilst as a Jew he suffered under the increasing anti-semitism of Poland in the thirties. He died in November 1937: lucky in a sense to escape by two years an incarnation of non-existence that outdid even the catastrophes summoned up by his prescient imagination. Only in recent years has Leśmian received the recognition due him as the greatest of twentieth-century Polish poets, although in the thirties he had the support of, among others, Bruno Schulz – whom he greatly influenced, and who knew many of his ballads by heart. Artur Sandauer has remarked that Leśmian's style is 'deliberately slapdash', but in fact he is a writer not of one style but of two: a nonchalantly neologistic fantasy style, and an exact style that carefully traces the contours of nature. His private mythology is a careful miscegenation of Slavonic folk lore and the aesthetics of negation. This duality nourishes his concern with doubles, mirrors and paradoxes, and grants him the fascinating, contradictory position of a popular Symbolist poet.

The Polish secondary literature on Leśmian's work teems with references to the polysemic nature of his poetry, but no analysis I have encountered ever proposes more than one meaning. One is tempted to say that such remarks merely pay lip service to works they simultaneously serve to repress. Polysemia constitutes a Romantic attack on the notion of authority. Too many critics, however, eager to shore up their own authority, suppress the dialectic of Leśmian's work and refuse to see it as an hallucinatory synthesis of diverse meanings and poetic movements, deemed incompatible elsewhere: a synthesis dictated by the imperative of charity that governs his work. Only a self-contradictory criticism can read him without repressing the vital diversity of his work. A good example of the polysemia of his images is that of 'the non-existent girl'. I can only mention some of the causes of her non-existence: the pregnant, mythical quality of her image provokes a strictly interminable reflection. She is the poet's anima or other; she is merely an imaginary projection, so that in ascribing a fictional character to her the verse hints at its own epistomology; unseen in the darkness in which the act of love conventionally occurs, she is everyone – and hence no one; she is the silent, idealised peasant girl of Young Polish iconography, and her taciturnity renders her no more than a screen for the poet's projections (a waxdoll upon whom his jealous vengeance on other women is wrought); she represents the impossible synthesis of Leśmian's wife and his mistress; and she is also – as Sandauer has suggested – the semi-real lover conjured by the onanist. Among other things, the essays below seek to examine some of her other meanings.

Finally, a word about my versions of Leśmian's poems – mere pallid shadows of the originals, their metrical feet sadly crippled. Leśmian's work is highly resistant to translation, not just because of its neologisms, but also because Polish critics have still not determined which words are archaisms, which neologisms, and which descend from peasant dialect. My versions are doubtless often merely 'hints and guesses'. But, if, in their deformity, they reflect some of the brilliance of an art whose greatness – like that of Kafka – involves viewing itself as deformed, they will at least have fulfilled some purpose.

TRANSFORMATIONS OF THE MIRROR IN THE POETRY OF LEŚMIAN

Figures in the theatre of the soul

W marzeniu moim puste na przestrzał komnaty,
Wbrew nocy rozjarzone spiekotą południa.
Cisza. W lustrach się dwoją i troją złe kwiaty.
Bije północ. Snu próżnia nagle się zaludnia.

Idą z mroku, na oślep, śpiesznie i kolejno,
Postacie, co swym chodem i bladością czynną,
Przypominają kogoś, co zmarł w beznadziejną
Noc, gdy wszystko, prócz niego, umrzeć było winno.

Czarną na białych płaszczach znakowane kresą,
Twarz ode mnie ku snowi odwracają pilnie,
Stąpając po podłodze wiernie i usilnie,
Jakby chciały pokazać, że są tym, czym nie są . . .

I nie tylko zwierciadła, ale ślepe sprzęty
Odbijają niejasno i niecałkowicie
Owych ludzi, co idąc z odmętów w odmęty,

Chętnie starliby ślad swój i swoje odbicie . . .

Wiem, że boją się chwili, która zewsząd kroczy,
A w której dłoń wyciągnę i pierwszego z brzegu
Wytrącę, jak sen jeden z reszty snów szeregu,
I zapytam o imię i zajrzę mu w oczy!

Ale który to będzie – nikt nie wie, nie zgadnie . . .
Przechodzą, los nieznany tłumiąc w płaszczów bieli.
A ja dłoń opóźnioną wyciągam bezradnie
Do tych, co już mijają i już przeminęli . . .

(In my dream, at both ends empty chambers are open.
Though it's night, they are sultry with heat of the noon.
Silence. In the mirrors evil flowers multiply.
Midnight strikes. Sleep's vacuum is peopled suddenly.

They steal from the shadows – blind, quick and successive –
Figures whose active pallor and gait
Recall a person who died in a hopeless
Night, when all should have died except him.

Their white garments bearing a black mark's insignia,
Their deliberate faces avert towards dream,
Moving across floors with a faith and a purpose
As if wishing to show they are what they are not . . .

And not only the mirrors, also the blind fittings
Reflect in a fashion vague and incomplete
These people who pass from abyss to abysses
And would like to erase their reflections and traces . . .

I know that they fear the moment closing in now
When my palm will reach outward and displace the first
From the ledge, the first dream in a dreamlike succession,
And ask him his name and gaze into his eyes!

But which it will be – no one knows or divines it . . .
They pass, their fates muffled up in coats of white.
And helplessly I extend my late hand now
To those who are passing, have already gone . . .)

In many of Leśmian's verses, the creator strives to hide himself. One may feel that he wishes to lose himself in what he creates. In 'Bałwan ze śniegu' (The Snowman), we read of the snowman, 'Ktoś go ulepił z tego śniegu, / Co mu na imię: biel i nic . . . ' (Someone formed him of this snow; / What can his name be? Nothing and white . . .),[1] and this someone is just as vague and just as much nothing as the snowman. It is later stated that the snowman is a god, but the withholding both of the reason for his divinity and of the identity of his creator engenders a silence, a namelessness, as oppressive as that of the snow. When one recalls that the figures in 'Postacie' (Figures), the poem quoted above, have the whiteness of the snowman – and are, even as he is, marked with a slash of darkness (in his case, this is a black stick piercing his side, like a Christ figure) – one may feel that the melancholy of Leśmian's verse is that of a man sensing God slip out of his reach. The invisible creator who forms an image with his own negative properties resembles the tautologically self-affirming creatures of many of Leśmian's other verses. These creatures personify momentary states: dusk (*zmierzch*) becomes a personality ('Zmierzchuń') and lives for the duration of the sunset. The unknown figures of 'Postacie' are like the mystery in Lesmian's 'Z rozmyslań o Bergsonie' (Thoughts on Bergson) 'whose face is unlike any human face'.[2] If this is so, then the narrator may fear to look into their faces as much as they fear to gaze on his. In 'Postacie' – Leśmian's programmatic introduction to a series of poems about fantasy figures, misfits banished out of existence to the realm of dreams – the figures turn away from the narrator as an expression of his own willingness to dispense with the sight of his own face: when he turns them back-to-front, he does the same for himself, lest he perceive in their deformity the image of his own. (Leśmian's own diminutive stature was often mocked – especially when conjoined with the daring and aggressiveness of his verse.) The effect is disquietingly akin to Magritte's painting of a man staring at the back of his own head in a mirror. He becomes his own fantasy image. The poem expresses the pain of a creator who lends his creatures autonomy in order to enable them to share his own freedom – and is then rejected by them. This is one aspect of God's inability to master a self-willed creation in other poems by Leśmian. Leśmian's figures remind him of a person who died in a hopeless night: their emergence reflects the death and rebirth of the narrator of the poem himself. Their coming into being is a dialectical event. Canetti has shown how the survivor imagines a crowd of the newly dead in order to relish the fact of his own survival, which thus acquires the sense of a victory.[3] Leśmian goes further and reaches the point at which the individual simultaneously destroys the world (it is midnight, all things are expected to die) and imaginatively prolongs the destroyed lives of its inhabitants. The figures are the dead, risen from the grave at his command. The survivor's isolation forces upon him a theatricalisation of the self: he is himself the crowd he has swallowed – alienated from humanity through having absorbed the whole of humanity. But for action to begin again in this solitude, for life to persist, the narrator must reinstate the otherness he has abolished. As he does so, the figures assume autonomous life and forsake him, turning his survival into a Pyrrhic victory.

For Leśmian, the soul is a theatre. 'Internal dialectic, the habit of thinking in opposites, was held by the Romantics to be the very germ of drama.'[4] Leśmian shares this belief. But he also shares the Romantic belief in the possibility of a fusion of spectator and actor, a momentary mingling of the opposites. In 'Tajemnicy widza i widowiska' (The Mystery of Spectator and Spectacle) he writes,

> The reader of Werther himself becomes Werther for a moment. Were that moment to be extended for months or even whole years, play would turn into responsible action; free will – into enforced necessity; art – into nature; and the failed actor – into a real suicide. Woe to those who do not know how to play![5]

Here 'Werther' has the same status as one of Leśmian's own figures. On the one hand, there is the Romantic fetishisation of the hero, who vicariously extends the bounds of the reader's experience; but on the other there is a commonsensical limitation of the degree of identification (identification should only be momentary). The actor's relationship with the public duplicates that between creature and creator in 'Postacie'. Thus,

> when Hamlet appears on the stage, in the darkness of the auditorium all hearts beat with the single synchronised emotion of a thousand Hamlets. The theatre becomes the arena of miraculous metamorphoses. . . . Stage and auditorium are suddenly detached from their moorings and exchange places, their fixity hitherto having been merely an illusion.[6]

The actor who faces the public is facing himself, split into a unanimous crowd: the underlying metaphor is that of a (splintered) mirror.

The pillar of light that accompanies the actor as he moves across the

illusionist stage – the figure crossing the floorboards in 'Postacie' –
lapped in darkness, renders him the fetish form of the drama: the part
that stands for the whole. Freud's essay on fetishism has broached the
possibility of identifying the fetish with a light that looks. It is thus akin
to a mirror.

> The fetish deriving from earliest childhood has to be read in English
> rather than German, the 'Glanz auf der Nase' [shine on the nose] was
> actually a 'Blick auf die Nase' [a look at the nose], and so the nose was
> the fetish which – whenever he wanted to – he endowed with a sheen
> invisible to others.[7]

Freud omits to add that in the case he is examining the fetish is also the
foreign language, a special hidden possession like the penis it represents.
Perhaps Freud overlooks this linguistic aspect of fetishism because his
own mode of analysis fetishises English ('the language of Shakespeare',
and Freud's own secret possession) in a similar fashion. The fetishist,
Freud argues, denies the female's lack of a penis in order to assuage his
own fear of possible castration: if one sex has lost its penis, so may the
other. Leśmian denies the demonic power of woman's otherness by
placing himself before the mirror, redefining otherness as a perverse
restatement of selfhood. The neologisms that dot his poems are fetish
words that seek to restore the penis, the power of fecundation, to the
castrated body of language: to the Polish language emasculated by the
partitioning powers, and to the poetic language of Romanticism,
cheapened by a century's blind repetitions.

Installed in a room, a mirror creates the illusion of extra light and
space. At the turn of the century the poetic image of the mirror stands for
the alternative 'world of art', which expands one's consciousness when
one fears that one's mind has become a trap. It is thus possible to see the
European Symbolist preoccupation with mirrors as a strategy to
prolong the fulfilment of the urge to colonise – to escape the confines of
one's own consciousness – once colonial initiatives had penetrated
virtually all the available lands. Further development can only occur in
the negative space of the imagination. In a sealed room, the mirror
creates the last illusion of a window open onto exotic otherness.

When Leśmian's apparently tautological beings affirm themselves
and their roles, they engage in a mirroring: tautology is a picture of one
word mirrored by another. When the barn barns,[8] spring springs,[9] and
the stream streams,[10] they are both performing an action and marking
time, imprisoned in the straitjackets of their own limited being. Their

affirmation of their own *haeccitas*, like that of Gerard Manley Hopkins, has something of the unalterable sterility of the priest (can one who is 'Manley' ever become one with woman?). The lives of these beings are both condemned to obviousness and totally unpredictable: spring 'springs', i.e. behaves as we expect spring to behave, but this may only seem to be so, the illusive result of the fact that linguistic codes require spring to be spring. Objects imitate the reactions expected of them by mankind to remain enigmatically apart behind an inscrutable mask. It may be that the net of language has garnered only its own tautological emptiness. Conversely, it may be that objects frantically deny the possibility of their own non-identity or change because change (in the form of industrialisation, for instance) spells destruction. They use tautology to strengthen their own uniqueness, but this defensive tactic also endangers them by cutting them off from the possible solidarity of other creatures. Self-affirmation becomes a whistling in the dark.

Violence and montage: satirical animals

The creator of 'Postacie' is both near to and far removed from his creatures (as is Leśmian's God: see the analysis of 'Urszula Kochanowska' in the next sub-section). This reflects the co-existence of theatre and *cinema* during this period, which is both an opposition and a confluence, as the Meyerholdian total art-work seeks to unify the arts under the aegis of theatre in order to defeat the cinema with its own weapons. If the figures turn their backs on their creator, it is to secede from the stage to the cinema screen. Benjamin writes that

> the feeling of strangeness that overcomes the actor before the camera, as Pirandello describes it, is basically of the same kind as the estrangement felt before one's image in the mirror. But now the reflected image has become separable, transportable. And where is it transported? Before the public.[11]

Leśmian's figures leave his presence just as the stage actor walks out of the theatre to become a passer-by, a potential film actor.

In 'Postacie' even the fittings are said to reflect the figures: this participation by objects is like 'the interaction of spirit and matter' noticed as characteristic of film by Karol Irzykowski.[12] As they dematerialise, objects leave traces (death masks) on the road by which they depart. It is likely that the notion of realistic mimesis gained such currency and achieved so hallucinatory an exactitude in the nineteenth century because art was perceived as the mirror that would preserve a photograph of vanishing nature. The mimesis participated in the destruction of nature by only permitting its continued existence within the gilded cage of an artefact, the art-work. The camera removed surface from its intimacy with depth just as mechanised agriculture and deforestation were removing the topsoil – and as the growing system of the world economy linked areas that had nothing in common. Realistic description eats reality away in the name of a blank potentiality. The process is re-enacted in the following poem, 'Przyśpiew' (Refrain):

> Wkosmacona w kwiat płytki,
> Łeb ująwszy w dwie chwytki,
> Pszczoła, nim ją porwie lot,
> W słoncu myje się, jak kot –
> I do naga z odwianych skrzydeł się rozbiera.
> Lada powiew – lada
> Płoszy wróbli stada,
> I psi rumian kreśli cień
> Ten sam niemal co dzień w dzień,
> I żuk brzuchem w niebiosy złudnie zaumiera.
>
> Staw obłokiem żegluje,
> Młyn mu kołem ojcuje,
> Spoza lasu szumi las,
> Spoza czasu szemrze czas,
> Droga roztopolona śni się nie do końca . . .
> Utrudą żałobny
> Koń, dozgonnie ksobny,
> Zaniepatrzył się na wóz,
> Przymknął oczy w cieniu brzóz,
> I krótkim kaszlem dudni, jak kobza, do słońca.
>
> Niech się dłuży cień ławy,
> Niech wypoczną w nim trawy!
> Z łbem na łapie chudy pies
> Śpi po łapy owej kres,
> Jakby na niej się świata kończyło bezdroże.
> Ziele w jarze, ziele!
> Skąd twoje wesele?

Niech się wzmaga wiew i żar,
Niech się wzmaga bór i jar,
I to wszystko, co jeszcze, prócz nich, stać się może!

(Furred into a shallow flower,
Head held in a double grip,
The bee, before it's seized by flight,
Washes in the sun, like cats –
Strips off its unwound wings to nakedness.
Any breeze now – any –
Would fright the gangs of sparrows,
And the dog flower draws the shade
Nearly the same shape every day,
And the dung beetle on its back plays dead.

The pond drifts with a cloud,
Its father the mill's wheel;
Forests murmur outside forest,
Time now whispers outside time –
The road strung out with poplars dreams, reaches no end . . .
Fatigue-melancholy,
The horse, forever harnessed,
Numbed unlooking at a cart,
Shut its eyes in the birch shade –
Its short cough drones like bagpipes at the sun.

Let the bench's shadow lengthen
For the grasses to relax in!
Head on paws, the skinny dog
Sleeps at paws' end like a log –
As if the trackless earth stopped at that point!
Herbs in ravines, O herbs!
Whence all your bridal mirth?
Let the heat and wind increase,
Forest and ravine increase,
Along with all things else which yet may be!)

The first stanza of this poem appears purely realistic, and although there are anthropomorphic metaphors (and an initial neologism), they give the scene a playful frisson, without displacing the surface reality. In the second stanza, however, ambiguous details begin to slip their contextual moorings: 'Młyn mu kołem ojcuje' suggests that the mill wheel is both accompanying the pond and the cloud like a guardian, and as it were fathering them, printing them out; 'Droga roztopolona śni się nie do końca . . . ' expresses the will to freedom of the open road, and also hints at a repression, whilst the pregnancy of the phrase tempts us to lift it out for meditation; similarly, the magical 'Spoza lasem szumi las', which suggests that the self-mirroring forest is also self-displacing (the conjunction with the verb 'roztopolić' in the next line reinforces the suggestion that self-propagation and destruction are one: the *roz-* prefix suggests both a dispersal and a destruction). The moving forest is as enigmatic as that in *Macbeth*. The movement of the whole poem is summed up in the centrally placed neologism 'zaniepatrzył się', a coinage that brings to mind an intensity of staring at an object that finally prevents one perceiving it, just as a word long-pondered dissolves into incomprehensibility. For by the end the invisible world has broken through the surface of the visible one: the last line intimates a nameless becoming akin to the abstract storm wind of the *durée* in Bergson. It both reinforces the pigments of being and washes them away. As when one repeatedly blows up a photograph, the real scene finally becomes a white potentiality sailing between archipelagoes of separate dots.

The process whereby the invisible rises from below the surface of reality and then displaces it is a variety of montage. It is thus that the cat emerges from under the bee in the first stanza of 'Przyśpiew', and that an abstract potentiality finally comes to wash over the entire pastoral scene of the poem. It is hardly surprising that Leśmian, domiciled in Kiev, should have employed methods reminiscent of the Russian cinema of the twenties. In his work, as in that of the Russian directors, montage has two aspects: a satirical one, and a mystical one. When Eisenstein juxtaposes Kerensky with a peacock, this is the satirical aspect of montage. Montage subverts the tastes of the average citizen, who, as Leśmian remarks in an essay on the theatre, 'dislikes rare and unexpected occurrences'.[13] Montage expresses the Revolution and is collectivist and reductivist: it demonstrates how little the human individual is worth by sweeping him away after a split second, as crowds (on a formal level: the inexorable torrent of a film's images) engulf him and/or infect him with 'the herd instinct'. In a silent film, man becomes bestial, for he is deprived of language, the one attribute that raised him above the animals: as his mouth moves and emits no sound, the result is frightening and grotesque. Montage reduces man to the level of the animals – or of ephemera, mere momentary epiphenomena in the unfolding of the wave of events. Montage thus effects a qualitative change. And here it loses its satirical function and becomes mystical. Eisenstein often likened the birth of an idea out of the collision of two images to the development of an Hegelian triad: it is mystical to assume that disconnected images can generate a concept, or enlightenment stem from pictures of the mystified world. The mysticism is the means whereby the animal is identified with – and allowed to humanise – the human: in *Strike*, Eisenstein cross-cuts between dying workers and beasts in a slaughterhouse. The cut both represses the fact of human death – this is 'only happening to animals' – and forges a solidarity between all the victims of creation. As the bee discards its clothes like a human being, ' "the dignity of man" – that arch-bourgeois concept – gives way to the healing recollection that man was fashioned in the image of the animals'.[14] When a grub makes love to the forlorn Jadwiga[15] in another of Leśmian's poems, the unity of man and beast is consummated.

Forms of the self-critical grotesque

The Grotesque is generally a means of making alienated and advanced elements socially acceptable.[16]

Leśmian's work is full of images that can only be termed 'grotesque': take, for instance, the events of such a poem as 'Piła' (The Saw), in which a demonic woman employs her saw-like spine to chop into segments the ploughboy to whom she makes love. But Leśmian's poems do not so much render the alienated elements of radical terror grotesque, in order to make them acceptable, as show how those elements stick in the throat of the art that tries to swallow them. In the grotesque, art grins and bears suffering, and the grin becomes a leer; in Leśmian's work, the suffering twists the grin into a grimace. His verse was not grotesque enough to win him popularity in his own lifetime (the popularity of Morgenstern's *Galgenlieder* [Gallows Songs], for instance). If his poems feed on images of terror, the terror remains visible, half-submerged, through the poem, whose shape it alters as a recently ingested animal distends the skin of a boa constrictor. In Leśmian's poems, two bodies occupy the space allocated to one.

According to Bakhtin, however, it is this very straining identity of two bodies that is characteristic of the Grotesque. Perhaps one should say that Leśmian's images are Grotesques in Bakhtin's sense, though not in

Adorno's. For Bakhtin, the Grotesque figure is so often overblown (as in the paintings of Stanley Spencer) because it contains more than one person: 'it represents two bodies inside one'.[17] This swollen body can occasion either joy or nightmare. Nightmare, for it is the looming human tower (the family or the mother), the cannibalistic womb that swallows up – refuses to release, give birth to – the individual. And joy: joy in the sense of unity with the other, at the way identity proves indestructible, and is even fortified by the otherness it has absorbed. The individual fears the Grotesque as the agent of a hostile totality that seeks to subsume him under a larger system. But the individual-as-member-of-a-crowd sees it as the personification of the crowd, as the image of the metonymic Father King or Matriarchal Queen who can refer to him- or herself as the nation (in Shakespeare, the King of France is 'France'). The two conjoined bodies Bakhtin refers to are the inseparable pairs who wander through Leśmian's poetry: 'Świdryga i Midryga', or the two Matthews (these are figures before a mirror), or the twelve brothers of 'Dziewczyna' (The Girl) (figures in a hall of mirrors). Bakhtin has criticised Wolfgang Kayser's theory of the Grotesque as nightmare:

> the Existentialist tone of this statement [by Kayser] asserts above all the existence of a total opposition between life and death. Such an opposition is completely foreign to the system of the Grotesque. In this system, death does not represent a negation of life (in its Grotesque sense of the entire body of the people). According to this system, death enters into life as an indispensable necessity, as the precondition of its endless renewal and rejuvenation.[18]

The Grotesque can be said to reconcile life with death because the collectivity of the nation includes all its inhabitants, dead or alive: the living are merely modulations, echoes, of the genes of the dead, and are not qualitatively different. Kayser, however, views the Grotesque from the standpoint of the individual: he reads as negative what Bakhtin views as positive. Bakhtin can adopt this positive view because 'the category of the subject was far less firmly rooted in an essentially pre-bourgeois Russia than it was in the West'.[19] Writing in Poland, but affiliated to Russian Symbolism, Leśmian is suspended between opposed traditions: democratic individualism and autocratic collectivism. Hence in his work the Grotesque acquires the self-critical ambiguity of a confrontation between Kayser and Bakhtin – between the individual's rights and those of the group. His neologisms – words that are not words, words of self-negation – dramatise this duality: the neologism contains two semantic bodies within the space of one. Leśmian's first published verses were in Russian – but they are of far less distinction than his Polish verse. Perhaps that is why the 'Polish' Leśmian chronicles the defeat of the 'Russian' Leśmian (of the Russian Symbolism at the heart of his work). (It is surely this defeat that his verse enacts – and not, as Sandauer has argued, the 'defeat' of Polish Symbolism by such movements as 'Skamander', which can in fact only be said to have *succeeded* it.) He may borrow from Russian folk lore the image of the holy beggar, consecrated by his sufferings, as both Artur Sandauer and Rochelle Stone have pointed out, but he does so in order to emphasise the reality of the beggar's earthly suffering rather than the transcendental privilege of which it is the signifier. This continual ambivalence *vis-à-vis* his own iconography causes his verse to destroy itself in its moment of birth. Like the Grotesque, it refuses to distinguish between its own life and death. (Similarly, the neologism refuses to distinguish between the life and the death of *language*.) But unlike Bakhtin it hesitates to place an optimistic gloss on the erasure of this border. One poem that insists strongly upon the simultaneous identity and non-identity of life and death, of heaven and earth, is 'Urszula Kochanowska':

Gdy po śmierci w niebiosów przybyłam pustkowie,
Bóg długo patrzał na mnie i głaskał po głowie.

'Zbliż się do mnie, Urszulo! Poglądasz jak żywa . . .
Zrobię dla cię co zechcesz, byś była szczęsliwa.'

'Zrób tak, Boże – szepnąłam – by w nieb Twoich krasie
Wszystko było tak samo, jak tam – w Czarnolasie!' –

I umilkłam zlękniona i oczy unoszę
By zbadać, czy się gniewa, że Go o to proszę.

Usmiechnął się i skinął – i wnet z Bożej łaski
Powstał dom kubek w kubek, jak nasz – Czarnolaski.

I sprzęty i donice rozkwitłego ziela
Tak podobno, aż oczom straszno od wesela!

I rzekł: 'Oto są – sprzęty, a oto – donice.
Tylko patrzeć, jak przyjdą stęsknieni rodzice!

I ja, gdy gwiazdy poukładam w niebie,
Nieraz do dzrwi zapukam, by odwiedzić ciebie!'

I odszedł, a ja zaraz krzątam się, jak mogę –
Więc nakrywam do stołu, omiatam podłogę –

I w suknię najróżowszą ciało przyoblekam
I sen wieczny odpędzam – i czuwam – i czekam . . .

Już świt pierwszą roznietą złoci się po ścianie,
Gdy właśnie słychac kroki i do drzwi pukanie . . .

Więc zrywam się i biegnę! Wiatr po niebie dzwoni!
Serce w piersi zamiera . . . Nie! To – Bóg, nie oni!

(When I arrived in Heaven's wilderness when I was dead,
God took a long look at me and He stroked me on the head.

Come closer to me, Ursula! You look the old live you . . .
Whatever you may wish for to be happy, that I'll do.

Make things – o Lord – I whispered – so that in Heaven's place
It's just the same as there – in Czarnolas.

But fearfully I halted there; my eyes looked up to test
He felt no anger over my request.

He smiled and gave the sign – and by God's grace
A house rose – brick for brick like Czarnolas.

Its furniture, its flowerpots, its herbs:
So much the same, my joy could know no words.

He said: Look – flowerpots and furniture.
Just wait and see, your yearning parents wil! be here.

And I, each time I rearrange the stars,
Will sometimes knock to see just how you are.

He left; I did my best to tidy up –
I cleaned the floor and put out all the cups –

My body in a bright pink skirt I drape –
Shake off eternal rest – and sit and wait –

The kindlings of the dawn are on the walls,
And I hear footsteps, knocking at the door . . .

I jump up. All across the skies winds toll.
My heart stops . . . No! It's God – not them at all.

For Ursula, the dead daughter of the great sixteenth-century poet
Kochanowski, the ideal future would be a regression to, and mirror of,
the past. Leśmian sympathises with her passionate attachment to the
things of this world. But the ambiguity of the mirror, and of repetition in
general, leads the poem from the fairy-tale simplicity of the beginning to
the intensely dramatic, shocking and enigmatically ambivalent close.
This ending is a variety of second death, which initiates Ursula into the
true meaning of her first death: the winds toll a knell, her heart stops, and
an unbridgeable gap yawns between the dead and the living (her
parents). What variety of God is Ursula dealing with there? The fact that
he appears instead of her awaited parents does not necessarily mean the
reunion she requested has been refused: after all, earlier on he was
willing to re-create the parental home. This God may be absent-minded,
he may actually intend to fulfil his promise, or he may be playing a
metaphysical joke upon Ursula: for indeed her parents will soon join
her – all flesh is dust – and, since in Heaven time is without meaning,
their coming may seem instantaneous. It is also possible, of course, that
God's control of the universe is only a partial one. As the poem
proceeds, the narrative distance created by the past tense melts away, the
repeated copula adds immediacy, and the poem moves from experiences
that are subject to control, open to narration, to those that sink under
the drift of silence. And drift is the right word: part of the horror and
hysteria of the poem lies in one's inability to put one's finger on the
moment at which things start going wrong (there may not even be such a
moment: according to this reading, the ending would not be a climax of
shock but a provocative anti-climax). Retrospectively, even the simplicity of the opening is booby-trapped. The cause of the horror is
suppressed, suggesting either that Ursula has over-reacted, or that the
impossibility of establishing causal and temporal relations is itself a
source of horror. For how many times has Ursula lived and died? If
Czarnolas can appear in Heaven, then so can her death: an infinite
regress opens up. The poem turns on the question of what Ursula has

asked for in wishing for the re-creation of her earthly abode. The request seems innocent, but is interrogated and revealed to be ambiguous by the poem. Has she, for instance, unconsciously wished death upon her parents? (And would this also entail a rejection of God the father figure?) The murderous implications of her wish may be the subconscious source of her initial fear and final desolation. All depends on the ironic metaphysical joke of the third line: on whether or not the dead can ever resemble the living. The masterful simplicity that moves from the casual opening to the shattering close takes one's breath away.

The Grotesque figure represents a superimposition of two bodies upon one another. Leśmian's identification with the other body within him is only partial, and that is why he often represses the force of the other into a position at the margin of the body: it becomes a virtually detachable fetish, like the hand of 'Ręka' (The Hand), which swells monstrously to cast a palm-like shadow, like the hump in 'Garbus' (The Hunchback), which preys upon the back of the hunchback, and like the wooden leg in 'Ballada dziadowska' (A Beggarly Ballad), which outlives the old man who wears it. When two bodies are linked at one point the result is a partially grotesque image that evinces a fear of the totally Grotesque: Siamese twins, rather than the overblown double body of the fully fledged Grotesque. Świdryga and Midryga are just such Siamese twins: the alien body has suffered an almost complete expulsion from the body it seeks to invade, and yet remains tied to it as a shadow is sewn to the feet. But of course the other cannot be expelled from the self, if only because it constitutes the shadow-side of the self: the night-self whose activities are feared at the end of 'Przemiany' (Transformations), in which the speaker asks himself where he was and what he did last night. The logical corollary of this distrust of the night self is a fear of the feminine principle within the self. Hence the theatrically exaggerated eroticism of Leśmian's love poems; hence also the mythical image of the 'non-existent girl' ('niebyła dziewczyna'), who haunts his verse. By identifying the female with the non-existent, Leśmian shields himself from it: on the one hand, it is merely the product of his imagination; on the other, it is self-negating. The feminine is allowed to exist (this concession is made to reality) but only on the condition that it assume a negative ontological status and submit at all times to the dictates of his poetic will.

The paradoxical, subversive status of the non-existent girl introduces a problem into the heart of Leśmian's famously explicit erotic verses: the demands of desire are fulfilled only in the space of fantasy, through intercourse with the vampirical living dead (the non-existent girl inhabits a vault), and so frustration infiltrates the language and transforms its power into bombast. During a nocturnal assignation, the body of the other 'Dla mnie się pokładło, bym je mógł całować / I znużyć – zużyć – i nie pożałować' (Laid itself down for me so I could kiss it / And use it – abuse it – and feel no remorse). The second line enacts the self-regarding drama of the libertine, its mechanical syncopations the mask of a yearning sigh. The internal rhyme grits its teeth as a reminder that even this climactic moment is only imagined. The body thus used then 'mdlało od nadmiaru niedoumierania' (fainted with an excess insufficiency of death):[20] the stress on failure directly after the mention of 'excess' is a tormentedly ironic dissonance. The theatricality stems from the imagination's inability to assuage a real frustration. The neologisms and internal rhymes of these lines demonstrate that even Leśmian's apparently 'interpersonal' poems are profoundly self-referential – shot through with the theme of the mirror.

Like all mythical figures, the non-existent girl derives her illusive being from contradictory emotions. Although subordinate to the poet – her theatrical conquerer on the mirror stage of his own mind – she is also his reflexive companion. And, unlike him, she never forfeits her self to a nightmarish sequence of metempsychoses (she cannot lose a self that has already vanished; that is why she is associated with the grave): she is always a girl, even if always only the shadow of a girl. Her male equivalent however suffers endless metamorphoses and becomes a 'Zmierzchuń' (Duskman), a 'Srebroń' (Silverman), an 'Alcabon': one notes that almost all Leśmian's fantasy figures are male. A variety of sublimated transvestism may prompt Leśmian to dream of occupying the body of a woman – a body that will be attractive, unlike his own. But he also fears this unification with the other: in 'Topielec' (The Drowned Man) a man allows himself to be seduced into primal verdure by the Demon of Green, and is there buried by the fertility principle of 'hundreds of springs'.[21] Moreover, even the dream of the other is reflexive – like the Polish verb to dream, *śnić się*. Dreaming provides a Romantic pseudo-unity of the active and passive principles. Leśmian is consistently aware of the delusive, Utopian nature of this unity. He indulges the dream, but underlines its dream character: the ontological barriers are never crossed. Thus the non-existent girl of 'Ballada bezludna' (Uninhabited Ballad) fails to extricate herself from the meadows and achieve her own bodily incarnation. Reflexive love betrays its identity with frustration: the girl in front of a mirror ('Dziewczyna przed zwierciadłem') may ask, 'Któż mnie kochać potrafi zgadliwiej / Niźli – ja sama?' ('who could love me more knowingly than myself?'[22]) but her successful self-love precludes the love of others, such as the poet–voyeur. Even the grub that makes love to the abandoned Jadwiga is akin to her alienated penis returning to her – not the truly other, but the alienated self as a mockery of the (im-)possibility of the other. For Leśmian – unlike Bakhtin, who would probably see 'the two-backed beast' as the primal embodiment of the Grotesque – man and woman are never 'one flesh'.

A non-existent girl is a denizen of Utopia: of a place that is 'no place'. If Leśmian is a writer of fantasies – among other things – the home of fantasy is the Utopia. In the artistic genre referred to as 'the Utopia' a non-existent place is evoked in the language of a given, known reality, whilst the incomprehensibility of the truly other place cripples and compromises the language that strives to encompass it. In such a Utopia as Samuel Butler's *Erewhon*, the frequent comparisons between Erewhonian and European traits are embarrassing: in consolatory fashion, they replace Erewhon with Europe and demonstrate unwittingly the degree to which Erewhon itself really is Nowhere. Butler's Utopia is truly a Grotesque in Adorno's sense: it serves to neutralise the otherness of fiction by turning it into a merely mechanical negation of the existing world. Leśmian is far more consistent. His neologistic language faithfully reflects the true otherness of the space in the mirror. It also knows the danger of purely negative space ('Pan Błyszczynski').

Tautology and paradox

> To the aesthetic eye, which sides with the useless against utility, the aesthetic, when severed violently from purpose, becomes anti-aesthetic, because it expresses violence: luxury becomes brutality.[23]

Tautology and paradox are notorious for their 'uselessness'. They represent the two aspects of the mirror: the one typifies identity; the other, non-identity. Since the Romantic movement, the point at which they have met – as in Leśmian's 'Przyśpiew' and his nature poetry in general – has been Nature. Leśmian speaks of flowers that look askance at him:[24] the natural world that observes us has assumed the features of culture. The notion of 'nature' itself is a construction that mirrors 'culture'. For Leśmian, nature mirrors man and seeks to seduce him by adopting the role of his (projected) other. Romantic anthropomorphism can be understood as a symptom of near-equality in the struggle between man and nature: man detaches himself from nature, which becomes a mirror, an empty sign awaiting his inscription. And so the flight to nature at the start and close of the nineteenth century can be seen as not just a rejection of industrialisation, but also as an expression of sympathy with the process that colonialised the otherness of nature. The imperialism of the mirror creates an anthropomorphised reality, reflecting the self. The Romantic love of wild and deserted places was fed by a desire to create such places as slag-heaps and open-cast mines, with the ruin of nature signifying the Sublime. The double man who stands before – and within – the mirror occupies two histories. Each image of the self does penance for the other: the figure on both sides of the mirror is *jenseits von Gut und Böse* (beyond good and evil). This is the reason for the interest in Hinduism in the *fin de siècle*: the next life is an escape clause in the previous one: its mirror image or *inversion*.

As the cycle of Karma is played out, the body of the Satanist Aesthete tastes different modes of existence, unwilling to commit or limit itself to any single one. It becomes polymorphous–perverse, and behaves in accordance with the laws of Sadian syntax formulated by Barthes: 'la première est une règle d'exhaustivité . . . toute la syntaxe sadienne est ainsi recherche de la figure totale. Ceci se rattache au caractère panique du libertinage; il ne connaît ni désemploi ni repos.'[25] The key words here are 'figure totale' for they permit one to correlate the desire for totality that underlies the conjunction of paradox and tautology with the sadistic love often found in Leśmian's poems of jealousy and rejection. Thus there is the directly sadistic context of 'Piła' in which the destruction of the body of a plough boy releases his members into the condition of separate beings, who both are and are not him: every part is kissed and thereby severed by the buzzing saw of the woman's teeth. As the separate members begin to act independently, the frenetic multiplication of the activities of the body becomes a form of 'libertinage'.

An intimate relationship between paradox and tautology, inversion and repetition, fantasy and realism – the two aspects of the mirror – can be found in the paradoxical tautology of the re-creation of Czarnolas in 'Urszula Kochanowska'. It can also be seen to structure one of Leśmian's greatest poems, 'Dziewczyna' (The Girl). Twelve brothers, believers in dreams, hear the voice of a girl on the far side of a wall and reach for their hammers in order to demolish it and free her. 'She weeps, therefore she is', they remark, with a poignant learnedness typical of Leśmian. But before they can break the wall down they die; their ghosts continue, but they too perish; and finally the hammers continue on their own initiative and succeed in breaching the wall. All there is on the other side is a void, the repository of a voice but no body. Leśmian's magnificent ballad has many meanings – the hammer fetishes are unable to pierce the virgin's vaginal wall; there is no 'person' behind any voice, not even that of the poet; compulsive repetition transforms action into the phantom of action – but the most remarkable thing about it is the way it combines paradox and tautology, disruption and monotony. The tautological hammering is the fruit of a series of paradoxical survivals; and life finally migrates into a single fetish, the hammer.

Tautology and paradox are often criticised as mechanical, boring and inhuman. They do violence to the poem by threatening to arrest it; their meaning is so unspecified that one may either apprehend them as 'full' statements transcending the text, pregnant objects of meditation, or as 'empty', black holes into which the text collapses. Both eventualities rupture the continuity of the text. This accords with Leśmian's aesthetics of the momentary. A tautological state of affairs presupposes the impossibility of movement, figures whirling on the spot in a single religiously awesome and endlessly frozen moment; on the other hand, paradox permits of a promiscuity of movement that does not even stop short of confounding opposites with each other. Tautology is the *reductio ad absurdem* of realism; paradox, the dead end of fantasy. In the former, language is crippled by the self-sufficient power of reality; in the latter, the vacuity of the real bestows omnipotence upon language. Their interpenetration in the work of Leśmian shows him to be more than a writer adept in the contrasting modes of 'nature poetry' and fantasy; it indicates the degree to which his descriptions of nature are impregnated with fantasy, and vice versa. The *locus classicus* for this is perhaps 'Przemiany' (Transformations). I should like, however, to consider another fine exemplification of this dialectic, in which the presence of fantasy is less obtrusive: 'W polu' (In the Field), an object lesson in how 'nature poetry' brings tragedy and Utopia under a single roof.

> Dwoje nas w ciszy polnego zakątka.
> Strumień na oślep ku słońcu się pali.
> W liściu, co trafił na krzywy prąd fali,
> Wirując, płynie szafirowa łątka.
>
> Nadbrzeżna trawa, zwisając, potrąca
> O swe odbicie zsiwiałą kończyną,
> Do której ślimak, pęczniejąc z gorąca,
> Przysklepił muszlę swym ciałem i śliną.

W przerzutnym pląsie zniknąwszy od strzały
Płotka się czasem zasrebrzy na mgnienie.
Pod wodą – spojrzyj! – prześwieca piach biały
I mchem ruchliwym brodate kamienie.

Czemu ci głowa na dłonie opadła?
To – pachnie trawa i ten piach pod wodą –
To – wód, polśnione smugami, zwierciadła
Parują ciszą, blaskiem i ochłodą.

Tych kilku dębow ponad brzegiem liście,
Podziurawione i przeżarte chciwie
Przez gąsienice, trwają tak przejrzyście
Nad własnym cieniem, co utkwił w pokrzywie.

Z tej tu pokrzywy czar dębowych cieni
Zgarnę ku piersiom, co na słońce dyszą,
Ustami dotknę bezmiernej zieleni
Stęsknionej do mnie swym sokiem i ciszą.

Do kwiatów przywrę rozpalone czoło,
Wsłucham się w bąki grające i brzmiki,
I będę patrzał, jak lepkie goździki
Wśród jaskrów lśniącą, ociekają smołą.

I będę patrzał, jak maki i szczawie
Mdleją, ciał naszych odurzone wonią,
I będę wodził twoją białą dłonią
Po wielkiej trawie, nie znanej nam trawie.

(The two of us in this field's corner seclusion.
The stream burns blindly towards the sun.
On the leaf that cut across the waves' current
An emerald damsel fly's travelling, whirling.

The grass at the river's bank, hanging down, touches
Its own reflection with its greyed tip,
To which a snail, bulging with the heat,
Has stuck its shell with its body and slime.

Darting, turning, swifter than lightning:
From time to time, silver slivers of roach.
Look! Underwater white sand shines
And stones with beards of moving moss.

Why has your head dropped into your hands?
There's the scent of grass and the water's sand –
There's the water's mirror – brightly lined –
Exhaling haze of peace, glare, cool.

These oak leaves above the bank of the river –
Caterpillars' greed gnawed them, holed them
To lace – keep their gauze ever-hanging
Above their own shadows, which nettles have fixed.

From these nettles I scoop up the spell of oak shadow,
Lift it up to my breast, which heaves in the sun;
My lips now touch the boundless green
Whose juice and silence yearn for me.

I press my flushed brow to the flowers,
I hear the droning horseflies, gnats,
And I will watch the ooze of cloves
Among the glares, dripping bright pitch.

And I will watch the poppies and sorrel
Grow faint beneath our bodies' perfume,
And I will trail your white hand through
The grass expanse, the unknown grass.)

The syntax of this poem progresses with drugged carefulness, as the
relative clauses create a sense of expectation and mingling, and the often
isolated participles embody timeless actions in another world, perceived
through a keyhole in this one. The world is weighty and one has to work
to grasp it. This weightiness is apparent in the characteristic downward
movements of the poem: the grass hangs down, the head droops, is
pressed against flowers; one moves from the leaves of the oak to the
shadow below it. The stickiness of summer is richly present: the mention
of sweat, slime and tar stress the adhesiveness of a world stunned into
immobility by the sun. The world's feast challenges the senses' power of
ingestion. And yet it is shot through with signs of frustration: the objects

that weigh down the eyebeams are blind, the stream burns blindly towards the unattainable sun (blinded itself by the sun, by the light reflected in it, its light groping upwards); the objects that relate to the fullness of their own being (the grass grazes its own reflection, trees touch their own shadows) exclude the observer; the two lovers (?) are silent, as if the natural plenitude were merely an imaginary compensation for the (real, mental?) absence of the other, which drives the poet to direct his attention to nature above all. When the poet speaks of running the white hand of the other across unknown grass, a strange transference of meaning occurs: the hand itself becomes 'unknown'. And since emotions are projected – the flowers are said to grow faint with *our* scent – it is more than likely that the yearning of the grass is the speaker's own in projected, mystified form. As the description of nature hovers between objectivity and magical anthropomorphism, it teases and torments us: is its silence empty or golden? The recurrent images of reflections and shadows suggest that 'the two of us' may be a single divided mind. The plenitude of nature may be coded eroticism, or it may indicate that when human relationships are frustrated nature becomes full: the poet bestows on nature the love he is too shy to offer the other, as it were. The richness of nature feeds on the absence of man: thus in 'Ballada bezludna' the girl fails to emerge out of the meadow and her non-existence is celebrated by a singing carnival of insects at the end. The last few lines of 'W polu' express both the promise and the impossibility of the future, the impossibility of even knowing the things one can touch. The final outstretched hand recalls the desolate, reaching fingers at the end of 'Postacie'. The poppies and sorrel are said to be numbed with the fragrance of the lovers' bodies: this inversion of actuality, of the expected sentence, displaces the state of ideal unity into a fantastic Utopia in which plants have consciousness. This quiet displacement is one of the key links between the fantastic, the erotic and the realistic imagination in Leśmian. Within the poem different planes of consiousness are impacted. The resultant multivalence is born of the impossibility of choice, of the desire to create a 'figure totale' – to possess the other in all its forms (nature, woman, one's reflection). Like the mirror – that image of man's multiplicity, of the potential others he contains – it opens the door to another world and places there the doorkeeper of Kafka's famous fable.

Imagism, tautology, metaphor

In *L'Évolution créatrice*, Bergson states that the notion of the void arises when consciousness lags behind events.[26] The early twentieth century was a period when consciousness was seen to be doing just that: it could no longer keep step with the rapid motion of technological change. I intend in the next section to consider the relationship between a mutability too rapid to be registered and the negative tropes of Symbolist verse.[27] For the moment, however, I should like to consider its correlation with the theme of *metamorphosis* in Imagism. (Metamorphosis is of course an eminently Leśmianian concern: as in his poem 'Przemiany'.) P. N. Furbank has written perceptively of a series of Imagist poems in which the two terms of a comparison become interchangeable, such as HD's 'Whirl up, sea', in which it is impossible to discern whether the subject is a sea compared to a forest, or vice versa.[28] HD is concerned here with the mechanisms of metamorphosis, which are also thematic in the early Cantos of Pound. Furbank goes on to mention the characteristic 'overlapping of planes' in Imagism. I would interpret this as the overlapping of rapidly successive objects, which seem to melt or metamorphose into each other. The Imagists' phenomenological isolation of the object can be seen to attempt to establish clarity within the vertiginousness of endless metamorphosis – either by eliminating and forestalling the transformation, or by concentrating upon one in a series of transformations. The degree to which this is merely a holding-operation can be illustrated by the following quotations from Pound and HD:

> ply over ply, thin glister of water
>
> > (Pound, Canto IV)

> where rollers shot with blue
> cut under deeper blue
>
> > (HD, 'The Shrine')
>
> each leaf
> cuts another leaf on the grass,
> shadow seeks shadow
>
> > (HD, 'Evening')

In each case, an object overlaps with *itself*. There are several reasons for this. First, factory mass production is beginning to influence the imagination; secondly, the attempt to hold the object fixed and still is seen to fail and so the next best alternative, its repetition (change masquerading as the same) is adopted; thirdly – this second look at the object is itself Utopian, for the rapid processes of modern life have already removed it into an endless flux. The repetitions employed here by HD and Pound are similar in function to the tautologies of Leśmian: because the isolated object is presented in dual form – mirrored, negated, alongside its shadow, as it were – the meaning of its isolation alters. It becomes a pseudo-isolation: a euphemism for, or an evasion of, metamorphosis.

If – as Furbank contends – Imagism dispenses with the metaphor in order to solve the problem of duality and relationship which is posed by comparison, it does so in reflection of a Bergsonian world of incessant movement, where nothing can be held still long enough to serve as a point of comparison, an anchor. The two terms melt into each other, and their superimposition annihilates the blank space of inbetweenness metaphor serves to create. The resultant unity-in-duality overwhelms the conscious mind and prevents it distinguishing what is being transformed into what. (An effect very close to that of Symbolist verse.) Whence the impressiveness of the 'image', which can stand unexplained because it defies all explanation. Its double meaning incubates a polysemia. And so the Imagists' ostensibly rational reduction of events to their basic atoms is revealed to be a chimera: the image has the unified duality of a myth, and stands mysteriously at the end of the work like the statue of a god by the altar at the end of a temple.

SYMBOLISM, FEMININITY AND NEGATION: THOUGHTS ON TWO POEMS BY LEŚMIAN

Piła

Idzie lasem owa zmora, co ma kibić piły,
A zębami chłopców nęci i zna czar mogiły.

Upatrzyła parobczaka na schyłku doliny:
'Ciebie pragnę, śnie jedyny – dyny moje, dyny!

Pocałunki dla cię, chlopcze, w ostrą stal uzbroję,
Błysk – niedobłysk na wybłysku – oto zęby moje!

Oczaruj się tym widokiem, coś go nie widywał,
Ośnijże się tymi snami, coś ich nie wyśniwał!

Połóż głowę na tym chabrze i połóż na maku,
Pokochaj mnie w polnym znoju i śródleśnym ćmaku!'

'Będę ciebie kochał mocą, z którą się mocuję,
Będę ciebie tak całował, jak nikt nie całuje!

Będę gardził dziewczętami, com je miał w swej woli,
Bo z nich każda od miłości łka, jak od niedoli.

Chcę się ciałem przymiarkować do nowej pieszczoty,
Chcę się wargą wypurpurzyć dla krwawej ochoty!

Chcę dla twojej, dla zabawy tak się przeinaczyć
Abym mógł się na twych zębach dreszczami poznaczyć!'

Zazgrzytała od rozkoszy, naostrzyła zęby:
'Idę w miłość, jak chadzałam na leśne wyręby!'

Zaszumiała ponad nimi ta wierzba złotocha –
Poznał chłopiec, czym w uścisku jest stal, gdy pokocha!

Całowała go zębami na dwoje, na troje:
'Hej, niejedną z ciebie duszę w zaświaty wyroję!'

Poszarpała go pieszczotą na nierówne części:
'Niech wam, wy moje drobiażdżki, w śmierci się poszczęści!'

Rozrzuciła go podzielnie we sprzeczne krainy:
'Niechaj Bóg was pouzbiera, ludzkie omieciny!'

Same chciały się uciułać w kształt wielce bywały,
Jeno znaleźć siebie w świecie wzajem nie umiały.

Zaczęło się od mrugania ległych w kurzu powiek –
Nie wiadomo, kto w nich mrugał, ale już nie człowiek!

Głowa, dudniąc, mknie po grobli, szukająca karku,
Jak ta dynia, gdy się dłoniom umknie na jarmarku.

Piersią, sobie przywłaszczoną, jar grabieżczo dyszy,
Uchem, wbiegłym na wierzchołek, wierzba coś tam słyszy!

Oczy, wzajem rozłączone, tleją bez połysku,
Jedno brzęczy w pajęczynie, drugie śpi w mrowisku.

Jedna noga popod lasem uwija się w tańcu,
Druga włóczy się na klęczkach po zbożowym łańcu.

A ta ręka, co się wzniosła w próżnię ponad drogą,
Znakiem krzyża przeżegnała nie wiadomo kogo!

(*The Saw*

Through the forests strolls that nightmare with its saw-like waist,
That draws boys on with flashing teeth and knows the charms of
graves.

And she espied a ploughboy walking on the sloping valley –
'I yearn for you, you are my sole dream – o you, dilly dilly.'

I will arm bright kisses for you, boy, in harshest steel:
Ever threshing, gleaming white, my teeth are never still!

Just look and gloat on what you've never seen!
Dare dream the dreams you never yet have dreamed!

Lie down in knapweed and in poppied rest,
In the sweat of your brow and forest gloam – let me feel your caress!'

'I'll love you with the strength of one who fights,
I'll kiss you as no man has kissed as yet!

I'll chuck the girls who tread upon my heels
And moan with love as if they'd fallen ill.

My body wants to test itself against a new caress,
My lips – to crimson with blood's eagerness!

For your sake, just for fun, I will create another me,
To thrill against your teeth with shudderings of ecstasy!'

She ground her teeth and sharpened them for joy –
'As once I set about a tree, I go to love a boy!'

Above them a willow tree waved its golden tresses;
The boy learned the strength of loving steel when it caresses.

Her love bites bit him into ones and twos:
'Ha! More than one soul will come out of you!'

Her kisses tore him into little bits –
'O little ones, I hope in death you have a good time of it!'

She divided him up and flung him to opposite lands:
'Let God collect you again, offal of mankind!'

Bits tried to scrape their well-known shape together,
But in the wide world could not find each other.

To start with, eyelids blinked amidst the dust.
Quite *who* blinked – no one knew. No man, at least!

Bumping swiftly down a dike, the head was looking where
Its neck was – like the pumpkin you can't catch at the fair.

Ravines employ a borrowed chest – breathe deep;
Willows listen with ears that flew into trees.

Eyes decay, divorced, grow lustreless:
One buzzes in a cobweb; one sleeps in an ants' nest.

Beneath the trees one leg twists itself into a dance;
The other drags itself kneeling across the corn's stands.

And the hand upraised in vacancy over the road
Made the sign of the cross where nobody stood.)

Ballada bezludna

Niedostępna ludzkim oczom, że nikt po niej się nie błąka,
W swym bezpieczu szmaragdowym rozkwitła w bezmiar łąka.
Strumień skrzył się na zieleni nieustannie zmienną łatą,
A goździki spoza trawy wykrapiały się wiśniato.
Świerszcz, od rosy napęczniały, ciemnił pysk nadmiarem śliny,

I dmuchawiec kroplą mlecza błyskał w zadrach swej łeciny,
A dech łąki wrzał od wrzawy, wrzał i żywcem w słońce dyszał,
I nie było tu nikogo, kto by widział, kto by słyszał.

    Gdzież me piersi, Czerwcami gorące?
    Czemuż nie ma ust moich na łące?
    Rwać mi kwiaty rękami obiema!
    Czemuż rąk mych tam na kwiatach nie ma?

Zabóstwiło sie cudacznie pod blekotem na uboczu,
A to jakaś mgła dziewczęca chciała dostać warg i oczu,
I czuć było, jak boleśnie chce się stworzyć, chce sie wcielić,
Raz warkoczem się zazłocić, raz piersiami się zabielić –
I czuć było, jak się zmaga zdyszanego męką łona,
Aż na wieki sił jej zbrakło – i spoczęła niezjawiona!
Jeno miejsce, gdzie być mogła, jeszcze trwało i szumiało,
Próżne miejsce na tę duszę, wonne miejsce na to ciało.

    Gdzież me piersi, Czerwcami gorące?
    Czemuż nie ma ust moich na łące?
    Rwać mi kwiaty rękami obiema!
    Czemuż rąk mych tam na kwiatach nie ma?

Przywabione obcym szmerem, wszystkie zioła i owady
Wrzawnie zbiegły się w to miejsce, niebywałe węsząc ślady,
Pająk w nicość sieć nastawił, by pochwycić cień jej cienia,
Bąk otrąbił uroczystość spełnionego nieistnienia,
Żuki grały jej potrupne, świerszcze – pieśni powitalne,
Kwiaty wiły się we wieńce, ach, we wieńce pożegnalne!
Wszyscy byli w owym miejscu na słonecznym, na obrzędzie,
Prócz tej jednej, co być mogła, a nie była, i nie będzie!

    Gdziez me piersi, Czerwcami gorące?
    Czemuż nie ma ust moich na łące?
    Rwać mi kwiaty rękami obiema!
    Czemuż rąk mych tam na kwiatach nie ma?

        (Uninhabited Ballad

Beyond the reach of human eyes, where nobody could tread,
A meadow's emerald seclusion infinitely spread.

A stream lit out with ever-altered patches through the green,
And from behind the grass the cloves blossomed like cherry trees!
The jaws of the dew-bloated cricket darkened with foam.
Milk-drops topping slivers of stalks: the dandelions shone . . .
The meadow breathed heat's live ferment, fermented and breathed,
And there was nobody around to hear a thing or see.

> Where are my June-warmed breasts?
> Why does my mouth not exist?
> Why have I no hands there on the meadow
> To gather the flowers up where they grow?

Out of the midst of hemlock something wondrously divined,
A girlish sort of mistiness in want of lips and eyes.
And one could sense her painful will to self-create, to incarnate,
Just once – wear golden-braided hair, display a breast of white.
And one could sense the anguish heaving, panting, in her womb –
Until her strength gave way for ever – left her unbecome!
But just there where she might have been some whispers of existence
Kept a blank space for that soul – for that body, a fragrance.

> Where are my June-warmed breasts?
> Why does my mouth not exist?
> Why have I no hands there on the meadow
> To gather the flowers up where they grow?

Attracted by strange whispers, every herb and insect came apace,
Converging there in ferment, scenting an unheard-of trace,
The spider set his net in nothingness to catch her shadow's shade,
The bittern trumpeted the feast of fullfilment of the unmaid,
Dung-beetles played a passing, and crickets a welcome, song;
Ah! flowers wound themselves in wreaths to lie her grave along.
Collected on that sun-soaked spot, they all observed the festival –
Except for her, the might-have-been, who never came and never will.

> Where are my June-warmed breasts?
> Why does my mouth not exist?
> Why have I no hands there on the meadow
> To gather the flowers up where they grow?)

Foreign words and embarrassment

In Leśmian's verses, as in those of Mallarmé, George and many other Symbolists, the reader often encounters strange-sounding words. In his case, these are neologisms, archaisms and fragments of peasant dialect. Criticism has still not yet determined which words belong to which categories, and as a result his poetry becomes – in the strictest sense – untranslatable. The versions presented above are merely approximations. The difficulty of categorisation blurs the difference between the various kinds of outlandish words, which exotically intertwine, and permits one to define them as literally 'out-landish': as *Fremdwörter* (foreign words), in the partly metaphorical sense of Adorno.[29] For him, these words provide windows onto an otherness blocked by the familiarity of the words that surround them: they are like transparent panes surrounded by stained glass, at least as far as the revelation of alterity is concerned. In a thesis that has been heavily criticised in Poland itself, Rochelle Stone has considered the problematic status of these words in Leśmian's poetry, the possibility of their derivation from Russian, and their relation with the Russian Symbolists' and Futurists' search for a primordial Slavonic tongue (the *zaum*).[30] The possibility of Russian derivation is less outlandish than it would seem and than fiercely patriotic Poles might wish: Leśmian was brought up in Kiev, wrote some of his first published poems in Russian, and even when living in Poland inhabited the former Russian partition. But, although the juxtaposition is potentially illuminating, Dr Stone stretches her thesis to the point of situating Leśmian unproblematically in the force field of Russian Symbolist poetics. She ignores Leśmian's simultaneous dependence on the Polish tradition: on the neologisms and silences of Norwid, on peasant songs, and on Słowacki's vision of the Ukraine.[31] Worse still, she overlooks the correspondences between Leśmian's estrangement of language and the distrust of words the modernist displays. An attitude of suspicious scrutiny of language is just as characteristic of modernism as belief in the magical force of the hermetic word. The modernist distrust of words was doubtless intensified in Leśmian's case by the spectral after-life the Polish language led in the Russified schools of the late nineteenth century, under the pressure of Czarist revenge for the 1863 uprisings. During Leśmian's youth, 'Poland' was as non-existent as his negative beings. Like them, it had sunk into the soil: a magical vanished village. Its persistence was strongest in peasant idiom: doubtless one reason for the 'peasant mania' of the *fin de siècle* intelligentsia.[32] It is surely significant that Esperanto was devised by a

Pole and that by the end of the nineteenth century it had become possible for one of the greatest of all Polish writers – Joseph Conrad – to compose in a completely alien tongue.

One may ask what all this has to do with the image of the feminine and its links with negation during the *fin de siècle*. The connection is forged by the *femme fatale's* status as a *foreign* (or declassed) woman. Because she falls outside the co-ordinates of one's own society's map, one cannot know how to defend oneself against her. And because one's desire for her is free of social elements – of marriage to gain position, for instance – it is desire in its naked form. Whence the appositeness of the casting of Louise Brooks, an American, in the role of Lulu in Pabst's film of *Die Büchse der Pandora* [Pandora's Box]. For the male, often homosexually inclined, authors of the *fin de siècle*, the feminine was Other, linked with the foreign; and the foreign is experienced as the *negation* of one's own culture. (Especially in this pre-war period of intense nationalism.) She is the non-existent girl of 'Ballada bezludna' in her aspect of destroyer (the woman of 'Piła'): one fears annihilation by the creature one has oneself annihilated, whose existence has been repressed by the myth of male superiority. *Femme fatale* and *Fremdwort* have the same magnetism:

> the early yearning for foreign words is similar to the desire for foreign and (if possible) exotic girls; it draws one on by a process of linguistic exogamy which seeks to step out of the closed circle of repetition, to lift the curse of the thing one is and immediately recognises. Foreign words provoked one's embarrassment like the uttering of an especially cherished, unspoken name.[33]

The name is that of the non-existent girl of one's adolescence: a name that embarrasses because of its referent's absence.

The embarrassment the *Fremdwort* provokes is that of the man exiled within his own tongue, the man whose language is non-communicative. This blush also appears on the face of a man who senses that women writers are eroding his exclusive right to use his own tongue and who imports foreign words to counter them: the embarrassment he feels is that of one who shores up failing powers with mystification. In the case of the Polish writer, however, the foreign word is also embarrassing in its embodiment of the non-referentiality, the non-instrumentality, of his speech in a country governed by others. The blush appears on the face of the writer sceptical about the value of writing whenever someone catches him red-handed – his hands coloured red by the face he is striving to cover – in the act of writing. This reaction is common amongst the split or commonsensical Romantics, such as Leśmian or Keats. A fragment of 'The Eve of St Agnes' was transcribed in such haste that the word 'garlanded' became 'gardneded':[34] this untoward haste may be a major source of neologisms (our century's flurry may explain its writer's neologistic penchant) and may stem from the writer's desire to finish as soon as possible: the Romantic cult of action entails that he live rather than write, whilst the torment of inspiration may be feared as undermining selfhood. (The privileging of the short poem by the Symbolists as part and parcel of the hurry of the modern age?) Neologisms have more affinities with the fluidities of everyday speech than with the codified formality of writing: they can have a demagogic, hustling, crowd-pleasing air, as they do when uttered by Uncle Sam in Robert Coover's novel *The Public Burning*. This populist aspect of the neologism is in Leśmian the ally of his sympathy for folk ballads. But the imitation of demotic idiom also expresses the writer's yearning for the immediacy of speech and stems from the tale-teller's fear that in the modern age of mass production and urbanisation his audience has evaporated. It is most embarrassing to write without an audience (the ghost in the textual machine known as the 'implicit reader' is hardly a substitute). The subconscious seeps through the text written in haste and the resultant disfigurement of his words causes the writer further embarrassment. The modern difficulty in believing in the purposefulness of writing is reflected in the problematic status of the neologism. In his fascinating book *Keats and Embarrassment*, Christopher Ricks has formulated a series of hypotheses that can be applied equally well to Keats and to Leśmian: both diminutive men whose verses' compensatory sensuous luxuriance provoked embarrassment in their readers. 'I believe that a good many of Keats's mis-spellings are Joycean or Carrollian acts of imagination, their portmanteaux hastily packed', Ricks writes.[35] The mention of Joyce should indicate that, for all my remarks about the potential populism of the neologism, it cannot be purely and simply populist. It also embarrasses the reader by subverting his claim to know 'his own' language, to have a language of his own. But neologisms are not invariably the products of haste: they can be the result of a quasi-scientific experiment with language; and science is of course one of the main sources of neologism. Neologisms can either free words from the chains of orthographic standardisation, so reintroducing into the language the variability it had lost to lexical exactitude, or they can be the result of science operating upon language. They can be 'irrational' (sorting well with the vitalism Leśmian shares with much of the *fin de siècle*) or 'rational'. Their Janus status illustrates the degree to which rationality is steeped in myth.

Negative space

At one point in his essay on Leśmian's 'poetics of negation', Professor Michał Głowiński remarks that researchers have noted a tendency in the French language

> to employ negative formulae in contexts in which equivalent positive formulae could equally well appear. A similar phenomenon is evident in Polish, above all where value judgements are concerned: one says 'not nice' rather than 'nasty', 'incorrect' rather than 'wrong' or 'false'. This is connected with the question of euphemism, which is more or less marginal in the case of Leśmian.[36]

Głowiński is right to mention euphemism here, but he fails to perceive how crucial a role it plays in Leśmian's poetics of pity. The absence of any dualistic distinction between good and bad (or good and bad taste) in his verse is owing to his classification of 'negative' traits as declensions of positive ones, as genetic variations within the same family. The euphemistic definition by negation expresses frustrated expectations: the condemnatory word one was ready to apply is displaced by the presence of a higher authority (fear of reprisals – hence the use of euphemism may well be more common in a subjugated culture, such as that of late-nineteenth-century Poland; conscience; 'reality') that enforces a softening of the dualistic judgement. One often uses language in a euphemistic fashion during a first fleeting encounter with a person or thing: only later is the holding action of the negative (I know what it isn't . . .) replaced by a crystallised judgement. In Leśmian's world, everything is ephemeral – Sandauer writes memorably of his 'momentary mythology'[37] – leaving only enigmatic traces. The girl of 'Ballada bezludna' is but the whimsy of a moment. 'The notion of emptiness is born' – Henri Bergson writes – 'when consciousness, lagging behind itself, remains attached to a past state even though a different one is present.'[38] This emptiness is the void the *fin de siècle* fills with mist: the atmospheric equivalent of euphemism. Here euphemism is language blushing with its self-conscious awareness of its helplessness to register the new reality of technical and industrial change, the events that whirl past in the city street.

After the partitioning of the body carried out by 'the Saw', the *femme fatale*, it is no longer able to act. Action goes on only in the negative space of the imagination: the space in which the hand makes the sign of the cross where nobody stands. If the hand has the last word, it is a sign that writing will continue. It will however be writing suspended in a void, like the hand itself. The negative forms that live there embarrass both reader and writer. For, if silence is to be more eloquent than words, why does the poet not retreat into silence? If the meadow of 'Ballada bezludna' is imperceptible to human eyes, then how did the speaker of the verse come to perceive it? The existence of the poem becomes as absurd as that of the unmanifest girl. This experience of seeing events at which one is not actually present is akin to the experience of the cinematic audience; it is surely no accident that Leśmian's poetry is the fruit of an era when cinema was coming into being. A cinematic action is both present and absent: technology splits the atom of the phenomenon and isolates sight, sound and touch from each other. (The *Gesamtkunstwerk* attempts to reunite them.) Cinema renders the experience of voyeurism a general one. The close-ups of the severed portions of the farm boy's body resemble cuts in a film: the poem thus identifies with the cutting mechanism of the female 'Saw'.

If one returns to the earlier comparison of Leśmian with Keats, one notes how the voyeurism of 'Ballada bezludna' is anticipated in the scene in 'The Eve of St Agnes' in which Porphyro covertly watches Madeleine's dress slide down to her feet, wreathing round them like seaweed. The inviolate distance between the onlooker and the observed is the voyeurist poet's confession of inability to step physically into his fantasy. This is very like another poem by Leśmian, 'Sen wiejski' (A Village Dream), which depicts a poet dreaming of milkmaids returning home, and the milkmaids discussing the poet who dreams their existence: the two ontological planes (fantasy and reality) are mutually exclusive. Porphyro's exclusion in 'The Eve of St Agnes' also corresponds to Keats's own position *vis-à-vis* the literature of his own time: his verses represent the point at which Romanticism discards the eighteenth-century remnants it retains even in Byron and Wordsworth and advances (in time, not necessarily in aesthetic merit) towards the Tennysonian, as Bagehot was to realise when he dubbed Keats the most modern of the Romantics. The voyeur is looking into the future, which may well be unattainable (Keats's unconscious intimation of his own brief mortality?) and is in any case perceived as qualitatively *other*. Yeats's sarcastic image of Keats as a small boy with his nose pressed up against a sweet-shop window inadvertently encapsulates the poignancy

of his exclusion from the fair domain of luxury, which compels him to
eat words as tactile substitutes. The modern ideology of the word as
concrete entity (rather than something both abstract and concrete)
betrays the same compensatory bias. And Leśmian in his poetic lifetime
was just as much an exile as Keats. The ruling poetic powers – the
cabaret poets of 'Skamander' – paid mere lip service to his eminence,
although Uniłowski rightly noted in his *roman maudit* of the thirties,
Wspólny pokój (A Shared Room), that their technical devices were
mainly inferior copies of those of Leśmian. His poems anticipate later
poetic practices. The recurrent theme of jealousy in his work reflects the
feelings of the voyeur observing pleasures he cannot attain to in
person – and who, even when he does partake of pleasure, is so
embarrassed by his body as to feel he is watching somebody else, his own
double. The position of the voyeur is embarrassing, for it is that of an
adult shrunk to the level of a child. The embarrassment felt by a writer
incapable of writing plays, of matching the Romantic model of genius –
who is Shakespeare (both Keats and Leśmian wrote plays of little
interest) – is the fruit of the solitude which prevents him imagining
credibly the voice of another. To compensate for this, the place of the
other is usurped by the image of the self-alienated self, the self trapped in the
mirror. The internalisation of this pseudootherness engenders self-
negation. That is why the girl is unable to enter existence in 'Ballada
bezludna': it is also why the self is unable to identify with and enter into
the words it uses but is forced to hold them at arm's length, in the tongs
of euphemism and dramatic monologue, cancelled in advance by a
negative prefix. The tautologous self-affirmation engaged in by the
inhabitants of Leśmian's universe is the final cause of their destruction,
as they wear themselves down and thin into phantoms. They are not
renewed by any contact with others: their only companions are doubles,
i.e. themselves in an earlier frame from the film of existence. The real
absence of others drives them to self-repetition.

The voyeur is a projection of the exhibitionist. According to Freud,
the exhibitionist identifies with the voyeur and so comes to share his
pleasure.[39] Teresa Skubelanka has written of the exhibitionist features
of the language of Leśmian's erotic verse.[40] At the heart of projection is
the experience of standing before a mirror. The person who occupies two
places at once – his own and the place 'in' the mirror – fights himself for
his own being until his strength fades and he disappears.[41] Whence the
seemingly paradoxical theme of non-existence in verses that are
exhibitionist: the figure in front of the mirror follows the dictates of
Sartrean 'bad faith' and ceases to identify with his own body (or

language). He can then chop it up, as in 'Piła' or annihilate it, as in 'Ballada bezludna'. The Romantic identification with the child conceived of as other leads to a simultaneous dissociation and fusion of the periods of child and adult life. The image of the adult, of the self as it has become, is attacked through a refusal to believe that it is the necessary future of the child: this disavowal, strictly fetishistic ('I know this is so, but . . .' is the fundamental form of fetishism), seeks to restore the lost potentiality of childhood. The adult annihilates himself by first identifying with the child and then, on the strength of this identification, refusing to admit that the (deformed) image in the mirror is his own.

In the published preface to *Endymion*, Keats remarks that 'the imagination of a boy is healthy, and mature imagination of a man is healthy; but there is a space of life between in which the soul is in ferment'.[42] This state of ferment prevails in 'Ballada bezludna', which discloses the link between embarrassment and the Sartrean analysis of viscosity cited by Ricks, who applies it to Keats: the girl is sucked into unbeing by the viscosity of the empty meadow, its marshiness. Keats defines adolescence by means of a double negation that corresponds to the duality of the figure before the mirror. The adolescent observes himself (in the mirror) because he is alarmed by the biological changes unfolding within him. Goffmann remarks of embarrassment, a condition generally deemed typical of adolescence: 'by showing embarrassment when he can be neither of two people, the individual leaves open the possibility that in the future he may effectively be either'.[43] Sandauer has correlated the mirage of the non-existent girl with a decision on Leśmian's part to camouflage the theme of onanism.[44] Inheriting the tradition of nineteenth-century Romantic spiritualisation of sexuality, Leśmian is forced to veil this theme. Moreover, the habit of camouflage is reinforced by the Polish tradition of writing allegorically in order to outwit the censor. In voicing the relationship between non-existence, voyeurism and auto-eroticism, Sandauer seems to echo Byron's complaint that the erotic images of Keats were the sterile fruit of 'mental masturbation'.[45] The blush blushes at itself: at the displacement of the rush of blood from the penis to the face. Yet it is also a masochistic wound that creates the illusion of blood – self-sacrifice on the altar of convention – which persuades the enemy that sentence has already been executed, and so preserves the blusher from punishment. The word that cancels itself as it emerges is masochistic and self-protective in this very way. The embarrassment that is rampant in the late nineteenth century reflects a growing disparity between private experience and the public modes of self-expression: it occurs as society centralises and draws to its centre provincials ill at ease with the established codes. Provincials such as Keats – or Bolesław Leśmian, a denizen of the far-flung edge (what is known in Polish as the *krańce*) of Polish literary culture.

The neologism appears as outlandish within the normal sentence as the provincial stunned by the bustling city street. Neologisms are fresh blood. They are symptoms of a disease in the language against whose greyness they stand out. This disease is 'the new'. Sickness can be defined as a condition in which one part of the body is opposed to the others, acting as a brake on the functioning of the entire system. The paradox and dilemma for the body politic of modern society lie in the fact that the force encapsulated within the new – the neologism – is necessary to maintain the growth of the system. The workings of the literary and social systems are homologous in this respect: just as peasants are recruited from the land to the cities and the big industrial factories, so the poet from the *krańce* is received into the heart of literary culture, so the neologism is admitted into literary language. The non-instrumentality of the neologism mirrors the provincial poet's lack of expertise in working the levers of the literary system. Thus his innovations are received and appropriated, whilst he himself is refused due recognition: the poets of 'Skamander' plundered Leśmian's repertoire, diluting it to the ends of their own literary politics. Because of the multiplicity of meanings compacted within it, the neologism becomes the material form of the silence (or gap) that almost always expresses the sexual act (in the form of euphemism): the neologism fills that gap, but leaves it opaque all the same. The neologism does not so much transcend history as suffer extradiction from it: the neologistic writer can be passed over in silence – because of the scandalous (sexual) nature of his preoccupations, (neologism as a literary equivalent of orgasm), because of his provincial origins, and because of the genuine difficulty of his work. He is plunged into often sentimental isolation. Such was the exemplary fate of Leśmian, Joyce and Celan.

Like the neologism, the negation is a materialisation of silence. Language deprived of its ancient right to act upon matter – language stripped of its instrumentality – exacts its revenge by assuming the place of matter itself: it solidifies into an opaque material sign that shrugs off all referents. Masochistically, it denies meaning and cultivates a resemblance to the most non-identical of arts: music. Music was accorded a special privilege in Symbolist aesthetics, but it was less music that achieved this status than the melody that courses below the libretto in the the operas of Wagner: in his operas music represents the mythical silence of the ancestors that underlies, and gives the lie to, the speech,

presence and individuality of the performers. That is: the elevation of
Wagner as a yardstick was intended to demonstrate that speech had
become non-identical with itself through its sacrifice of its musical
elements to a self-sufficient and autonomous realm known as music. It
has been remarked that the non-conceptuality of music is bound in with
its status as the only art in which a child can be a master: its structures
antedate experience and thus have something in common with the
blindness of life in the womb. The blind poet is the poet as musician – as
Eliot noted when writing of Joyce. Thus music, negation and neologism
all belong together.

In Leśmian's poetry, negation and neologism are virtually interchangeable: most of his neologisms are formed through the insertion of
a negative prefix (usually *nie*; one could render this in English as 'un-', as
'not-' or as 'non-'). Bergson defines the negation as an assertion to the
second power: 'It affirms something of an affirmation which itself
affirms something of an object.' [46] Bergson stresses the possibility of
extracting two words or statements from the word equipped with a
negative prefix. This is perhaps too positive a view. For the dialectical
nature of the negation can mean that – to quote Chesterton on
Browning – 'the word with two meanings seems to mean rather less, if
anything, than the word with one'. [47] The overload of signification in the
neologism and the negation can cause the system to short-circuit.

The majority of negative prefixes in Leśmian's work are parasitic
upon abstract nouns – that is, upon nouns such as 'being', 'time',
'world', 'hope', 'flowering', which become 'unbeing', 'nontime', 'unworld', 'nonhope' and 'unflowering'.[48] Even where these words are
relatively concrete ('unflowering' for instance), their generalised form
('unflowering' is a statement about everything that flowers) impels them
towards abstraction. This strategy underlines the difference between the
word that denotes a specific object and the word that has drifted so far
away from its metaphorical base as to tend towards abstraction – and
non-existence. 'When the end draws near, there are no images left, only
words remain', writes Borges. As the end draws near the world drains
away from the words that once represented it. The total severance
between world and word transforms the word itself into a material thing:
the dialectical reversal that transmutes spiritualising idealism into
materialism. Thus the neologisms possess the same concrete force as the
strips of real newspaper affixed to Cubist paintings. In this respect,
different levels of linguistic history co-exist in Leśmian's work: the
solidity with which speech begins and the nullity in which it concludes;
the magic of the hermetic word, and abstract philosophy. If neologism is

'an erotic act' (Barthes), its multiple meanings are the multiple times and gathered genetic possibilities of past and present co-existing in the sperm. In the case of Leśmian, this linguistic eroticism is soaked in necrophilia, aflame with a lust for dead words. Neologisms violate language's grave once its headstone has become illegible.

As a footnote to this essay, it may be interesting to note a link between the private mythologies of Leśmian and Proust. It is evident in the coincidence between 'Ballada bezludna' and the following passage from *À la recherche du temps perdu*:

> Parfois à l'exaltation que me donnait la solitude, s' en ajoutait une autre que je ne savais pas en départager nettement, causée par le désir de voir surgir devant moi une paysanne que je pourrais serrer dans mes bras. Né brusquement, et sans que j'eusse eu le temps de le rapporter exactement à sa cause, au milieu de pensées très différentes, le plaisir dont il était accompagné ne me semblait qu'un degré supérieur de celui qu'elles me donnaient. Je faisais une mérite de plus à tout ce qui était à ce moment-là dans mon esprit, au reflet rose du toit de tuile, aux herbes folles, au village de Roussainville où je désirais longtemps aller, aux arbres de son bois, au clocher de son église, de cet émoi nouveau qui me les faisait seulement paraître plus désirables parce que je croyais que c'était eux qui le provoquaient, et qui semblait ne vouloir que me porter vers eux au plus rapidement quand il enflait ma voile d'une brise puisante, inconnue et propice. Mais si ce désir qu'une femme apparût ajoutait pour moi aux charmes de la nature quelque chose de plus exaltant, les charmes de la nature, en retour, élargissaient se que celui de la femme aurait eu de trop restreint. Il me semblait que la beauté des arbres, c'était encore la sienne, et que l'âme de ces horizons, du village de Roussainville, des livres que je lisais cette année-là, son baiser me la livrerait; et mon imagination reprenant des forces au contact de ma sensualité, ma sensualité se répandant dans tous les domaines de mon imagination, mon désir n'avait plus de limites.[49]

In Proust's passage, the motif of the non-existent girl accompanies that of crossing a border: a constant theme in Leśmian's work, and one that recurs in the first two lines of 'Ballada bezludna'. It is perhaps no accident that Proust's remarks appear immediately after a meditation upon the incapacity of language to render the meaning of experience, with the implicit postulate of the need for a new language; or that they precede the fragment in which Marcel is the voyeur of Mlle Vinteuil.

Voyeurism, the new language, the non-existent girl: in Proust, as in Leśmian, these form a constellation. And, as in Leśmian, the fullness of nature is steeped in erotic longing for the non-existent to manifest itself. The new language postulated by Proust would probably be composed of neologisms, pronounced by Adam the magician in a second Garden (like the garden of Pan Błyszczyński) – drawing forth a girl from the womb of the earth. But, although he wishes, as it were, to charm dryads out of their tree-trunks, he is forced to superimpose the objective fact of their non-existence upon the *fata morgana* conjured by the imagination:

> Je fixais indéfinement le tronc d'un arbre lointoin, de derrière lequel elle allait surgir et venir à moi; l'horizon scruté restait desert, la nuit tombait, c'était sans espoir que mon attention s'attachait, comme pour aspirer les créatures qu'ils pouvaient recéler, à ce sol sterile, à cette terre épuisée . . . '[50]

Only in imagination does nature respond to the culture that has exhausted it – that has transported it into the negativity where it only persists as a thought.

FURTHER ASPECTS OF LEŚMIAN

The object whose action is a tautology – the stream that streams – is its own father. That is, it enacts the fantasy known as the Oedipus complex, that fundamental experience of Leśmian's epoch, as documented by Freud. Similarly, the name change carried out by Bolesław Lesman indicates an existentialist desire to give birth to himself – perhaps an attempt to cut the cords linking him to the dark yellow star of a Jew's fate. And yet the new name, Leśmian, is almost identical with the old: again, the structure of identity is tautologous. Joining in the Expressionist revolt against the fathers, he becomes his own father. Expressionism rejects realism on the grounds of its servile reproduction of a world established before the child's birth. The anti-realistic rebellion employs tautology to negate the existence of a previous generation, to erase the signs of its otherness; moreover, tautology mimics the form of argumentation used by the fathers and so magically appropriates their existence. For the fathers, however, tautology is a structure of nouns ossified in self-evidence: a stream is a stream. But for the usurping sons it is active, a verbal as well as a nominal construction: the stream streams.

It is possible that the colonial energy of Britain derived in part from the frequency of this grammatical form in English, which permits the object to act out its being: it is as if the object (like England itself, and like the noun that assumes the role of the verb) has an innate tendency to overrun its own borders. (Is it an accident that this grammatical form first becomes current in Shakespeare, that son of the colonising Elizabethan era?) Perhaps this is why the poetic theory of active tautology was formulated in England by Gerard Manley Hopkins, on the basis of his meditations upon the notion of *haeccitas* in the philosophy of Duns Scotus: this whirling on the spot, unable to shed the self, is the source of Hopkin's own torment in the 'terrible sonnets'. Leśmian's active tautology founds an hermetic world of youth, and represents modernism in its active phase, before it fell victim to old age.

Leśmian's verses have the animistic content of folk ballads, but their form is imposed by the fragmentariness of city life. The contradiction is resolved by the modernist experience of the city as an alien jungle, no longer comprehensible to the isolated individual.

> It would seem that his unusually intimate relationship with nature derives from a great love of it, from continual intercourse with it. And yet Leśmian was not fond of it. Throughout his life he behaved with indifference towards flowers, verdure, landscapes. His character was that of a town-dweller engrossed in the flux and specific nature of town life.[51]

An acquaintance of Leśmian, Helena Wiewiorska, enlarges upon this:

> Apropos flowers – in his private life Leśmian was completely indifferent to their charm (Sophia alone tended them) and to landscapes, forests, mountains etc. Whenever we went on an excursion in the car Leśmian never accompanied us. Faced with his poetry, it is hard to believe such indifference possible.[52]

The negative prefixes attached to objects in Leśmian's verse are signs that *they have not been seen*: they only exist in the lexicon, in the imagination. The element of Green is important for Leśmian because it is only from a distance that nature appears to be exclusively green, as the following excerpt from one of his versions of a tale from *The Arabian Nights* confirms:

Firuz Shah looked down and noticed that something was turning green below the clouds. He took heart, for he realised it was the earth that was turning green. It couldn't be seen at all: all one could see was the distant, miraculous colour of green.[53]

Leśmian's poem 'Przemiany' underlines the fact that neither he nor Nature trust one another. During the sultry night of desire evoked by the verse, lower forms of being seek to appropriate the positions of higher and more complex ones: the cornflower becomes a deer; the poppy becomes a cockerel; and the barley husk crushes itself into the form of a hedgehog. In so far as man also seeks to transcend himself and – in this Nietzschean period – supplant God, Leśmian sympathises with this revolt, which is a corollary of the cripple's protest at God's deforming ordinance in his other poems. But, in so far as his own being is threatened by Nature's clamorous desire for the evolutionary leap (Nature's love for man in Leśmian's verse in general is steeped in a will to occupy the place humanity occupies), he seeks to quell the revolt. That is why he finally returns from the anarchic confusion of the night to the conservative clarity of day; and also why the night's attempts to bring forth a thunderstorm end in frustration. Thus the ecstatic aggression whose level rises from verse to verse is in every case braked by the stabilising, shuddering arrest of the final distych. This rhythm of a growing enthusiasm ending in sudden silence and defeat is characteristic of many of Leśmian's poems, which progress from careful openings into ever denser thickets of ambiguity: it is evident in 'Urszula Kochanowska', for instance. When the barley (*jęczmień*, a word which also suggests *jęk*, a groan of pain) crushes itself into a hedgehog (*jeż*) the transformation ceases to be motivated by visual similarity and is generated instead by the acoustic resemblance between the two words: thus language, and hence man, is implicated in the fomenting of the uprising. Hence the transition to the mention of the human subject in the following stanza is a logical one. Whereas in the third stanza language aids the ferment in nature, the final stanza is eager to exonerate man by opposing him to a Nature possessed of fuller knowledge: the speaker seeks to deny his ownership of a nocturnal, other self, such as all the poem's other protagonists possess. He retreats from Nature, whose violence is really his own in projected and disavowed form, and returns to civilisation. (See pp. 184–7 for the text of this poem.)

Leśmian is drawn to folk lore because demythologisation has robbed it of its function, because its alienation mirrors that of the writer. Gabriel Josipovici acutely notes that 'modern writers seem to be drawn to myth more by a sense of its alienness than of its naturalness'.[54] The grotesques that dot Leśmian's work are images of the absurdity of myth following the Enlightenment; and even as he proclaims the value of fairy tale and legend (in his 'Z rozmyślań o Bergsonie') he implicitly criticises it by dispensing with its moral dualism and by writing lines so playfully symmetrical as to anticipate Propp's reduction of the fairy tale to a functional binary machine.

The groups of two or three pregnant dots with which Leśmian and many other Secessionist writers often conclude their lines drop hints both of a repression and of the emergence of new life – the unnamable, the 'something too deep for words'. In 'Z rozmyslán o Bergsonie' Leśmian writes, 'zastaniemy prawdę w połowie zdania' (we meet with truth in the middle of the sentence). The other half of the sentence remains unwritten – the writer is torn away, his pen leaving a few tell-tale dots on the page, the *signs of a crime* – like the unwritten half of the *Tractatus* Wittgenstein deemed more important than the part actually completed. Language collapses, shrugs its shoulders, because of the failure of its attempt to grasp everything: the failure of the totalisation attempted in the *Gesamtkunstwerk*. 'With the decline of the Church, "the gods" cease to be its exclusive property', Leśmian writes. The result, however, is that everything becomes divine. But, if everything is sacred, nothing can be touched, and so the impotence of the imagination incapable of choice is justified. The reality tautologously doubled in photography is self-alienated: photography broadcasts the fact of that alienation. Leśmian's tautological ontology both frantically denies that reality has become displaced from itself and re-enacts the displacement: if everything were really what it is, there would be no need to say so. Tautology is its own worst enemy.

5 Flowers of Nothingness: the *Spätwerk* of Paul Celan

HÖLDERLIN, RILKE, CELAN: TOWARDS AN UNDERSTANDING OF THE LATE WORK

Theodor Adorno has interpreted the parataxis and 'harte Fügung' (harsh articulation) of the late Hölderlin as a sign of tenderness in the poet – of unwillingness to impose an order upon the discontinuous objects of his perception. The late work of Celan, however, demonstrates that parataxis is as violent as it is tender: it is not merely broken, but jaggedly provocative too. As Celan finds himself sucked towards vortices of imbalance, he discovers consolation and bleak auguries in the career of Hölderlin, surely the greatest of schizophrenic poets. Celan's 'Tübingen, Jänner' takes as its theme the relation with the work of Hölderlin:

> Zur Blindheit über-
> redete Augen.
> Ihre – 'ein
> Rätsel ist Rein-
> entsprungnes' – ihre
> Erinnerung an
> schwimmende Hölderlintürme, möwen-
> umschwirrt.
>
> Besuche ertrunkener Schreiner bei
> diesen
> tauchenden Worten:
>
> Käme,
> käme ein Mensch,

käme ein Mensch zur Welt, heute, mit
dem Lichtbart der
Patriarchen: er dürfte,
spräch er von dieser
Zeit, er
dürfte
nur lallen und lallen,
immer-, immer-,
zuzu.

('Pallaksch. Pallaksch.')

(Eyes, talked / over to blindness. / Their – 'what / comes forth
pure / is enigma' – their / memory of / swimming Hölderlin towers,
circled / by gulls.
    A drowned joiner's visitations / to these / deep-delving words:
    If there came, / if there came a man, / if there came a man, to the
world, today, with / the patriarch's / beard of light: he could
only, / were he to speak of this / time, he / could only / babble and
babble / con-, con- / tinually, -ally.
    ('Pallaksch. Pallaksch.')

The importance this poem held for Celan himself is evident from the
word 'Jänner' in the title: for this is the date given at the beginning of
Büchner's *Lenz*, of which Celan spoke at length round about the time
this verse was composed, in his speech entitled 'Der Meridian', on
accepting the award of the Büchner Prize. In this poem he explicitly
situates himself on the poetic line – the meridian – that issues from
Hölderlin. The poem effects a strange double maneouvre. On one level it
establishes the necessity of a non-communicative mode of discourse,
whilst on another the very comprehensibility of its argument refutes its
own thesis that the modern poem can only be a stammering. (Metaphors
of stammering are very frequent in Celan's late work.) On another level,
however, the poem occupies various time scales: the temporal multiplicity signalled by the references both to Hölderlin and the patriarch.
The poem has at least three temporal co-ordinates – the separate times
of Hölderlin, the patriarch, and Celan himself – and perhaps also a
fourth: the apocalyptic time of revelation, which goes beyond time. This
multiple temporality invalidates the interpretation of the poem as a
statement of response to the gradual historical darkening of modern
poetry. The eye is said to have been 'talked / over' to blindness: as

Benjamin noted in his essay on Kafka, those who listen hard do not see. It is as if the 'blinde Sänger' of Hölderlin's late odes has lost his sight through sole concentration upon language (or internal visions): hence the poem's visual images are blurred (like the tower shimmering in the water). The poem demonstrates that nothing can in fact be 'Reinentsprungenes': there are traditions from which one is perpetually quoting. Celan inverts the meaning of this quotation from Hölderlin's Rhine hymn by depicting time and tradition and the complexity of the relationship of times – rather than that which emerges pure and independently of time – as the source of the enigma. Each of the poem's time scales is visible to the others, and yet each is sealed off, as surface reality is sealed off from that which lies underwater. The river, abode of reflections, is the alternative, nocturnal world revealed by Celan's verses. 'Ein Rätsel ist Reinentsprungenes' because, among other things, the water never surrenders the thing it has absorbed: the reflection of the joiner becomes his drowned figure, unable to emerge from the Rhine, the river upon whose name Hölderlin puns. It is the underworld, and the site of Celan's own future death (surely of relevance in the context of the poem's open time scales). The prophet – Hölderlin – Celan himself: each is a splintered image of the absent figure who lies between them, like the true humanity seen through a glass darkly in the words 'käme ein Mensch'. Christoph Theodor Schwab reported in 1846 that during the period of his madness Hölderlin used the word 'Pallaksch' to signify yes and no interchangeably. Uttered twice, it signifies both, and is also eerily suggestive of the sound of lapping water. Quotation is understood here as the ripple generating further ripples that cancel each other out, blur the specificity of each others' forms. The incomprehensible final word is a *material form of silence* (the 'Rätsel' mentioned earlier in the text): an 'Atemkristall' (breath crystal – *AW*, 27), it stands in for a language that does not yet exist.

The main representative of the Hölderlinian hymnic tradition in twentieth-century German verse is of course Rilke. So intense is the elective affinity between Rilke and Celan that many critics have interpreted Celan's work as a form of Rilke parody. Thomas Mann's remark that parody expresses an artist's love for a mode that has ceased to be viable ought however to help one understand the nature of Celan's 'debt'. A primary resemblance can be seen in the way both authors combine a seductive musicality with mannerist conceits that defy one to surrender to the flow of the words. Their most important shared theme, however, is the metalinguistic one. A late poem by Rilke makes this apparent:

Ausgesetzt auf den Bergen des Herzens. Siehe, wie klein dort,
siehe: die letzte Ortschaft der Worte, und höher,
aber wie klein auch, noch ein letztes
Gehöft von Gefühl. Erkennst du's?
Ausgesetzt auf den Bergen des Herzens. Steingrund
unter den Händen. Hier blüht wohl
einiges auf; aus stummen Absturz
blüht ein unwissendes Kraut singend hervor.
Aber der Wissende? Ach, der zu wissen begann
und schweigt jetzt, ausgesetzt auf den Bergen des Herzens.
Da geht wohl, heilen Bewusstseins,
manches umher, manches gesicherte Bergtier,
wechselt und weilt. Und der grosse geborgene Vogel
kreist um der Gipfel reine Verweigerung. – Aber
ungeborgen, hier auf den Bergen des Herzens . . .

(Cast out on the heart's mountains. See, how small there, / see: the last habitation of words, and higher, / but also so tiny, one last / farmstead of feeling. Recognise it? / Cast out on the heart's mountains. Rock ground / under the hands. Something / doubtless blooms here: from the dumb precipice / an ignorant plant is flowering singingly forth. / And the person with knowledge? Ah, the one who began to know / and is silent now, cast out on the heart's mountains. / Doubtless many a thing walks there / with a clear consciousness, many a safe mountain beast / wandering, lingering. And the great secure bird / circles around the summit's pure renunciation. – But / insecure, and here upon the heart's mountains . . .)

Rilke's poem begins starkly, without a verb. One can find similar openings in Celan's late poetry – which also dispenses with titles (wishing to retain the openness of the poem's experience) – particularly 'Weggebeizt' (*AW*, 27: see below, pp. 154–6), which appears to allude to this poem by Rilke. Such openings embody a condition in which events have shuddered to a halt; they flower at the edge of an abyss. Rilke's location of words as part of the landscape is also a feature of late Celan. There is, however, a slight but crucial difference between the two poets: where Celan habitually depicts objects as part of an allegorical inscription upon nature, as in 'Bei Tag' (By Day – *NR*, 60), in which a wing is said to 'write' on the hare-pelt of the sky, Rilke is more likely to consider language as a speech act and term his poems 'songs'. For him

'Gesang ist Dasein' (Song is being) – and vice versa. Rilke's use of the word 'song' is of course suspect: even in his day the poet had ceased to be a 'singer'. What is more, Rilke spins out his linguistic metaphor with a leisureliness suspended between allegory and whimsy, whilst the late poems of Celan are urgent and paratactic. Much of the vocabulary of this poem is echoed in Celan's work. 'Gehöft' anticipates Celan's posthumous collection *Zeitgehöft*, whilst the words 'unwissendes Kraut' surely underlie Celan's injunction in 'Die zweite' (*FS*, 43): 'beiss dich als Wort in den wissenden, / sternlosen, / Halm' (bite as a word on the knowledgeable, / starless, / blade). The verb 'to bloom' is a key one for both authors. (Moreover, Celan had an encyclopaedic knowledge of flowers.) Rilke's etymological play with 'Bergen' (mountains) and 'geborgen' (secure) points backwards to Hölderlin's poem 'An Eduard' and forwards to the Heideggerian theme of the loss of ontological security (*Geborgenheit*), and of course the etymological puns of Celan himself.

Celan's poetry draws conclusions from the fact that for many the Rilkean idiom has become irrevocably compromised. The late work in particular practises systematic doubt *vis-à-vis* the Rilkean key words and themes of his own earlier poetry: breaking up the long musical line, attaching elemental key words such as 'heart' and 'eye' to non-poetic modern terms, replacing the narcissism of Rilke's philosophy with a repertoire of quotations that indicates the fragmentation of a multiple personality. In Rilke's poetry the mirror restores the self to itself: the Angels draw their own beauty back into themselves. For Celan, the reflected image is an index of an unquenchable self-alienation. In the work of Celan, Rilke's assertion that the individual has a personal death is blown apart by the terrible impersonality of the Jews' annihilation in the Nazi concentration camps. If life and death interlock in the work of both poets, for Celan this means that one consents to live on by breathing the airborne ashes of the crematoria. (Upon which one's conscience chokes. See 'Deine Augen im Arm' [The Eyes in Your Arm] – *FS*, 17.) Where Rilke deems art the repository of truth (at the beginning of the *Neue Gedichte* the statue of Apollo convinces the spectator he must change his life) Celan depicts truth as situated somewhere beyond the 'Metapherngestöber' (the metaphors' swirlings). In the poem in question, 'Ein Dröhnen', Celan alludes to Rilke's poem entitled 'Gong' (the gong Rilke describes as the 'Summe des Schweigenden, das / sich zu sich selber bekennt' [the sum of that which keeps silence / affirming itself]) in order to contradict it. The sound of the gong becomes the 'Dröhnen' (rumbling) of truth, which has come down to humanity, in the midst of 'das Metapherngestöber'.

These swirling metaphors rage throughout Celan's final collections. He accumulates them furiously so that the speed of their coloured whirling will finally generate the whiteness that contradicts them. Truth does not enter the world as the Logos ('Ein Dröhnen' parodies the beginning of the Gospel of St John) but in the form of white noise. The mannerist metaphors of Celan's late work are not Rilkean indicators of the grotesquely self-sufficient and often tasteless ingenuity of the author, but stand for the contradictions of reality. In Rilke's work negative experience underpinned a metaphysic and an aesthetic: the negative was positive inasmuch as it constituted the precondition of poetic imagination. Since – as Sartre notes – one can only imagine that which is absent, it becomes possible for Rilke to interpret the experience of loss as an induction into the non-possessive possession represented by a purely imaginary 'grasp' of the object, the *Ding* (thing). For Celan, however, negative experience yields no such dialectical consolation, and this is because his theme is the wounding and death of the human being, not the loss of the *Ding*. (When Rilke says of the objects we possessed once 'nie erholen sie sich ganz' (they never quite recover), the anthropomorphisation is surely etiolated.)

If Celan's early poetry is rich in Rilkean phraseology, his later work contaminates it with scientific terms and colloqualisms or vulgarisms. But, if this ravaged late language is dark, it is not because it cherishes a lone solitude but because it speaks the lament of defeated causes. These include those of the Spartakists, of the Republicans of the Spanish Civil War, and – of course – of the Jews during the Second World War. A Romanian Jew, living in Paris, writing in German, Celan was deeply scarred by the disruptions and compulsory relocations of this century. Much of his significance stems from his decision not merely to write 'after Auschwitz' (of which he had far closer experience than any of the 'extremists' touted by such a critic as Alvarez) but to manage its traumas through the oblique ciphers of a high and mannered art. For to have given a simply documentary impression of the horror of the events he survived (the most common means of rendering both the events and the helplessness of the artist confronted with their often unimaginable bestiality) would have been to imply that these appalling events could be considered with an objective eye. The documentary approach (even at its most crystalline and shocking, as in the stories of Tadeusz Borowski) suggests that the suffering is bound to a single moment, that it has a half life, and that after 1945 it gradually recedes. Celan knew this was not so: the terror of the Third Reich lives on in the lives and political orders it damaged, and the roots of fascism are still too ill comprehended for one to deem it a thing of the past. They are perpetuated, for instance, in modern anti-semitism. Celan rethinks Mallarmé – rethinks Rilke – and transforms the art of the inexpressible into the art of the unspeakable. In this respect he is Kafka's heir. The enormous resonance of his work is the result of its fusion of politics and Symbolism – a combination so unusual as to pass unmentioned in most considerations of the poems. The closest parallel is surely with the work of Adorno. English exegetes of Celan tend to repress the politics of his poetry, and to deem its obscurity necessarily apolitical. Its politics are susceptible of repression, however, because they are problematic, not because they are non-existent. They become clear when one realises that, like Adorno, Celan lived and wrote in the prolonged shadow of the concentration camps. For both men the hermetic verse, the verse that is difficult and provokes meditation, opposes the fatal ease of exchange that degrades both a language and its users. Celan's later poetry in particular can be seen to practise shock therapy upon the German language: in rendering it virtually 'unreadable' – so much so that some Germans accuse him of having forgotten his German through residence in Paris (in fact he used his life in Paris as a means of alienating the German language from itself, to express its own self-alienation in and after the Nazi period) – he asks what it means to speak it – what it means to speak at all – in the aftermath of the wordlessness of one's horror.

EIGHT POEMS

Psalm

Niemand knetet uns wieder aus Erde und Lehm,
niemand bespricht unsern Staub.
Niemand.

Gelobt seiest du, Niemand.
Dir zulieb wollen
wir blühn,
Dir
entgegen.

Ein Nichts
waren wir, sind wir, werden

wir bleiben, blühend:
die Nichts-, die
Niemandsrose.

Mit
dem Griffel seelenhell,
dem Staubfaden himmelswüst,
der Krone rot
vom Purpurwort, das wir sangen
über, o über
dem Dorn.

(No one kneads us anew of earth and clay, / no one conjures our
dust. / No One.
    Praised be You, No One. / For Your sake / we will
bloom, / towards / You.
    A Nothing / is what we were, are, and will / remain, blooming: / the
nothing's, the No One's / rose.
    With our pistil soul-bright, / our stamen heaven-ravaged, / our
crown reddened / by the purple word we sang / over, O over / the
thorn.)

'Psalm' is enunciated by a chorus that includes the living, who are dead,
and the dead, who are alive. The present tense functions very interestingly and very bitterly in the first three lines: it sucks the futurity of
resurrection or a second creation back into the present and so insists that
any after-life must be one of this body, this earth. It denies the soul –
body dualism of Christian thought (there is no basis for this dualism in
Judaic tradition). The time of these lines is a limbo-like unity of the
beginning, middle and end of temporality: the reference to the creation
of Adam out of the dust introduces the beginning, the present tense
embodies the interim period, whilst the hints of resurrection invoke the
end. In its desolation the verse surveys all time and then discards it,
subverting the very mythology it evokes.
    The tripartite reduction of the first verse unit is repeated in the three-
part movement of the second one. At first the 'we' praises No One; then
it voices a wish to flower for His sake; finally 'Dir / entgegen' has
overtones of opposition or defiance. The last two lines are apparently
ambiguous (meaning both 'towards you' and 'against you'), but the
lineation tips the balance towards the latter possibility by infusing the
words with an insolent coolness or deliberation, as if the 'we' is staring

the No One out. Blasphemy is concealed beneath an ambiguity that fools no one (No One?).

The triple temporality of the opening lines reappears in the third group of lines: 'Ein Nichts / waren wir, sind wir, werden / wir bleiben'. By juxtaposing within a single line the verbs for past, present and future Celan indicates their uniformity: time is unchanging. Thus it is hardly surprising that although both the line break after 'werden' and the congenital optimism of the future tense suggest the imminence of change, the verb 'bleiben' instantly undermines our faith in the purposiveness of forward movement and sends us back to the previous line (a sort of poetic snakes and ladders: the move forward sends one back). 'Die Nichts-' parallels the earlier 'ein Nichts' and the force of the parallel is such as to turn it into a separate word, to counteract its subordinate status as part of a compound word (the lineation that grants it a position on its own simply accentuates its self-sufficiency): as such, however, it represents an absurd denial of grammar. And also of sexuality: just as all time is filled with the same emptiness of experience, so there is no sexual differentiation: 'Nichts' can be both masculine and feminine here, androgynous, like the flower of the final stanza. 'Nothing' is as it were the neuter state between the sexes. The androgyny is the correlative of the sense of sterility that dominates the verse. 'Blühend' is a timeless participle and so reinforces the mocking uniformity of the unaltering state. In the light of these lines the 'Dir / entgegen' of the previous verse assumes the intonation of a threat: 'waren wir, sind wir, werden / wir bleiben' is like a declaration of intent to bloom as a bitter eyesore before 'Niemand': condemned by Him to an endless nullity and death, yet still somehow persisting. This determination is embittered still further by the fact of His non-existence: so there will be no witnesses to the blooming of the 'we': 'Niemand / zeugt für den Zeugen' (No one / witnesses to the witness – *AW*, 68). Yet 'Niemand' is both the unnamable God of negative theology, referred to only in circumlocutory form, and a real absence of persons. The self is observed as the flower that testifies to, and causes oblivion of, the fact that people underlie it: the dead who push poppies, push roses.

Because of the unchanging sky that hangs above the poem there is no verb in the final section: only an inescapable state. The Rose is a mystical symbol, seldom visualised in the poems that employ it. Celan however demythologises the pseudo-religious, Rilkean incarnation of the Rose, the 'Niemandsrose': 'Psalm' alludes to Rilke's famous epitaph for himself, 'Rose, o reiner Widerspruch, / Lust, niemandes Schlaf zu sein / unter so viel Lidern' (Rose, o pure contradiction, / wish to be no one's sleep / under so many eyelids). Celan inserts into the rose the thorn that gave Rilke blood-poisoning. He evokes the pain the poet feels through the thorn. The thorn of the last lines is somehow inserted into the rose, like a knife or a needle. 'Über, o über' gasps for breath as if speaking through gritted teeth in despite of suffering, and if the song transcends pain just as the rose itself is higher than ('über') the thorn, the intonation also suggests a sardonic appraisal of this transcendence. This is because the speakers of 'Psalm' are trapped between death and resurrection. Having suffered something akin to a crucifixion (Christ's death is suggested by the 'Krone', the 'Dorn' and the mocking 'Purpur', the purple robe of the King of the Jews); having transcended the pain of the thorn ('sangen' is in the past tense – as if the song of transcendence over the thorn were a different one from the bitter 'Psalm' of the perpetual present, in which time is unchanging and nothing is ever preterite) – the speakers are condemned to a dual exile, unable to either live or die. They are material ghosts, the living who are only at best 'undead'. Spoken from the grave, the poem looks to a second life and sees that no one (No one? the birth of religion out of despair?) will provide one. The song of release from the nightmare of the first life – the song that was a rose in the desert (Isaiah) – has become a psalm to 'The nightmare Life-in-Death' (Coleridge). Negative theology and blasphemy prove to be one.

Weggebeizt

Weggebeizt vom
Strahlenwind deiner Sprache
das bunte Gerede des An-
erlebten – das hundert-
züngige Mein-
gedicht, das Genicht.

Aus-
gewirbelt,
frei
der Weg durch den Menschen-
gestaltigen Schnee,
den Büsserschnee, zu
den gastlichen
Gletscherstuben und – tischen.

Tief
in der Zeitenschrunde
beim
Wabeneis
wartet, ein Atemkristall,
dein unumstössliches
Zeugnis.

(Cauterised from / the raywind of your language / the bright chatter of ex- / perience – the hundred- / tongued false / poem, the noem.

Whirled / out, / free / the way through the human- / shaped snow, / the penitents' snow, / to the hospitable / glacier chambers and tables.

Deep / in time's crevasse, / by the / honeycomb ice / there waits, a crystal of breath, / your incontestable / witness.)

The first lines of this poem oppose a cleansing raywind to a hundred-tongued poem, but the opposition is also an apposition, for the Pentecostal allusion links the two. It may have been Celan's intention – as Michael Hamburger has noted – to polemicise with low mimetic varieties of poetry, but the ambiguity of the 'du' compels one to see the invective as directed inwards as well as outwards. For even if 'Mein- / gedicht' is an intended allusion to *Meineid*, a false oath, it still has the literal meaning of 'my poem'. Celan's polemic opposes the facility of a writing based on 'das An- / erlebte': the enjambement after the 'An-' sardonically rips off what is merely an accretion to the *tabula rasa* of silence towards which the poem tends. Hamburger translates 'Mein- / gedicht' as 'pseudo / poem' and explains that Celan himself rejected 'my poem' as a feasible version, but in the original German the distinction ceases to exist: the claim to own a poem itself declares it a pseudo-poem, and Celan undercuts the sanctity of property by alienating the self into 'du' and by virtually eliminating all personal and possessive pronouns from the poem.

Celan's poem opens with a cluster of alliterations and assonances that ricochet crazily within the confined space of the short lines, evoking a clangorous atmosphere of conflict. The initial verb vibrates like a spear hurled challengingly into the heap of substantives below it, in which it is mired. The double-barrelled formations and the breaking-open of words are shocking and generate immense energy. They are disturbing: two words are locked in combat for a single place, as are the poet's self and his anti-self. With the second verse and the reference to the penitents' snow the poem acquires a certain positivity, yet the description of the 'Gletscherstuben' as 'gastlich' has a satirical ring: it parodies the world of those who find alienation comfortable and anticipates the 'Schneekneipe' of 'Lila Luft' (*SP*, 9). There is a constant tension in the poem between the rhetorical and the Symbolist modes. The only element that is unequivocally positive is the silent vigil at the end. The poem is able to close here because its tension has been exhausted: the price it pays for this is an access of sentimentality, a certain sloganeering quality. For the last verse is far less interesting than the two previous ones – it is safer, less poetically daring. It is glad to overcome its own mixed feelings in the stupored weariness that follows the climb to the upper reaches of the mountain. This climbing above words and subsequent passage into the sheltering openness of the mountain echoes Rilke's 'Ausgesetzt auf den Bergen des Herzens', which also opens with an arresting adjective. Celan does, however, achieve an airy sense of release in this final stanza: in the assonances of 'beim / Wabeneis / wartet', for instance, and this partly compensates for the weakness of the final stanza. There is a grace and a singing sweetness alien to the poem hitherto.

In the light of 'Weggebeizt', one can say that the poems of Paul Antschel (Celan's real name) are not 'Meingedichte', for they are attributed to Paul Celan. The dialectical triad ends outside language, in a realm of crystallised breath, of frozen pre-language. The poem enacts a dialectic of self-cancellation and self-transcendence, and comes to rest in the snowy whiteness of the page. The future will witness to the poet: in choosing silence now he declares his allegiance to its non-existent language.

Ich kenne dich

(Ich kenne dich, du bist die tief Gebeugte,
ich, der Durchbohrte, bin dir untertan.
Wo flammt ein Wort, das für uns beide zeugte?
Du – ganz, ganz wirklich. Ich – ganz Wahn.)

((I know you: you are the one bowed deeply, / I am the pierced one, subject unto you. / Where does a word flare out as both our witness? / You – quite, quite real. And I – mad through and through.))

'Ich kenne dich' evokes the absurdity of speech in a world of failed communication. The placement of the poem in parentheses underlines the absurdity. The parentheses isolate their contents, patronisingly but also ambiguously: they demonstrate that the poetic (whose signifier is rhyme) has to be insulated from a reality that suffers impoverishment in its turn through the loss of the poetic. Absurdity arises from the elimination of context: the parenthetical text requires an accompanying text, a commentary, the absence of which makes a mockery of its meaningfulness. By removing from their contexts such words as 'die Gebeugte' and 'der Durchbohrte', Celan creates an interpersonal suspension of properties, of mysterious elective affinities. The scene is a *Pietà*, but superimposed upon this 'original' scene are the Crucifixion and the piercing of Mary's breast by the swords of her sorrows. For both Christ and Mary are pierced (the one by nails and a spear, the other by the sword of grief), and both are 'servants' (Christ as the servant in Isaiah, Mary bent over the broken body of her son). The 'bending' mentioned in the first line may recall either the Catholic image of Mary interceding for unworthy souls (Gretchen's 'Ach neige, / Du Schmerzenreiche, / Dein Antlitz ab zu meiner Not' in *Faust*; O you, rich in sorrows, bend your countenance to my distress), or Christ's willingness to divest himself of the Godhead and assume mortal form. Hence 'die tief Gebeugte' and 'der Durchbohrte' fuse into a single androgynous figure which, expelled from its cultural, social and religious contexts, is on the verge of crumbling away.

This crumbling is the fundamental experience of the modern era. Benjamin termed the destruction of context in modern society, whose elements are mingled ever more promiscuously, a destruction of 'aura'. If, however, the kaleidoscope of shifting images is held at one point as two or more images pass over and eclipse each other, the result is a new kind of 'aura', the aura Celan's poem possesses; the aura of mystery. One peers into the darkness of the image by pressing one's eyelids, forcing dancing colours out of obscurity. Thus 'Ich kenne dich' suggests an image of George and the dragon as well as a *Pietà* and a Crucifixion: several types of religious image are impacted within it. (The linking of speech and flame in the third line helps suggest this semi-formed image, which one should not take too seriously, just as one should not read too univocally the earlier references to the *Pietà*.) Press the eyelids again and one perceives an image of Celan's relationship with his mother: her suffering and death in a concentration camp (here the bending has far different implications) fuse with his sense of having died with her, the piercing stab of grief, and self-hatred for having survived.

'Ich kenne dich': the statement is comprehensively ironised by the unknowability of the personalities that move within the poem. For the poem is not 'about' the Crucifixion, the *Pietà*, or the death of Celan's mother, though the latter is the main source of its poignancy. The parentheses, and perhaps even the additional thematic levels, are the means whereby Celan defends himself against the unmanning power of his emotion. The parentheses say the poem is an image of all that is not the case; they insist that its words can never be the Word, the word of witness (Celan alludes to and contradicts Gottfried Benn's 'Ein Wort', in which the poetic word is a fire illuminating the darkness around 'Welt und ich'[world and I].) Nevertheless, the confidence with which reference is made to 'die tief Gebeugte' (the periphrasis implies shared knowledge of her identity) evokes trust in the existence of an order of reality in which the words are comprehensible. It brims over with an unfocused faith. The longing for the world within the parentheses, for the poetic order of rhyme, is yearning for lost time, for lost worlds. The parentheses are clamps that hold it in place to prevent it dissolving in tears.

Give the Word

Ins Hirn gehaun – halb? zu drei Vierteln? –,
gibst du, genächtet, die Parolen – diese:

'Tartarenpfeile.'
        'Kunstbrei.'
              'Atem.'

Es kommen alle, keiner fehlt und keine.
(Sipheten und Probyllen sind dabei.)

Es kommt ein Mensch.

Weltapfelgross die Träne neben dir,
durchrauscht, durchfahren,
von Antwort,
       Antwort,
             Antwort.
Durcheist – von wem?

'Passiert', sagst du,
      'passiert',
           'passiert'.

Der stille Aussatz löst sich dir vom Gaumen
und fächelt deiner Zunge Licht zu,
          Licht.

(Cut to the brains – half-way? or three quarters? – / you give,
benighted, the passwords, these ones:
'Tartar arrows.' / 'Artificial mash.' / 'Breath.'
Everyone comes, no man or woman missing. / (The siphets and the
probyls are all there.)
There comes a man. / World-apple-big the tear by your
side, / tumultuously   shot   through / with   answer, / answer, /
answer. / Iced through – by whom?
'Pass by' you say, / pass by, / pass by.'
Still leprosy lifts itself from your palate / and fans light in your
tongue's direction, / light.)

The title of this poem is a quotation from the scene in *King Lear* (IV.
vi) in which Lear accosts Edgar and Gloucester near Dover and, with deep
dramatic irony, asks them to 'Give the word' as a sentry would. His
madness has stripped him of his identity as king: he is merely a sentry,
with no castle to guard. The opening line translates Lear's earlier cry
that he is 'cut to the brains'. But his language of pain and excess is
questioned, rendered absurd, bombastic, by the interlocutor who takes
it literally: how deeply have they cut you, he asks? Have they cut through
half your brain? Or as much as three-quarters? The questioning voice is
also an internalised one; it is Celan's echo of the Fool. The benighted self
(the word 'genächtet' may seem to allude to the 'Umnachtung' of
Hölderlin's madness) is exposed to a buffeting storm without and
within. The absurd sequence of question and answer continues in 'Es
kommen alle, keiner fehlt und keine', in which the second half of the line
and the sentence in brackets suggest disbelieving mock agreement ('Oh
yes, they all come now you've lost your crown', the Fool might say). It is
as if the Fool is deriding the King's pretensions to be able to convoke an
assembly of the entire realm. Only parodic, inverted prophets and
sibyls – 'Sipheten und Probyllen' – could present themselves at the scene
of such mental suffering, their bizarre names akin to appellations of
demons.

At this point, however, the poem changes gear, from jeering to
solemnity. 'Es kommt ein Mensch' has a disillusioning starkness: the
speaker has only a man for company, not the arcane powers of the
universe. All that comes is a bare fork'd animal. But the phrase also

inaugurates a pathos, an apocalyptic and hieratic mode of speech that dispels the earlier bitter torment. It is the axis on which the poem turns, both ludicrous (if everyone has come, how can there be any new arrivals?) and solemn (the 'Mensch' is like the true and Utopian human being envisaged in 'Tübingen, Jänner', and resembles the biblical 'Son of Man'). True humanity can only be revealed at the edge of derangement. The poem's passage from bitter allusiveness to a grand style of solitude is relatively frequent in Celan's work (cf. 'Weggebeizt'): the allusions are a chaos of voices from which the speaker's own voice only gradually disengages itself. The weightiness of 'Weltapfelgross' reinforces the altered rhythm (the comparison between world and apple recalls both Enzensberger's 'nänie auf den apfel' (Elegy for the Apple) and the biblical conceit of the apple for which the world was lost). The adjective is doubly apt: a world-moving tear is of great significance, and a tear the size of an apple is of unusual magnitude. The fact that the 'Träne' is said to be 'neben dir' prompts one to ask its provenance. The phrase may be an inversion of the statement that the self is close to tears. But there may be another present – Edgar, the Fool – whose tears are the only adequate, because mute, answer ('Antwort, Antwort, Antwort') to the sight of extreme human pain. The tear is also shed by the self, which finds relief in tears from its blind bellowing pain at the outset: the advent of a person with compassion as it were allows the self to break down and cry like a child, as the sympathetic other weeps. The mystery of encounter is that with the arrival of the other the self itself becomes other. Whence the question 'von wem', the haziness of the identity of 'du'. But, if light dawns in the tongue at the end, it may be because the mind remains in darkness.

Landschaft

Landschaft mit Urnenwesen.
Gespräche
von Rauchmund zu Rauchmund.

Sie essen:
die Tollhäusler-Trüffel, ein Stück
unvergrabener Poesie,
fand Zunge und Zahn.

Eine Träne rollt in ihr Auge zurück.

Die linke, verwaiste
Hälfte der Pilger –
muschel – sie schenkten sie dir,
dann banden sie dich –
leuchtet lauschend den Raum aus:

das Klinkerspiel gegen den Tod
kann beginnen.

Landscape with urn beings. / Conversations / from smoke mouth
to smoke mouth.
They eat: / the madhouse-inmate truffle, a piece / of disinterred
poetry, / encountered tongue and tooth.
A tear rolls back into its eye.
The left-hand, orphaned / half of the pilgrim's / scallop – they gave
it to you, / and then placed you in bonds – / lights up the space as it
listens:
The clinker-game against death / can begin.)

In the poetry of Celan the eye has been 'talked / over to blindness'
(*NR*, 24). Where the eye is sightless one learns to look with one's ears. As
they attend to a verse by Celan, the ears perceive shadow senses that
scurry along inbetween the lines. The eye may perceive the link between
'Stück' and 'zurück' (establishing that the weeping is for the object of the
previous verse, for the 'Tollhäusler-Trüffel'), but the ear will see other
connections. Take the word 'Urnenwesen'. The poem begins in a
landscape of urns: the combined presence of landscape and urns a dual
sign of the absence of human beings. But ghosts of meaning emerge from
this landscape and from the word 'Urnenwesen'. 'Urnen' is almost akin
to a stammer, the form of speech Celan programmatically favours in
'Tübingen, Jänner'. It contains two prefixes, 'ur' and 'un' (in the form of
'u . . . n'): 'Ur' designates the primeval, 'un' a negation. 'Ur . . . wesen'
and 'U . . . n . . . wesen' become one in the suggestiveness of a word
that links primeval death, urn burial and the *Unwesen* of the landscape
of a concentration camp. For 'Landschaft', like most of Celan's
verse, circles round the experience of the Nazi concentration camps. To
say this outright is to risk sounding implausible or brutal or both: and
yet a whole series of touches in the poem point to the presence of the
theme. There is the 'Rauchmund', so like a chimney in the
crematoria, the 'Rauch', which for Celan represents the wandering
homeless forms of the dead (cf. 'Todesfuge' (Fugue of Death)), the
reference to the 'Tollhäusler' – the 'degenerates' exterminated by the

Nazis – and of course the expunging of all signs of humanity from the
verbless first line. This beginning, an apparent end, is followed however
by a defiant flashback to that which preceded the initial *nature morte*.
Like *Nuit et brouillard*, Alain Resnais's film about the concentration
camps, 'Landschaft' begins by presenting them as they now appear to
us: neutral, overgrown landscape, still life, *nature morte*. The reminder
of death implicit in the notion of the *nature morte* and the sense of
continued being contained in '*still* life' give Celan his cue to resurrect the
dead, to play 'das Klinkerspiel gegen den Tod', and to penetrate the
impassive surface of the first line to reveal the tortured thicket of
traumas that underlies it. The second line speaks of conversations: these
are held, as it were, between the dead who have risen into the sky as the
smoke of the gas ovens, who address each other with 'smoke mouths'.
But this conversation, this dialogue, is also enacted within each and
every image, which is subjected to an overdetermination that renders it
dialectically at odds with itself. Thus 'Rauchmund' is both the speaking
mouth of the dead and the chimney from which the wreaths of smoke
arise. The second stanza in its turn indicates the ambiguity of the mouth
(the poem is a network of apertures): it both creates and
destroys, generates dialogue and consumes, is both 'Zunge' and 'Zahn'
(for, if 'fand Zunge' suggests a positive breakthrough from silence into
speech, 'fand . . . Zahn' carries far more disturbing connotations of
being eaten alive). If the 'Urnenwesen' of the beginning can also be seen
to recall the characters of a Beckett, trapped in their terrible
selfhood, then 'Zunge und Zahn' conveys some of the violence of the
Beckettian speech act: the combination of tooth and tongue in *Not I*, for
instance. The 'Tollhäusler-Trüffel' would seem to be the poor lunatics
consigned to the camps by the Nazis. The ugliness of the compound
noun has the ring of a quotation from fascist utterance ('a tasty
morsel'), rather like the words 'die Sau' used of Rosa Luxemburg in 'Du
liegst' (*SP*, 8): in fact, the whole second verse unit constitutes a series of
transformations of clichés. (Apart from 'fand Zunge' there is also 'ein
Stück / unvergrabener Poesie', which recalls the vocabulary of sub-
Romantic literary criticism.) The poetry may be said to be unburied
because the dead who float up into the sky have no earthly place of rest
(this is one of the associative links between the first and second verse
units). With bitter irony Celan terms the dead 'truffles': truffles are
always disinterred, and exist to be eaten. Celan mocks the 'Poesie' (an
etiolated term for poetry) that discerns anything positive in this terrible
sequence of events. If poetry is immortal and people are mortal, all the
worse for poetry, he seems to be saying.

If 'look with your ears' is a possible epigraph to this poem, 'the ear of man hath not seen' is perhaps an even better one. The symbiosis of hearing and sight is a fundamental theme of Celan's poetry. The first lines of 'Du liegst' address a subject outstretched in the midst of snow 'im grossen Gelausche' (in a great listening): the conjunction of the whiteness of snow and the theme of listening recalls the 'leuchtet lauschend' of 'Landschaft'. In 'Du liegst' the snow lights up the darkness, erases the boundary between night and day, creating a white night of hallucination and epileptic vision, and so persuades the self to walk out into the trauma-laden dreamscape of the Berlin night world as if it were day. The connection between the last lines of 'Landschaft' and the opening line of 'Du liegst' is cemented by the appearance of the word 'beginnen' in the very last line: it suggests the possibility of continuation in a later poem (and also forms part of the underground sense of the Beckettian in this poem: 'in my end is my beginning' is the quintessence of Beckett).

In the second half of 'Landschaft' (each half begins with a single line standing on its own, the absolutism of which is subsequently relativised and as it were conjugated by the sequence of lines with enjambements that follows it on each occasion) an addressee for the poem emerges. He/she is termed 'du' and is said to hold the left-hand portion of a pilgrim's scallop shell. 'Linke', the adjective used of the shell, has connotations of lucklessness that are far stronger in German than they are in English. ('Verwaist' may also refer to Celan's own orphaned condition. In fact, he is doubly an orphan. Not only did he lose his parents in a concentration camp; he was also an only child, and the degree to which he suffered under his isolation can be felt in the force of his obsession with the image of the sister – which may be one reason why Trakl was a congenial influence. 'Verwaist' and 'Hälfte' are linked and may remind one of the fairy tales in which two lovers, or a brother and sister, live in separation, each holding a matching half of an object. Are these the two halves of the poem itself?) The half shell that illuminates space is also a clinker ('linke' and 'Klinker' rhyme and are very nearly anagrams of each other: their connection is seen by the ear that itself is present in the poem as the 'Muschel'). Why is this half shell said to be 'lauschend'? Because the 'Muschel' is also that of the ear, and because it is listening for the arrival of its complementary half. The word 'Muschel' can be seen to enact the same dialectic as was present in 'Rauchmund': both seashell and ear, as a seashell it listens to its own alienated sound (song, this poem?). The ear exists by itself: it is singular. And because of this singularity it anticipates a later poem by Celan, in which – as in 'Landschaft' – the verb *schenken* and the ear are associated: the poem in question, 'Mächte, Gewalten' (Powers, dominions) (*FS*, 103), ends with the statement that 'Vincents verschenktes / Ohr / ist am Ziel' (Vincent's / gift of an ear / finds its goal). In 'Landschaft' the enjambement 'Pilger- / muschel' re-enacts the halving of the shell, the severing of Van Gogh's ear. The ear, a pilgrim, consecrates space by its listening search. The searching-out of space by the ear is reflected in the echoing *au* sound of 'leuchtet lauschend den Raum aus', which moves outwards in concentric circles and culminates in the sense of release of the 'aus' (the game is 'aus', both finished and lost: the mention of beginning in the final line is in tension with this 'aus'). In mentioning the ear at this point the poem completes its three-stage passage from one sense organ to another, from the mouth to the eye to the ear. The fact that the 'du' of this verse unit is both the recipient of a gift and a figure bound suggests that, on one level of the poem's shifting veils of significance, he is identical with Van Gogh, who in his madness is both self and other, both the recipient of the posted ear and the one who has lost it and whose head wound needs to be bandaged (one sense of 'dann banden sie'). 'Dir' and 'dich', the dative and the accusative, form a grim semantic rhyme that brings out the duality of relationship: it renders one both the recipient of a gift and a victim. (The combination of gift and binding may also recall the last favour granted the victim tied to the stake.)

The last line of 'Landschaft' speaks of an imminent beginning: of a game with death in which clinkers are moved like pieces on a board. As it refers to the fact of beginning, it sends one back to the start of the poem – a frequent feature of Celan's work – which thus forms a circle, a whirlpool of signification in which all meanings are co-present in one and the same state of timelessness. The persistence of suffering from age to age, like the co-existence of opposite meanings within a single word (such as 'Rauchmund') renders time's succession senseless. Celan's primary empathy with the dead of the concentration camps opens out – in accordance with his aesthetics of the 'open' poem – into an outraged lament, banishing its tears (l. 8: a line which also alludes to Dante and the impossibility of tears in the Inferno), for the objects of judicial murder and incarceration, the marginal figures, of all the ages: for the damned, the insane, the Jews and Van Gogh. For if there is a single prevailing spirit in the poem it is that of Van Gogh: 'Tollhäusler', 'Landschaft' and ll. 9–13 can all be associated with him. For Celan's poem too, like the paintings of Van Gogh, is a still life, a *nature morte*, that rages with energy, exuding compassion and madness.

Helligkeitshunger

Helligkeitshunger – mit ihm
ging ich die Brot-
stufe hinauf,
unter die Blinden-
glocke:

sie, die wasser-
klare,
stülpt sich über
die mitgestiegene, mit-
verstiegene Freiheit, an der
einer der Himmel sich sattfrass,
den ich sich wölben liess über
der wortdurchschwommenen
Bildbahn, Blutbahn.

(Hunger for brightness – with this / I climbed up the bread / step, / under the bell / of the blind:
    it, the water- / clear one, / inverts itself over / the climbed-to, climbed- / away freedom, upon which / one of the heavens guzzled itself, / the one I had allowed to arch over / the word-swimming / image track, blood track.)

The ambiguity of Celan's conception of freedom through negativity lies at the heart of this poem: in 'Der Meridian' he had instructed the poet to enter into his most private straits in order to set himself free ('Geh mit der Kunst in deine allereigenste Enge. Und setzte dich frei'). This law of contraction is the motive principle of the development of his work as a whole. Nevertheless, I think one should understand this statement as a means of making a virtue of his own terrible personal suffering. One should resist the tendency to discover concealed affirmations below the surfaces of negation. The negative remains negative, without any sophistic consolation.

In 'Helligkeitshunger' freedom is limited at every level. First, it is circumscribed by Rilke's 'Der Turm' (The Tower), a poem whose long and syntactically complex climb into the light it reenacts, even as it amends its meaning. It is impelled upwards by a 'Helligkeitshunger', a hunger for real and metaphorical light, that cannot be stilled by the 'Brotstufe' (the stage at which bread alone suffices, as it were). The hunger, however, permits the sky to limit its freedom: 'den ich sich wölben liess' embodies a desire for self-limitation in which the sky is both real and other and a projection in the imagination. Between the words 'ich' and 'sich' is played out a dialectic of self-identity and otherness in which the reflexive verb allows the sky to be itself whilst at the same time absorbing it into the poetic self. What is more, the freedom the self achieves is 'mitgestiegen, mit- / verstiegen': it was lost on entry to the tower, regained on climbing its steps, lost and gained on arriving at the top (one lost the ability to keep on going, whilst the eye was liberated to survey the surroundings). But the sky itself is an extension of the tower over which it is suspended. One experiences it as such because the bell suggested by the 'Blindenglocke' (which blinds one by covering one, which is a clock for the blind, who hear its chimes whilst unable to perceive its face) – as well as by the words 'stülpt sich' – is rendered akin to the sky by the adjective 'wasserklar', which serves to make enclosure transparent – like blue water – and the transparent a form of enclosure. For all the elements of beauty and release the poem invokes, the fusion of sky and bell is a painful one: the metaphor of the bell-like sky is beautiful but imprisoning. Once the poet has reached the top of the tower he has exhausted the possibilities upon which his blind, isolated imagination had fed. He has ceased to be a poet, his passage out of the darkness having entailed renunciation of the status of 'der blinde Sänger' (Hölderlin's blind *seer*): he has been talked back from the blindness of 'Tübingen, Jänner' to sight. But at the same time the world of images for which he has renounced his words is horrific and meaningless: the 'Bildbahn' is also a 'Blutbahn' (which sounds like a 'Blutbad' – a bloodbath). Rather than perceive the world, the self transforms the sky into a bell beneath which it can hide. For, although the poem may enact a passage out of the ivory tower, it remains trapped in its own words and horror of words. Obedient to injunctions from the Rilke it also amends, it goes blind round the images within it.

Pau, später

In deinen Augen-
winkeln, Fremde,
der Albigenserschatten –

nach
dem Waterloo-Plein,
zum verwaisten

Bastschuh, zum
mitverhökerten Amen,
in die ewige
Hauslücke sing ich
dich hin:

dass Baruch, der niemals
Weinende
rund um dich die
kantige,
unverstandene, sehende
Träne zurecht-
schleife.

(*Pau, Later*

In your eyes' corners, stranger: / the Albigensian shadow –
towards / the Waterloo-Plein, / the orphaned / bark shoe, the /
hawked amen thrown in too, / and into the everlasting / house-gap
my song / directs you:
that Baruch, the never- / weeping / may grind to fit round you / the
angular, / uncomprehended, visionary / tear.)

Some of the facts one needs to know comprehend this poem's field of
reference have been supplied by Marlies Janz (*Vom Engagement
absoluter Poesie* (On the Committedness of Absolute Poetry), p. 185).
The Waterloo-Plein is the Amsterdam flea-market, situated in the old
Jewish quarter of the town; the gap in housing marks the spot where the
Nazis pulled down Jewish dwellings. As a Portuguese Jew, Baruch
(Spinoza) has a special relationship with the Waterloo-Plein: in the
adjoining synagogue the orthodox Jewish community pronounced him
anathema. One need only add to these details from the history of
Amsterdam the knowledge that Pau is a French town near the Basque
country, one of the strongholds of the Albigensian cause, and one is
almost able to comprehend the poem.

But Janz's reading, fine as it is, is only a partial one; and in general in
her book she tends only to perceive one allusion where in fact several are
compacted within a single poem. Thus Baruch is not only Spinoza; he is
also the historian mentioned in the Old Testament, the secretary of
the prophet Jeremiah. Inasmuch as he is Spinoza, 'Baruch' is
'niemals / Weinende' because his pantheist philosophy excludes the

problem of negativity or evil. But, inasmuch as he is the exile of the Old
Testament (again, a 'Fremde' −1.2), he sheds no tears because he is the
author of 'The Book of Comfort', an interpolation into the Book of
Jeremiah consistently attributed to him by Jewish tradition. This
interpolation includes two verses that seem to have sunk particularly
deeply into Celan's awareness, for they are alluded to elsewhere in
'Nah, im Aortenbogen' (Nearby, in the arch of the aorta)
(*FS*, 96), where he writes, 'Mutter Rahel / weint nicht mehr' (Mother
Rachel / weeps no more). In the Revised Standard Version these verses
read as follows:

> Thus says the Lord: 'A voice is heard in Ramah, lamentation and
> bitter weeping. Rachel is weeping for her children; she refuses to be
> comforted for her children, because they are not.' Thus says the Lord:
> 'Keep your voice from weeping, and your eyes from tears.' (Jeremiah
> 31: 15–16)

The Lord and Baruch act as comforters.

In Celan's poem Baruch is to file the tear until it be of the right
dimension (one recalls that Spinoza earned his living by grinding lenses).
The tear is said to surround the 'du', and this motif of the tear that lies
near or around the self occurs several times in Celan's late work (for
instance, in 'Give the Word' – see above, pp. 158–60). It evokes the
dissolution of identity in the moment of overmastering grief. If the tear
has to be reshaped, it is in part in order to control the excessive grief that
had led the poet to term the 'Hauslücke' everlasting. (The reference to
Spinoza shows that the Jews cannot be cast in the role of perennial
historical victims *tout court*: they too are capable of persecution, just as
they ostracised Spinoza, the Jewish 'Albigensian' of the first line. The
reference reins in the boundlessness of sentimental regret by emphasising that they too share in the guilt of history.) At the same
time, however, the language that speaks of an 'ewige Hauslücke' is not
excessive: as often in Celan, a phrase that is open to criticism on one level
of poetic meaning justifies itself on another: the poem is dialectically self-
critical. The 'ewige' is polysemically suggestive: it states that memory
should never fail, that the house-as-gap is a link with another world and
that this place is also the grave, the place of non-existence. As part of the
vocabulary of religion, the adjective suggests the religion that exists no
longer on this spot: it stands in metonymically for the world of Orthodox
Jewry. In Celan's poem the 'Fremde' is both a stranger to be sung into a

realisation of the magnitude of the Jewish tragedy and a person who, because he is perceived as 'strange', already suffers that holocaust. The 'Fremde' is thus both sympathetic and other. He is also Celan himself, singing himself into the abode of the dead like a child who sings in the dark.

If the second section of the poem insists on the persistence of past suffering within the present – its *Ewigkeit* – on the persistence of the pain of Amsterdam in the mind that has known it, even when the mind's owner is elsewhere, 'later', in Pau – then the third section aspires to a just grief founded on the realisation that all history is a catastrophe. The weighing-up and balancing is thematic in the vocabulary: 'rund' matches 'kantig', 'unverstandene' and 'sehende' are in equipoise within a single line, and 'zurecht- / schleife' promises a lament that will be just, fitting (its enjambement stresses the degree to which the grinding *changes* the tear). The 'I' may be as homeless as the Albigensians, as Baruch going into exile in the Jewish captivity, as Spinoza, as the wartime Jews deported by the Nazis; but it is no more homeless than they are. Memory of oppression tempers self-pity. Yet it may be that the required balance is unattainable: although it is suggested in the judicious equilibrium of the adjectives, the conditional tense shows that the tear has not yet assumed proper proportions. The misunderstood tear of the eye that stares at empty space, the eye of the apparently blind seer, is the only optical instrument capable of doing justice to the past – though it is an instrument requiring adjustment before it can see with exactitude. In contemplating the succession of historical disasters, which are fused in the catastrophe that is History itself, the speaker loses his own sense of crushing isolation. For the 'Albigenserschatten' stretches throughout history and darkens other lives than his own.

Es wird

Es wird etwas sein, später,
das füllt sich mit dir
und hebt sich
an einen Mund

Aus dem zerscherbten
Wahn
steh ich auf
und seh meiner Hand zu,
wie sie den einen

einzigen
Kreis zieht.

(There will be something, later on, / that fills up with you / and lifts itself up / to a mouth
    From the splintered / delusion / I rise up / and stare at my hand / as it traces the one / lone / circle)

The beginning of this poem speaks of the future; the second half, however, is cast in the present. This change in tense indicates a movement back from the conjured realities of the imagination to the present reality of the hand that is writing this poem. Yet there is a parallel between the two parts of the poem: between the 'something' that rises and the self that stands up. The two parts are further linked by the suggestion that the something is a glass, raised to the lips, chiming against the (glass?) splinters of 'zerscherbt'. Within the poem the death instinct and the instinct of self-preservation are intertwined: the projection that engenders the initial vision of the future, of survival, seems also to entail self-alienation, transformation of the self into 'dir'. The lateness, the self-alienation, the one and only circle: all suggest the symbolism of death. And this circle (the shape of a life rounded out, of the rim of a glass) is also the form a razor blade might trace round a wrist: which may be the reason why only one hand is seen in action. (The sinister hand, countered by the hand that writes?) The subject of the first half of the poem is something akin to a glass of blood, symbolically brimming with the alienated self which has drained its life blood into it. The poem's place in the collection, *Zeitgehöft*, lends plausibility to this hypothesis: it is preceded by a work about drinking wine from two glasses (again, the duality) (*ZG*, 46).

The two halves are contrasting: the first, vague and suggestive; the second, more concrete and precise. The second half appears to correct the first one. The 'Wahn' it leaves behind is the mysteriously de-personalised atmosphere of the first four lines, whose reflexive verbs enact the self-sufficiency of action unto itself. The second half dispels the 'Wahn' – shatters the glass ('zerscherbt'), as it were – and renders the self aware of the present action it has been carrying out whilst fixated on the trance of futurity. Returning to self-awareness, it recovers the ability to say 'I' ('ich'). In so doing it implicitly denies the seductive temptations of a world of purely impersonal occurrence, a reality from which the self is absent (in which it is dead, or at best transformed into a 'du': when speaking in the future tense, Celan's verse almost never mentions the self) (cf. the impersonal futures that conclude 'Tübingen, Jänner' and 'Du liegst'). At first the self-levitating object appears to indicate a future transcendence. It is later seen to result from the removal from the picture of the human subject that lifts it. The poem first accepts and then rejects the blandishments of suicide. The hand that writes says 'Not yet' to the sinister hand.

Krokus

Krokus, vom gastlichen
Tisch aus gesehen:
zeichenfühliges
kleines Exil
einer gemeinsamen
Wahrheit,
du brauchst
jeden Halm.

(Crocus, glimpsed from the / hospitable table: / sign-feeling / tiny exile / of a shared / truth, / you need / every blade.)

'Krokus' turns on the symbiosis of the words 'gastlich' and 'Exil': for to be a guest is to be in exile, even when one feels at ease, 'at home'. This polarity generates all the details of the verse: there is a comforting shared truth, but there is also the desperate isolation that clutches at every blade – as if at a blade of straw – just as Wordsworth clasped hold of a tree to assure himself of a reality beyond the self. If the crocus is a sign, an allegorical image that points away from itself, it is akin to the self that looks beyond the hospitable table to the world outside. It is because the self is a guest, anomalous at the communal table, that it drifts away mentally towards the otherness of nature. The exile is small, on the one hand because so is the crocus, towards which the speaker feels tenderly, and on the other because his own isolation is mitigated by human company. The syntax is such that the addressee may be either the crocus or an *alter ego*. Even in its isolation, speech links the self to a community in search of a shared truth; even within this community it is isolated by the nature of its use of language, which is 'zeichenfühlig', feeling for signs, exploratory. The self hangs in suspension between nature and mankind. And at the festival of nature man is but a guest.

ALLUSIVENESS AND THE HERMETICISM OF THE OPEN POEM

One poem that has become a focus of discussion of the importance of external knowledge for an understanding of Celan's poems is 'Du liegst', which appears in the posthumous collection *Schneepart*. If 'Du liegst' is one of Celan's greatest and most haunting poems, as I believe it is, it is because of the power of its magical fusion of Symbolism and political engagement. This has rendered it a stumbling-block to critics disturbed either by its formalism or by its Marxism. German critical debate has formulated the problem in terms of the degree to which the reader is expected to recognise its various political and autobiographical allusions. Gadamer, for instance, lists some of the allusions whilst ignoring others.[1] He is even accused by Marlies Janz of deliberate repression of some of them. Janz herself lists the allusions in detail, but seems also to have projected at least one (an implicit criticism of Swedish models of socialism) onto the poem.[2] Perhaps the best point of departure is Peter Szondi's fine unfinished essay describing the biographical circumstances of the poem's gestation.[3] But first the poem itself:

> Du liegst im grossen Gelausche,
> umbuscht, umflockt.
>
> Geh du zur Spree, geh zur Havel,
> geh zu den Fleischerhaken,
> zu den roten Aeppelstaken
> aus Schweden –
>
> Es kommt der Tisch mit den Gaben,
> er biegt um ein Eden –
>
> Der Mann ward zum Sieb, die Frau
> musste schwimmen, die Sau,
> für sich, für keinen, für jeden –
>
> Der Landwehrkanal wird nicht rauschen.
> Nichts
>   stockt.

(You lie in the great listening, / snowflakes, bushes, surround you.
  Go to the Spree, to the Havel, / to the meat hooks / and to the red

apple stakes / from Sweden –
There comes a table, gift-laden, / deflected by an Eden –
The man became a sieve, the woman / was forced to swim, the
sow, / for herself, for no one, for everyone –
The Landwehr Canal will not make a sound. / Nothing / halts.)

Peter Szondi has compiled a list of the allusions to a visit Celan made to
West Berlin: invited to give a reading over the Christmas period, he
visited Ploetzensee (where the participants in the abortive bomb plot
against Hitler had been hung from meat hooks), went to the exhibition
hall near the radio tower, where a Christmas market was being held,
including stalls with items from Sweden, and stayed in the Hansa
district – near the Berlin Wall – with a window overlooking dense
shrubbery. The reading-material Szondi lent him whilst there included
an account of the murders of Karl Liebknecht and Rosa Luxemburg,
who spent their last hours in the Hotel Eden. By the time of Celan's
arrival it had been converted into a night club. The brutal references to
the sieve and the sow are quoted from the cheery badinage of the
assassins once their work was completed. Rosa Luxemburg's body was
hurled into the Landwehr Canal.

The fulcrum of the poem, as Szondi notes, is the word 'Eden', which is
also embedded in the rhyme words 'Schweden' and 'jeden'. This is Eden
as the scene of the primal sin; as the paradise in which Liebknecht and
Luxemburg become a new Adam and Eve; as the false paradise of the
modern night club; as the source of apples whose redness reminds one of
blood. The conjunction of Christmas snow and Eden suggests the
magical air of a fairy tale or ballad, and recalls Celan's own earlier ballad
'Eis, Eden'. The universal, despecified nature of lines such as 'Es kommt
der Tisch mit den Gaben' or 'Der Mann ward', belong to the poetics of
the ballad – as does the musicality of the work. This balladic element
also suggests the German street ballads about 'the corpse in the
Landwehr Canal' or about the death of Walter Rathenau, 'der
Judensau'. Thus the seemingly escapist ballad form nourishes the
poem's political purposiveness.

The balladic form, however, also has nightmarish connotations. Its
very universality implies an endless typology of fearsome events – from
the biblical Eden to the present. Celan is horrified to see that 'Nichts
stockt': that life glides on regardless, shrugging its way round the crime.
The short sentence 'Nichts stockt' itself falls apart as a sign of trauma.
By doing so it attempts to rupture the bad circularity of a repeated
nightmare: the circularity of the compulsive 'Eden' – 'Schweden' –

'jeden' rhyme, of the echo of the opening 'Gelausche' in the 'rauschen' of the end (the sound the night is waiting to hear will never come), and of the reverberating sound patterns of 'Havel', 'Haken' and 'Staken'. This circular pattern is established brilliantly in the first line: the *l–g* of 'liegst' is reversed and mirrored in the *g–l* of 'Gelausche'.

'Du liegst' begins with an apparent opposition between a self safely shielded from the winter, and the cold outside. The opposition is, however, illusory, and the transition to the second stanza inevitable: for, although 'Gelausche' may suggest that all outside space is a listening ear in the uncanny quietude of snow, it is also, as it were, the listening posture of the self, apparently 'lauschig' – comfortably enclosed – but really awaiting instructions. A voice then exhorts it to be born into the contradictions of the world outside, which also form the tragedy of Berlin. The world is a slaughterhouse bristling with signs of an absent paradise. The lost paradise is, among other things, the lost possibility of a German revolution: the murder of Liebknecht and Luxemburg as the first step towards the 'Staken' and 'Haken' – and *Hakenkreuze* (swastikas) – of Nazi rule. The poem arranges various times and events in a typological series in the hope that this will bring time itself to a halt, to the point at which it 'stockt', and reflects upon itself. The reference to the Landwehr Canal in the suddenly desolating close gains some of its eerie power from its futurity: the uncanniness of a future once open in a past that is now closed. But the futurity is also instinct with premonitions of Celan's own coming death by water (like the ending of 'Tübingen, Jänner'). The water invites the body, accepts it in silence. And this is because it is dead water: frozen water: the water of the river of oblivion, as Janz remarks.

Peter Szondi lists the biographical details surrounding the poem's gestation, whilst equivocating over the degree to which its comprehensibility depends upon the reader knowing them. He then evades the problem by diverting his energies into a refutation of the possible objection that the biographical details are 'random', and hence meaningless. There can be no doubt, however, that Celan's juxtapositions are significant: one need only consider the rich semantic complex of the word 'Eden'. Moreover, although critical discussion of the problem of extrinsic knowledge has been focused on this poem, it is perhaps a misleading candidate for a *locus classicus* in this respect. For all the autobiographical allusions the poem makes are swallowed up in allusions to a political history every German ought to know: that of the early Weimar Republic. What is more, the poem is fortunate in its chosen setting – Berlin – to think of which is, inevitably, to be jolted into political reflection and regret. The problem of allusion and the necessary knowledge presumed in the reader does not so much arise with regard to this poem as to others, such as 'Mapesbury Road', which, Janz informs us, alludes to the attempted assassination of Rudi Dutschke. Although she may be right, no reader could possibly deduce this fact from the poem. The result is that 'Mapesbury Road', unlike 'Du liegst', is a failure: it fails to fuse private allusions with public ones. Moreover, the opacity of many of the later poems may lead one to suspect that they were composed neither for the benefit of Celan himself nor for us, but for a God who may not exist: they send messages to him in bottles,[4] for only he could intuit the occulted allusions and make the correct associations. In writing as if the resurrection had already occurred, as if all hidden and repressed facts had been brought to light, Celan is seeking magically to bring the Last Day nearer: to force into existence a painfully absent God. He, as it were, tries to compel the ideal (implicit?) reader into existence by acting as if he already existed: a despairing poetic equivalent of Anselm's argument. Yet he is also, of course, seeking to protect the integrity of the poem by forestalling the possibility of interpretations that would see through it to its occasion. The suppression of notes and titles to poems may have been a reflex of the paranoid traits in Celan attested to even by friends and acquaintances. It is the paranoia of the man in hiding, the man society no longer wants: the Jew.

ETYMOLOGY, LINEATION AND PLAY

In her study *Nonsense*, Susan Stewart defines the etymological use of language as the generator of an infinite regress:

> This is the etymological situation of Alice, who learns from the White Knight that the name of a song is called 'Haddock's Eyes', the name is really 'The Aged Aged Man', the song is called 'Ways and Means', and the song really is 'A-Sitting on a Gate'. The language event is thus caught up in an historical regress. What the song 'really is' becomes only one of its possible aspects through the history of use. The 'object' comes to be through a succession of situations.[5]

This etymological movement is the movement of play. Celan's etymological play often proceeds by breaking words down into their components. It is the lineation above all that carries out this process: thus in 'Weggebeizt' one encounters 'des An- / erlebten', and in 'Zur

Nachtordnung' (To the night's order), the words 'Über- / gerittener, Über- / geschlitterter' (he who rode over, he who sledded over). The movement of lineation is potentially endless. This is one of the reasons why *Die Niemandsrose* and *Atemwende*, the volumes in which Celan first applies this analytical use of lineation on a large scale, contain a number of very long poems; it is also why, later on, even the short poems are arranged in sequences that transform them into sections of one long poem punctuated by respiratory pauses. The theoretically infinite movement enacts a dialectic of association by contradiction; and the play of contradictions, like language itself, is never-ending. Chomsky's famous nonsense sentence, 'Colourless green ideas sleep furiously', as arranged into lines by Susan Bassnett-MacGuire, can serve as a simplified example of such association:

Colourless
green ideas
sleep

furiously.

Bassnett-MacGuire adds that when the sentence is laid out thus on the page 'the apparent lack of logical harmony between the elements of the sentence could become acceptable, since each "line" would add an idea and the overall meaning would derive from the association of logical elements in a seemingly regular logical structure'.[6] The logic here is that of dissonance: each word reminds one of the opposite it fails to encompass, of language as perpetual lack. Celan's lineation extends his poetics of absence. Of course, his use of lineation is far subtler than the Chomskyan example, but it operates according to a similar mechanism: it draws one step-by-step into a universe of the absurd by inducing acceptance of its elements one by one, until the reader is trapped inside the decentred labyrinth of the text. (This is also a way of rendering neologisms more palatable, of registering the seismic shocks they evoke in the reader whilst allowing him to continue nevertheless. And it may be the lack of such lineation that makes *Finnegans Wake* so difficult to read: Joyce's book refuses to recognise the 'du', the addressee inscribed at the heart of even the most seemingly impenetrable of Celan's poems.) Since the associative logic proceeds by generating an ever-renewed absence, it can only conclude when the sense of lack is removed. This is what happens in the poems each time the components of a contradiction meet in a paradox or a repetition (for instance at the end of 'Du liegst' [You lie] and 'Das angebrochene Jahr' [The Dawning Year] – *SP*, 8, 11); or whenever the poem sentence concludes by echoing its beginning (see the use of 'Wundgeheilt' [wound-healed] in 'Hafen'[Harbour] – *AW*, 47–9). In using such a phrase as 'the play of contradictions' to describe the movement of Celan's lineation, I hope to suggest the extent of its ambiguity. On the one hand there is Utopian play, play with infinity, opposed to the world of instrumental statement and utility. On the other, the logic of the play itself duplicates the very mechanism of contradiction that inflicts so much pain in the extra-poetic world: even the apparently formalist game is steeped in suffering. In this respect, Celan's poems are like no other 'nonsense verse' before or since.

The play of contradictions is evident in Celan's etymologies. Susan Stewart, one recalls, talked of etymology as initiating an infinite regress. In Heidegger, it provides a privileged means of access to a supposedly essential past, a determining origin. In Celan's poems, however, it does not convey one through time to a 'beginning' but suspends temporality: the different meanings of different ages revolve in a linked constellation. The result is language for all time and no time, language-as-music. And this language is musical in another sense than that of a counterpoint of dancing associations. Henriette Beese has shown how Celan's rhythmic readings of his own poems tie successive separate words into a single wordknot. This composite, rhythm-born word becomes a line within the line. (It is thus one of the motive forces of the fragmented presentation of the later poems on the page.) Thus his reading of 'Nächtlich geschürzt' has an effect Beese renders as follows: 'er-graut / das Moos, / er-schüttert / der-Stein'(greyed – the moss, Shattered – the stone).[7] In German, *Wort* can mean both an isolated word and a sentence, a statement. Here Celan makes sentences of single words, single words of sentences. He turns separate words into communities (perceived etymologically, they already are pluralities, assemblies of disparate meanings). The breaks within words undermine the notion of an object's identity with itself.

THE AESTHETICS OF QUOTATION

The person who quotes is vulnerable: he surrenders his own voice for another's. To quote is to emphasise both the possibility of survival and its extreme unlikelihood: only this small shred of a past text lives on. Indeed, that text has been destroyed by the process of quotation itself, which reconceives the past text as an assembly of detachable parts, a montage of fragments, rather than a totality. To quote from a text is, of course, to deconstruct it. So great is our alienation from the texts of the past that only moments, which are lifted out and christened 'epiphanies', speak to us still. The quotation stands for the text the poet is unable to write: it renders his silence *pregnant*. Thus in the poems of Celan, as Böschenstein notes,

> a system of images that has not yet been replaced cancels itself out in favour of a future world, reports of which can only be formulated by negation. Of necessity the poem situates itself in the non-place and non-time between two worlds.[8]

So the quotation is also a negation: evidence both of the destruction of the past and the absence of the future.

The text that quotes is self-confessedly intertextual, a place at which discourses meet and interpenetrate each other. Celan's work strives to approach this place of *Begegnung* (encounter). In 'Der Meridian' he writes, 'Das Gedicht will zu einem Andern, es braucht dieses Andere, es braucht ein Gegenüber. Es sucht es auf, es spricht sich ihm zu' (The poem wants to approach an other, it needs this Other, it needs an opposite. It seeks it out, speaks its way towards it).[9] To quote is to be mindful of the Other – and of the dead. If 'tief' and Schnee' are keywords in Celan's vocabulary this is because they point to the need to unearth a reality concealed below the present one: to remember that nature is a graveyard, and that the dead whirled away by the winds as dust or crematorium smoke (the sky is a grave, and 'da liegt man nicht eng' (there's lots of room there) – 'Todesfuge') may be present anywhere; to be mindful of the hidden world whose underlying forms are traced by the snow as concrete abstractions. Schulz has remarked that in the final phase of Celan's poetic development, which commences with *Die Niemandsrose*, poems become increasingly porous to quotation.[10] These quotations are a sign of receptivity towards the dead on the part of the living: the poem itself as a cipher of future remembrance, the carrier of the hope of a resurrection. Fearing the abstract storm-wind of the future, the poem gathers together the threatened remnants of obliterated events: the words of precursors and mentors, of Kafka, Hölderlin, Freud, Michaux, Meister Eckehart, among others. Thus the grass that is 'auseinandergeschrieben' (written apart)[11] at the start of 'Engführung' (Strette) is real grass seeking to cover a tomb with oblivion, but parted, its movement thwarted, by the process of writing, which reveals the presence of the anonymous dead. Without the writing that is inscribed upon it the tombstone would revert into nature and unbeing. But the poem does not simply quote the words of the dead in order to preserve them. It does so out of trust in the promise enunciated in the words of Mandelstam, as translated by Celan himself, 'Dreimal selig, wer einen Namen einführt ins Lied! / Das namengeschmückte Lied / Lebt länger inmitten der anderen (Thrice blessed he who brings a name into a song! / The song adorned with names / lives longer amidst the others).[12] In quotations, the poet's own breath inflates the life raft of another's words. The poet accommodates himself to death as a death mask does to a face. Indeed, a quotation can be said to be a mask. In one respect, this is the theme of the following poem:

> Aus Verlornem Gegossene du,
> maskengerecht,
>
> die Lid-
> falte entlang
> mit der eignen
> Lidfalte dir nah sein,
> die Spur und die Spur
> mit Grauem bestreun,
> endlich, tödlich.

(You, poured out of lost things, / as just as a mask, to be near to you / with my eyelid folded / along your eyelid, / to bestrew this and that trace with grey, / finally, in deadly fashion.)

Here the mask embodies the presence of the absent, a justly exact imprint. There is a desire to be as close to the other, as finally close, as a death mask. Various parallelisms establish the contemplative stillness in which face and mask interlock: 'Lidfalte' matches 'Lidfalte', 'Spur' matches 'Spur', 'endlich' meets 'tödlich'. Among all masks, only the death mask is 'gerecht': it does not distort the living movements of a face, as other masks do. It reflects the final shape of the face it conceals. To dream of a reconciliation between the face and the mask – the living and the dead – the words of the poet and the words he quotes – is to dream of the end of time. For the end of contradiction would entail the end of temporality. It occurs in the clearing of the text where the poet is silent and the words of the dead are resurrected in the form of a quotation.

In the multi-place governed by the law of quotation, the history of the self is a chronicle of migrations. This is the place where 'du / kommst nicht / du / dir' (you / fail to / come to / yourself – *LZ*, 27), where 'sie schulen dich um, / / du wirst wieder / er' (they re-educate you, // you again become / him – *LZ*, 7). Here one must admonish the other 'Du sei wie du, immer' (Be as you are, always – *LZ*, 101), lest he, she or it alter, just as German itself is transformed within this very poem, which is a network of High German, Middle High German and Hebrew. 'I' and 'you' mingle in the act of reading, of *Begegnung* – Celan's readings of other writers, our reading of Celan – as the seductive processes of identification persuade us to introduce into the textual 'I' that which from its position is 'you'; or to read its 'you' as a covert 'I'. Celan's poems are open, as he wished them to be: the vacuum of reference draws us into them. This process of identification with a text that uses personal pronouns almost interchangeably (as at the start of *The Waste Land*) is underpinned by a certain narcissism, and a certain paranoia. Narcissism: for the familiarity of the pronouns establishes an atmosphere of family romance; but paranoia: for the extreme difficulty of the poem transforms this sense of belonging into a feeling of entrapment within an infernal textual machine. One projects oneself into a text whose floating pronouns function as bait. We identify with the 'I' of the other because we are already divided and other than ourselves: for 'I', the shifter, is our name, and yet nobody's name.

NEOLOGISMS AND NOLOGISMS[13]

At the beginning of his study *Zur Lyrik Paul Celans* (On the Lyric Poetry of Paul Celan), Peter Horst Neumann draws a distinction between neologisms of the type of Nietzsche's 'Bildungsphilister' (culture philistine) and the coinages found in Celan's poems, which he is reluctant to term 'neologisms'. This dissatisfaction with the term 'neologism' is shared by the majority of Celan scholars, who favour the neutral definition *Komposita*: compound words. Their caution is hardly surprising when one realises that many of the ostensible neologisms in Celan's work are really scientific terms extracted from their original contexts, estranged by quotation. But perhaps even 'compound words' is a misnomer, for the nature of the German language renders it extremely difficult to distinguish the neologism from the word formed by assembling existing words into new combinations. For any and every German can, and daily does, form 'new words' by coupling two old words together, with the same ease with which one would place an adjective before a noun in an English sentence. It is more than likely that Celan exploits this aspect of German to infiltrate into everyday words the strangeness of the neologism: to break down the barriers between what is and is not 'German'. Nevertheless, Neumann's distinction is potentially significant. Analysing the coinage 'Herzbuckelweg' (the heart's humped way – NR, 80), he states that it 'evokes something that exists only through this invocation and remains attainable *through this word alone*'.[14] Such a coinage bestows a local habitation and a name on airy nothing: it hints that absence may be a form of presence, that nothingness may be something. It is instinct with a sense of possibility. Non-instrumental in nature, it refuses to intervene in any extra-poetic debate or even world, as does Nietzsche's deliberately provocative formulation. It inhabits a world of juxtaposed simples (*Herz, Buckel, Weg*), not the arena of intellectual debate summoned up by *Bildung* and *Philister*.

Although Neumann's remarks are illuminating, they have a fatal defect: they fetishise and reify the neologism, simply deeming it a mediator of the current of 'the poetical',[15] and failing to perceive its function in its original context. It is salutary, for instance, to replace 'Herzbuckelweg' in its context, which runs as follows:

> Brich dir die Atemmünze heraus
> aus der Luft um duch und den Baum:
> so
> viel
> wird gefordert von dem,
> den die Hoffnung herauf- und herabkarrt
> den Herzbuckelweg . . . .

(Break the breath-coin / out of the air that is round you and round the tree: / so / much / is required of those / whom hope wheels up and down / the humped way of the heart . . . .)

In this context, 'Herzbuckelweg' is less an opaque instantiation of 'the poetic' than a comprehensible condensation of various aspects of the experience of wearisome travel, vain expectation and hobbling hunched under duress: the way of the heart is a winding one, and every turning frustrates hope. What is more, the word is a polemical reformulation of Rilke's 'Herzwege'. So much for the absolute distinction between the instrumental and non-instrumental neologism! Rather than refusing all communication, 'Herzbuckelweg' oscillates between the poles of polemical revision (of Rilke's 'Herzwege') and invocation of non-presence (Utopia). In fact, all Celan's coinages can be said to occupy points on a graduated scale between the extremes of polemic and opacity: within the same poem, 'Atemmünze' is closer to the pole of opacity, whilst 'Ver- / freundung' is in a satirical register: as often in Celan, the enjambement is sarcastic, unmasking, for the word suggests friends who are friends no longer but rather a *Verfremdung* (estrangement).

Thus Celan's word assemblages have dialectical force, and are both polemical statements and self-instantiations of the poetic. Neumann's dualistic distinction overlooks this ambiguity. It also fails to note the political rationale of the neologism in Celan's work. Adorno once stated that to continue writing poetry after Auschwitz would be barbaric; the unspoken corollary is that to do so in *German* would be even more barbaric. Celan resolves the dilemma of the German writer after Auschwitz by writing a German that outrages everyday notions of German, and by contriving to do so outside the German-speaking countries themselves.

The poetics of the compound word are, however, more complex than this. Compound words also mimic the pidgin formations of children, which are as mysterious to the adult as his own words are to the child. Such a word as 'Schlangenwagen' (snakewagon – *AW*, 23) resembles a child's coinage: it suggests a series of mutually cancelling images, such as a train, perhaps a train bound for Auschwitz, snaking along the tracks, ill-omened as a viper, heading for the world of 'Todesfuge' in which Death 'spielt mit den Schlangen' (plays with the snake).

The eruption of the neologism in Celan's late poetry corresponds to the break-up of the notion of a standard language in modern society: the proliferation of new technological concepts destroys even the theoretical possibility of the individual mastering 'his own' language. This is surely one of the reasons for the degree of acceptance accorded Lacan's notion of language as the realm of the unconscious. Every day new inventions, new products and advertisements mint new words or shake the fixed forms of existing ones in a lexical kaleidoscope. One's experience of language becomes increasingly akin to that of the child: it is language-as-coinage, still in a fluid state, impossible to master. The late work of Celan imitates the action of the infernal machine we no longer control – hoping to survive, inoculated, in the poisoned climate of horribly infinite, incalculable possibility.

Appendix: Some Versions of Poems by Leśmian

Topielec

W zwiewnych nurtach kostrzewy, na leśnej polanie,
Gdzie się las upodabnia łące niespodziewanie,
Leżą zwłoki wędrowca, zbędne sobie zwłoki.
Przewędrował świat cały z obłoków w obłoki,
Aż nagle w niecierpliwej zapragnął żałobie
Zwiedzić duchem na przełaj zieleń samą w sobie.
Wówczas demon zieleni wszechleśnym powiewem
Ogarnął go, gdy w drodze przystanął pod drzewem,
I wabił nieustannych rozkwitów pośpiechem,
I nęcił ust zdyszanych tajemnym bezśmiechem,
I czarował zniszczotą wonnych niedowcieleń,
I kusił coraz głębiej – w tę zieleń, w tę zieleń!
A on biegł wybrzeżami coraz innych światów,
Odczłowieczając duszę i oddech wśród kwiatów,
Aż zabrnął w takich jagód rozdzwonione dzbany,
W taką zamrocz paproci, w takich cisz kurhany,
W taki bezświat zarośli, w taki bezbrzask głuchy,
W takich szumów ostatnie kędyś zawieruchy,
Że leży oto martwy w stu wiosen bezdeni,
Cienisty, jak bór w borze – topielec zieleni.

Przemiany

Tej nocy mrok był duszny i od żądzy parny,
I chabry, rozwidnione suchą błyskawicą,
Przedostały się nagle do oczu tej sarny,
Co biegła w las, spłoszona obcą jej źrenicą –
A one, łeb jej modrząc, mknęły po sarniemu,
I chciwie zaglądały w świat po chrabrowemu.

Mak, sam siebie w śródpolnym wykrywszy bezbrzeżu,
Z wrzaskiem, który dla ucha nie był żadnym brzmieniem,
Przekrwawił się w koguta w purpurowym pierzu,
I aż do krwi potrząsał szkarłatnym grzebieniem,
I piał w mrok, rozdzierając dziób, trwogą zatruty,
Aż mu zinąd prawdziwe odpiały koguty.

The Drowned Man

Among the billowing fescue, amidst a forest glade,
Where a meadow's likeness rises unexpected from the wood,
Lie the remains of a traveller, a corpse that nobody needs.
He wandered the entire world, both head and foot in clouds,
Until impatient melancholy urged him suddenly
To stride in spirit through the Green of Greens.
The demon of Green, meanwhile, with the forests for his breath,
Enwrapped him when he halted by a tree along his path,
And lured him with a haste of ceaseless bloomings
And charmed with panting lips' secret unsmiling.
And tantalised him with the fragrant wrecks of the unbeen
To draw him deeper and deeper – into the Green!
And so he ran across the shores of worlds that ever differed,
Unmanning soul and breath amidst the flowers,
Until he stumbled on such berries in unsounding jugs,
On such a fern-dark, such a moundy hush,
On such a vegetable unworld, such an undawn's deafness,
On such a congregation of the last blizzards' whispers,
That he plunged down dead through abysses of hundreds of springs:
Shadowy, like woods in woods – a drowned greeny thing.

Transformations

This night past the sultry darkness panted with desire;
In instant dawnings of dry lightning cornflowers suddenly
Found a way through to the eye of this deer
Which fled into the forest depths, scared by its alien eye:
As they dye its head blue like the deer they flit by,
Gaze on the world with cornflowers' greedy eyes.

A poppy, finding itself lost in fields,
With a racket that no ear perceived as a sound,
Bloodied itself, purpled out with feathers, cockereled,
And shook its scarlet crest out wide until the blood dripped down,
And crowed in the gloaming, fear-poisoned, wide-beaked,
Until some real cockerels crowed an answer back.

A jęczmien, kłos pragnieniem zazłociwszy gęstem,
Nasrożył nagle złością zjątrzone ościory
I w zlotego jeża przemiażdżył się ze chrzęstem
I biegł, kłując po drodze ziół nikłe zapory,
I skomlał i na kwiaty boczył się i jeżył,
I nikt nigdy nie zgadnie, co czuł i co przeżył?

A ja – w jakiej swą duszę sparzyłem pokrzywie,
Że pomykam ukradkiem i na przełaj miedzą?
I czemu kwiaty na mnie patrzą podejrzliwie?
Czy coś o mnie nocnego wbrew mej wiedzy – wiedzą?
Com czynił, że skroń dłońmi uciskam obiema?
Czym byłem owej nocy, której dzis już nie ma?

Wieczór

Słonce, zachodząc, wlecze wzdłuż po łące
Wielki cień chmury, ciagnąc go na wzgórza,
Zetknięte z niebem, co życie, gasnące
Pod barw przymusem – w głąb marzeń przedłuża,
Aby dowidzieć poprzez dale puste
Jedyną wokol purpurową chustę
Dziewczyny, która swych dłoni oplotem
Kolana zgodnie wgarnęła pod brodę
I coraz bardziej pod niebos namiotem
Samotniejąca w tę dal i pogodę,
Od dawna ruchu i snu nie odmienia,
Chłonąc czar drętwy samego patrzenia
We wszystko naraz, w nic zasię z osobna . . .
Wpobok, zaledwo do siebie podobna,
Wyolbrzymiona wobec próżni świata,
Krowa się w świetle różowi łaciata,
Co jednym rogiem pół słońca odkrawa,
A drugim wadzi o daleką gruszę . . .
Sennych owadów nieprzytomna wrzawa
Umacnia pustkę i podsyca gluszę,
Wspartą na stogach, powiązanych w drągi.
Kolejne idą nad polem przeciągi
Tchu ziół dalekich, zaprawnego potem
Zoranej ziemi, co – tknięta wron lotem –

And barley, desire deep-gilding its husk,
Fearsomely spread out its aggravated spikes,
To a golden hedgehog crunchingly crushed
Itself, ran off spearing the herbs' fragile dikes,
And whimpered and pouted at flowers, hog-bristled,
And will what it experienced always remain a riddle?

And I – in what place was I stung, at what hour,
To make me creep by, through boundary strips, secretly?
Why is there suspicion in the eyes of the flowers?
Do they know of a night self of mine – unknown to me?
What is it I've done that my hands clutch my brow?
What thing was I last night, gone forever now?

Evening

The sun in its setting tugs across meadows
A large cloud's shadow, pulls it up hills
Which are knit with the sky – the sky which prolongs
Life guttering out when the colours compel,
Into depths of dream – to make seen from afar
The lone purple shawl of a girl around here,
Where her arms have gracefully gathered her knees
To her chin. Under heaven's tent she has grown
Ever more lonely in this clime and remoteness,
Having long preserved the same posture and dream,
Drinking in the numbed spell of just looking
At everything, and yet no single thing . . .
Nearby, scarce resembling itself,
Enormous against the vacuum of world,
A speckled cow grows red in the light,
Slicing half the sun off with one horn
As its other encumbers a distant pear tree –
The drowsy stupor and hum of the insects
Nourishes emptiness, feeds the solitude
That leans upon hayricks bound up inside poles.
Sucessive breaths of distant herbs
Pass over fields, bringing the seasoning sweat
Of fresh-ploughed earth, stitched up by the crows' flights,
Which heavily steams and cools gradually.

Paruje ciężko i chłodnieje z wolna.
Na widnokresie jakaś mgła dowolna,
Cień, nie mający przyczyn wśród przestworu,
Rośnie, by zwiększyć potęgę wieczoru,
I wśród rosnących z nim razem bezmiarów
Dziwnie brzmią zgiełki świerszczących komarów.

Marcin Swoboda

Z górskich szczytów lawina, Bogu czyniąc szkodę,
Strąciła w przepaść nizin Marcina Swobodę.

Spadał, czując, jak w ciele kość szaleje krucha,
I uderzył się o ziem ostatnią mgłą ducha.

Poniszczony śmiertelnie, chciał się z bólem wadzić,
Wokół bólu jął miazgę człowieczą gromadzić.

Dłoń złamana w niej tkwiła, jak nóż w ciepłym chlebie!
To się ciułał, to trwonił . . . I tak pełzł przed siebie.

I z trudem bezkształtnego ciała rozwłóczyny
Doczołgały się wreszcie aż do stóp dziewczyny.

Wargami, zszarpanymi o skały i krzaki,
Szeptały własne imię pewno dla poznaki.

Bocząc na się pełzacza, w ogrodzie bielała.
'Nie strasz kwiatów ranami! Precz, kałużo ciała!

Odkrwaw mi się od stopy! Szukaj leków w niebie!
Próżno szepcesz swe imię! Nie poznaję ciebie!' –

A Bóg z nieba zawołał: 'Wstyd, dziewczyno młoda!
Nie poznałaś? – Jam poznał! To – Marcin Swoboda!'

I pobladła dziewczyna i odrzekła: 'Boże!
Już to ciało Marcinem dla mnie być nie może! . . .'

A Bóg otchłań do niego przybliżył mogilną,

Along the horizon a fitful kind of mist,
A shadow for which the whole cosmos knows no cause,
Rises, to multiply the power of dusk,
And amidst the infinities growing apace
The gathered pipings of the gnats sound strange.

Martin Freedom

A landslide came injuring God from the hills;
Into the abyss Martin Freedom was spilled.

As he tumbled he felt his embodied bones' riot,
Crashed into the earth with his last mist of spirit.

Mortally shattered, he made to grapple pain,
And round pain began to collect his mash of man.

A smashed hand lodged there like a knife in hot bread!
It scrabbled, messed about . . . then crawled on ahead.

In this way the misshapen body's ulcered scrawl
Laboriously came to the feet of a girl.

The lips rocks had ravaged and thickets had bruised
Whispered out the name of the form so abused.

She baulked at this sore amidst orchards, and paled.
'Stop scaring the flowers with wounds, cripple! Away!

Bleed away from my feet! Seek physic in the skies!
No point mouthing your name. You are not recognised!' –

But God called down from Heaven, 'Fie, lady, for shame!
You don't know him? I do! Martin Freedom – the same!'

The girl paled and cried, 'By all things heavenly
This body cannot represent Martin to me! . . .'

And so God slid towards him a tomb's wide abyss

Aby ciału ułatwić śmierć już bardzo pilną.

I biedne, przez dziewczynę nie poznane ciało,
Poszeptawszy swe imię, w otchłań się przelało.

Pan Błyszczyński

Ogród pana Błyszczyńskiego zielenieje na wymroczu,
Gdzie się cud rozrasta w zgrozę i bezprawie.
Sam go wywiódł z nicości błyszczydłami swych oczu
I utrwalił na podśnionej drzewom trawie.

Kiedy zmory są zajęte przyśpieszonym zmorowaniem
Między mgłą a niebem, między mgłą a wodą –
Zielna zjawa swe dłonie zbezcieleśnia ze łkaniem
Nad paprocią – nad pokrzywą – nad lebiodą.

W takiej chwili Bóg przelatał, pełen wspomnień wiekuistych,
Ścieżką podobłoczną – właśnie, że tułaczą – .
I przystanął na zbiegu dwojga tęsknot gwiaździstych,
Gdzie się widma migotliwie bylejaczą.

Zaszumiało jaworowo, ale chyba wbrew jaworom –
Samym cisz zamętem, samą cisz utratą . . .
'Kto te szumy narzucił moim dumnym przestworom?
Kto ten ogród roznicestwił tak liściato? . .'

Cisza . . . Nikt nie odpowiada. Płyną chmury i godziny . . .
Wszelka dal w niebiosach – to dal zagrobowa.
Pan Błyszczyński w świat nagle z trwożnej wyszedł gęstwiny,
Szepnął: 'Boże!' – i powiedział takie słowa:

'Był w zaświatach – sen i wicher i zaklętej burzy rozgruch!
Boże, snów spełnionych już mi dziś nie ujmuj!
Jam te drzewa powcielał! To – Mój zamysł i odruch . . .
Moje dziwy . . . Moje rosy . . . Dreszcz i znój mój!

Przebacz smutkom i widziadłom, nie znającym rodowodu
I opacznym kwiatom, com je snuł z niczego

To bring nearer the death the body sorely wished.

And so the poor body the girl would not know
Gave a whisper – its name – and into the gulf flowed.

Pan Błyszczyński

Pan Błyszczyński's garden is greening in the outdusk
  Where miracle distends to horrid lawlessness.
He extroduced it with his flashing eyes from nothing's husk
  And fixed it under trees upon dreamt-up grass.

When the nightmares are all busy with a quickened maring
  Between the mist and the water, between mist and sky,
The hands of a green phantom disembody amid weeping
  Above where pigweed, nettles and ferns lie.

At some such time did God, deep in eternal recollection,
  Fly past – along a wandering undercloud.
He halted where two starry yearnings made an intersection
  Where gleaming ghosts have always anyoldhowed.

Things rustled there like sycamores, in sycamores' despite,
  With the very clamour of silence, of silence and loss . . .
'Who stamped his rustling mark on the creations of My might?
  Who disvoided this garden and this grass? . . '

Silence . . . Nobody replies. The clouds and hours drift past . . .
  All distances of heaven are the dead's.
Pan Błyszczyński stepped into the world through trembling grass
  And whispered, 'O my God!' – and then he said,

'The afterworld was full of dreams and gales and magic storms.
  Lord, do not take away my fulfilled dreams!
'Twas I gave body to these trees. My motions they, my thoughts . . .
  My wonders and my dews . . . we are the same.

These sadnesses and lineageless shadows – Lord, oh pardon
  The misformed flowers I spun from the void.

Moja wina! O, Boże, wejdź do mego ogrodu!
Do ogrodu! Do –mojego! . . . Do –mojego! . . .

Wyznam Tobie całą zwiewność, cała gęstwę mojej wiary
W życie zagrobowe kwiatów i motyli.
Wejdź do mego ogrodu! I cóż z tego, że czary! . . .
I cóż z tego, że ułuda nikłej chwili! . . .'

Wszedł w gęstwinę, co szumiała poza życia drogowskazem.
Sami byli teraz. Oko w oko – sami.
Nic do siebie nie rzekli i ciemniejąc, szli razem
Alejami – alejami – alejami!

Ogród śnił się . . . Tu i ówdzie dąb prześniony zżółkł i powiądł.
Każdy krzew sam w sobie miał zaświata wygląd.
Sporo było w gałęziach – cisz zbłąkanych i sowiąt,
Lecz nie było ani świerszczy, ani szczygląt.

Uciekały się niebiosy pod najdalszych gwiazd obronę.
Miesiąc złotym rogiem chmurę mgliście pobódł.
Trzepotały się w piachu dusze zmarłych, spragnione
Nowych zgonów i pośmiertnych w mroku swobód.

Coś złociście wyspowego w daleczyźnie alej pełga –
Można taką wyspę brwi skinieniem spłoszyć . . .
Świetlikami za chwilę północ w zieleń się wełga,
Niepokojąc gmatwaninę leśnych poszyć.

Pan Błyszczyński sprawdzał ogród, czy dość czarom jego uległ –
I czy szum i poszum jest dość rzeczywisty –
I czy liszaj na dębie – jadowity brzydulek –
Dość się wgryza w złudną korę i w pień śnisty?

Badał jeszcze, czy ptak-lilia dość skowrończo w przyszłość śpiewa,
I czy wąż-tulipan wiosny jest oznaką . . .
I spojrzeniem przymuszał przeciwiące się drzewa,
By do zwykłych podobniały jako-tako . . .

Drapieżniały zbyt cudacznie zdradnych kwiatów niebywałki,
A gałęziom ciążył złej wieczności nawał.

The fault is mine. Lord, come into the garden,
  The garden, which is mine, is mine . . . O Lord.

I confess that frivolously, densely, I believe
  In afterlives of flowers and butterflies.
Come into my garden, though mere magic gave it life . . .
  Though it be but the folly of a day! . . .'

He entered bushes busy rustling signs from life's beyond.
  They were alone – alone, and face to face.
Saying nothing, darkening, together they walked on
  Down alleyways that followed alleyways.

The garden dreamed itself . . . Here and there oaks withered, died –
    overdreamt.
  The look of afterworlds was on each bush.
The boughs were thick with owls and many wandering silences.
  No cricket and no finch ruffled the hush.

The heavens fled to seek protection with the farthest star.
  The gold-horned moon prodded clouds mistily.
Dead souls fluttered in the sand, desired
  Their deaths renewed and – in the gloom – posthumous liberties.

Something like a golden island crawls in alleys far.
  An island such as takes fright when brows raise . . .
In a moment midnight creeps into the green with glow-worms' stars,
  Disturbing the forest overgrowth's intricacies.

Pan Błyszczyński checked the garden for its magic fit –
  That sounds and after-sounds quite really seemed –
And that fungus on the oak, that deadly derelict,
  Bit deep into false bark and trunks of dreams.

He checked the lily-bird trill was a lark's,
  And that the tulip's snake-head indicated spring,
And with a glance he brought reluctant trees up to the mark:
  More or less the same as the real thing . . .

Unheard-of fallacious flowers ramped wondrously enough.
  A burden of bad eternity weighed down each bough.

Pod stopami przechodniów piach niepewny i miałki
Tyleż istniał, ile istnieć zaprzestawał.

Szli, aż doszli tam, gdzie w mrzonce zagęstwionej i niczyjej
Cień dziewczyny jaśniał oczu w dal rozbłystką,
A jej usta i piersi i ramiona i sny jej
Były takie, żeby właśnie kochać wszystko . . .

Rzęsy miała dosyć złote, by rozwidnić blaskiem rzęs tych
Dno zmyślonych jezior, gdzie mży śmierć zmyślona –
Warkocz łatwo się płoszył, więc skrzydłami fal gęstych
Wciąż uciekał i powracał na ramiona.

Bóg w nią spojrzał, kiedy właśnie wynurzona z mgieł spowicia
Urojone oczy w modre nic rozwarła.
'Kto ją stworzył?' – zapytał. 'Nikt, bo przyszła bez życia
I bez śmierci, więc nie żyła i nie zmarła . . .

Próżno szukam w jej warkoczu źdźbeł istnienia, snu okruszyn,
Próżno chcę ugłaskac pozłocisty kędzierz!
Tak mnie wzrusza ten niebyt, cudny niebyt dziewuszyn! . . .
Bądź miłościw niebytowi . . . Wiem, że będziesz . . .

Wyłoniłem z mroku ogród, oderwany od przyczyny,
Rozkwieciłem próżnię, namnożyłem ścieżek –
I już wszystko rozumiem, prócz tej jednej dziewczyny,
Prócz tej jednej, którą kocham!' Bóg nic nie rzekł.

'Znam usilność rzeczy sennych i znużenie rzeczy martwych.
Ogród mój chwilami wolałby – bezlistnieć . . .
Boże, nie skąp w obłokach błogosławieństw i kar Twych
Tym, co wiedzą, że ich nie ma – a chcą istnieć!

W Twych przestworach coś się stało . . . Mgła o cud się dopomina . . .
Z tamtej strony świata modlą się zawieje.
I w tych strasznych bezczasach taka nagła dziewczyna
Tak niebacznie poza życiem – cieleśnieje!

Zbliż się do niej, ciemny jarze! Zbliż się do niej, modra strugo!
Czemuż pies mój wyje na jej czar cichutki?

At the feet of passers-by, the sand's uncertain snuff
  Only existed as much as its being snuffed out.

Onward they trod, coming to the spot on which – rank fantasy –
  A girl's shade lit up, eyes far-glistening:
Her lips and her breasts and her arms and her dreams
  Were such that she loved everything . . .

So gold her lashes they could flash to light
  Dreamed depths of lakes, in which a dreamed Death glooms –
Her braids like waves upon the wings of fright
  Were always fleeing, and always re-meeting, her arms.

God watched as she emerged from swaddling haze:
  As on blue voids her dreamt eyes opened wide.
'Who created her?' 'No one; she was lifeless when she came,
  She has no death, she neither lived nor died . . .

In vain I've combed her braids for being's traces, crumbs of dream,
  In vain I yearn to stroke her goldern curls.
And her unbeing moves me. Wondrous maid of the unbeen! . . .
  Be good to the unbeen . . . I know You will . . .

I drew this garden from the dusk, detracted from the causal,
  Flowered the gulf about, and multiplied roads –
And now I comprehend all things, all things except this girl –
  This girl I love' The Lord said not a word.

'I know the toils of dreamy things, the dead ones' weariness.
  At times my garden would prefer – unleaving . . .
O God in heaven, when you bless and curse, be generous
  To those who know they aren't and wish for being.

Throughout your vast spaces something has happened: mists demand
  miracles . . .
  Beyond the world's far side the blizzards pray.
And in these terrible untimes, so suddenly, a girl
  Goes and bodies forth outside life – heedlessly!

Draw closer to her, dark ravine! And you, O stream so blue!
  Why does my dog so howl at her mouse-quiet charms?

Może zimne jej usta są ostatnią posługą
Dla tych właśnie, którzy wierzą tylko w smutki.

Znam niedolę wniebowstąpień! Znam wskrzeszonych ust niedolę!
I płacz wśród zieleni . . . I zgon sierociński . . .
I to wszystko mnie boli! . . . Ja – sam siebie tak bolę!' –
Wołał w bezmiar i ku Bogu pan Błyszczyński.

Ale Boga już nie było . . . Pustka padła wzdłuż na kwiaty.
Widma drzew szeptały: 'Zmiłuj się nad nami!' –
Błogosławiąc snom wszelkim, leciał w dalsze wszechświaty
Powietrzami, wstrząsanymi powietrzami.

Pewno widać było z nieba, że świat mija i przeminie,
I że snom przyświeca – woda na kamieniu . . .
Pan Błyszczyński zaszeptał w usta niemej dziewczynie:
'Błędny cieniu, marny cieniu, cudny cieniu!

Zabłękitnij – odbłękitnij . . . I mów wszystko i niedomów!
Czy tu jest ów wszechświat, gdzieś zgubiła siebie?
Może ci się należy wpośród innych ogromów
Inna zieleń – inna nicość – w innym niebie.

Nie zaczęłaś dotąd istnieć w żadnym półśnie, w żadnym grobie,
Dotąd stóp twych śladu nie stwierdziły kwiaty –
Podczas twego niebytu zakochałem się w tobie,
Naraziłem mroczne ciało na zaświaty!

Czy mam z tobą iść w głąb żalu, czy w tę inną głąb doliny,
Nim świat zginie śmiercią, niebem malowaną? . . .
I jak dążyc do ciebie – do niebyłej dziewczyny –
Ty – mgło moja, usta drogie, złota piano!

Oto resztki mych przeznaczeń: noc niedobra i dzień sępny –
Oto – popłoch czarów, gdy je miłość zrani!
Od nicości do ust twych – ledwo jeden krok wstępny,
Od otchłani poprzez dreszcze – do otchłani!

Śni się liściom – nieskończoność. Śni się wiosłom – dno i łódka.
Odtrącone zorze raz na zawsze blednąc . . .

Perhaps her cold lips bear the last rites to
   Those who trust only sadnesses and dooms?

I know ascension's woe, the woe of mouths that are reborn,
   The tears in forests green, the orphans' deaths –
And all this pains me! I myself am pain!'
   He cried to God and to the boundlessness.

But God was gone. An emptiness lay upon all the flowers.
   Tree phantoms whispered, 'Have mercy on us!'
With blessings for all fantasies, the air around aquiver,
   He flew on to some other universe.

From heaven one could see – that the world fades,
   That dreams are lit by – water over stones . . .
Pan Błyszczyński whispered to the dumb lips of the maid,
   'Poor shadow, poor sad shadow, wondrous one!

Shine bright blue – and then shed that blue . . . Tell all – and do not say.
   Is this the cosmos where your lost self lies?
Perhaps you own another green, a void, another sky,
   Somewhere in another immensity?

You haven't started being yet in any halfdream, any tomb,
   Your steps aren't yet recorded in the flowers.
Whilst you have been unbeing here I fell in love with you,
   Laying open an obscure body to the hereafters!

Should I go into pain's depths with you, or that other valley's depth
   Before earth dies the death scrolled in the clouds? . . .
And how can I get through to you, O unbeen girl – your breath
   So dear to me, my mist, my gold-mist-shroud!

Observe my destiny in rags: dark nights and carrion days.
   Observe the state of my magic: love-wounded, it flutters.
From nothingness and to your lips – is but a step away:
   From gulf – to gulf, amidst many a shudder.

The leaves dream – of infinity. Oars: of boats, waters deep.
   Once cast-off, dawns become pallid forever . . .

Czy śmierć w nic nas rozśmieje, czy nas z nowych łez utka –
Wszystko jedno, tchu ostatni, wszystko jedno!

Noc zabije nas nie mieczem, lecz jaśminem i konwalią –
I zaciszem mogił – i oddechem sadu!
Prędzej pochwyć treść nocy i ucałuj i spal ją,
Żeby po niej nie zostało ani śladu!

Wszystkim widmom chce się zginąć takim nagłym wielozgonem,
Żeby brak ich we śnie – był dla jawy ulgą.
A mój upiór śpi w jarze – na wybrzeżu zielonem,
Gdy go znajdziesz, pusty cieniu – zbudź i tul go!

Tam – wysoko i najwyżej – między niebem a nadrzewiem
Włóczy się srebrnawo – cisza i znikomość.
Tak o tobie nic nie wiem, tak cudownie nic nie wiem,
Że miłoscią, jest ta moja – niewiadomość!'

Umilkł nagle pan Błyszczyński i popatrzył w dal niecałą,
Świateł i przeznaczeń było coraz więcej.
A on kochał ją w usta, kochał w stopy, w pierś białą –
I minęło różnych czasów sto tysięcy!

Ramionami ją ogarnął, a ustami doogarniał,
Oczom z gwiazd przyrzucał patrzącego złota,
Lecz cień w jego objęciach wciąż samotniał i marniał
I nie wiedział, że to – miłość i pieszczota.

Noc z roziskrzeń, wróżb i mgławic promienisty splotła batog,
Żeby nim biczować nie dość chętne groby.
A w księżycu się jarzył wykres cieśnin i zatok,
Gdzie nic nie ma, prócz oddali i żałoby.

Mrok zaskomlał w pustym dębie, zagwizdała nicość w klonie,
I rozbłysła w księżyc – śmierć i pajęczyna . . .
Pan Błyszczyński zrozumiał i załamał swe dłonie
I pomyślał: 'W nic rozwieje się dziewczyna!' –

W nic rozwiała się dziewczyna i jej czar, poczęty w niebie,
I pierś, zakonczona różową soczystką.
I rozpadło się ciało na żal straszny do siebie
I niewiedzę o tym żalu! . . . I to – wszystko . . .

Whether death derides us into naught or sews us up
  To weep – no matter – last breath – there's no matter.

Night does not use a sword to kill us but a lily, jasmine,
  The hush of graves and what orchards exhale.
Seize, caress and then destroy the things the night contains,
  So not one single trace of it remains.

All phantoms yearn to die just some such sudden multi-death,
  Take leave of dreams and lift the cares of day.
My ghost he sleeps in a ravine, beside the grassy sedge:
  When you find him, vacant shadow, hold him, when he wakes.

On high, and on the highest heights – 'twixt sky and overtrees –
  In silver, fleetingness and silence rove.
So little do I know of you that somehow, wondrously,
  My ignorance is nothing else but love.'

Suddenly he halted, stared to where the distance stops.
  There was a teem of destinies and lights.
Meanwhile he loved her at her feet and at her breasts and lips
  Throughout a hundred thousand different times.

He clasped her up into his arms: his lips her figure traced.
  He gave her eyes the gold of watching stars.
The shade within his arms grew ever lonelier, more waste,
  Unknowing what love and caresses are.

Night wove a knout of omens, mist and sparks
  To punish any none-too-eager tombs.
The moon's straits and bays lit up on its chart
  Where there is naught but distance, mourning, gloom.

The void whistled through maples; in the hollow oak, dusk whined;
  The moon illumined – death and a spider's web . . .
Pan Błyszczyński understood, began to wring his hands
  And thought, 'She's slipping into nothingness.'

She blew to nothing, with all of the charms heaven wrought;
  Along with her breast, and the pink juiciness at its tip.
In terrible self-pity, the body fell apart –
  Half ignorant of that pity. And that – was it . . .

Nie umarła, lecz umarło jej odbicie w jezior wodzie.
Już się kończył zaświat . . . Ustał cud dziewczyński . . .
O, wieczności, wieczności,i ty byłaś w ogrodzie!
I był blady, bardzo blady pan Błyszczyński.

Pszczoły

W zakamarku podziemnym, w mieszkalnym pomroku,
Gdzie zmarły, zamiast dachu, ma nicość nad głową,
W pewną noc Wiekuistą, a dla nas – Lipcową
Coś zabrzękło . . Śmierć słyszy i przynagla kroku . . .

A to – pszczoły, zmyliwszy istnienia ścieżynę,
Zboczyły do tych pustek, jak do złego ula!
Rój się iskrzy tak obco, tak brzęcząco hula,
Że strach w mroku tę jurną ujrzeć pozłocinę! . . .

A zmarli w zachwyceniu, źrenice rozwiewną
Przesłaniając od blasku skruszałych rąk wiórem,
Tłoczą się cień do cienia i wołają chórem:
'To – pszczoły! Pamiętajcie? To – pszczoły na pewno!'

Przytłumione snem bóle na nowo ich trawią!
Wdzięczni drobnym owadom za zbudzoną ranę
Z wszystkich sił swej nicości patrzą w skry zbłąkane,
Co wzdłuż śmierci i w poprzek żywcem się złotawią . . .

Znali niegdyś te cudła złotego pomiotu,
A dzisiaj, zaniedbani w swych mgieł niedobrzysku,
Podziwiają skrzydlatą szaradę rozbłysku
I chyżą łamigłówkę brzęczacego lotu!

Ale drogę powrotną zwęszywszy w odmęcie,
Pszczoły lśnią się gromadą już co chwila rzadszą,
Już – w świat się przedostając, gasną na zakręcie –
Już ich – nie ma! – A oni wciąż patrzą i patrzą . . .

She did not die, but in the lake there perished her reflection.
The afterworld closed down with the girl's miracle . . .
Eternities, eternities, you too were in the garden.
And Pan Błyszczyński looked very, very pale.

Bees

In underground seclusion, in a dark and lived-in depth,
Where the dead man has no roof above his head but nothingness,
Upon a certain Night Eternal – round July for us –
Something buzzes . . . And Death hears and quickens up his step . . .

It's – bees, who have strayed from the pathway of being,
Sidetracked to wastes that are like malign hives.
So strange is the glittering swarm's humming jive
One is fearful of watching it eagerly gleaming! . . .

And the dead, quite delighted, eyes flickering wide,
Their dry stick hands raised up as shields from the glare,
Crowd shade upon shade and concertedly cry,
'They're bees! You remember? They're bees; that's for sure!'

The pangs sleep once smothered consume them anew.
As they thank each small insect for each wakened wound
Every ounce of their voided strength watches their light
Zig a gold into death and then zag out alive . . .

Once upon a time they knew this wondrous gold litter
But now, desolate, wrapped up in ungoodly mist,
They marvel over the winged charade's glitters
And over the speeding teaser's humming wisps.

But now in the void the bees catch at a scent:
The exit! And shine on in crowds that grow thinner.
On reaching the world their light dies at the corner.
All gone! And the dead watch and watch where they went . . .

Dziewczyna

Dwunastu braci, wierząc w sny, zbadało mur od marzeń strony,
A poza murem płakał głos, dziewczęcy głos zaprzepaszczony.

I pokochali głosu dzwięk i chętny domysł o Dziewczynie,
I zgadywali kształty ust po tym, jak śpiew od żalu ginie . . .

Mówili o niej: 'Łka, więc jest!' – I nic innego nie mówili,
I przeżegnali cały świat – i świat zadumał się w tej chwili . . .

Porwali młoty w twardą dłoń i jęli w mur tłuc z łoskotem!
I nie wiedziała ślepa noc, kto jest czlowiekiem, a kto młotem?

'O, prędzej skruszmy zimny głaz, nim śmierć Dziewczynę rdzą
   powlecze!' –
Tak, waląc w mur, dwunasty brat do jedenastu innych rzecze.

Ale daremny był ich trud, daremny ramion sprzęg i usił!
Oddali ciała swe na strwon owemu snowi, co ich kusił!

Łamią się piersi, trzeszczy kość, próchnieją dłonie, twarze bledną . . .
I wszyscy w jednym zmarli dniu i noc wieczystą mieli jedną!

Lecz cienie zmarłych – Boże mój! – nie wypusciły młotow z dłoni!
I tylko inny płynie czas – i tylko młot inaczej dzwoni . . .

I dzwoni w przód! I dzwoni wspak! I wzwyż za każdym grzmi
   nawrotem!
I nie wiedziała ślepa noc, kto tu jest cieniem a kto młotem?

'O, prędzej skruszmy zimny głaz, nim śmierć Dziewczynę rdzą
   powlecze!' –
Tak, waląc w mur, dwunasty cień do jedenastu innych rzecze.

Lecz cieniom zbrakło nagle sił, a cień się mrokom nie opiera!

The Girl

Twelve brothers who gave credence to dreams tested the wall out from
the dream's side.
For on its other side they heard a trapped girl as she cried.

They came to love her voice's sound, thought on her eagerly,
And guessed her lips' shapes from the way her song died mournfully.

They said, 'She weeps, therefore she is.' And that was all they said.
They bade farewell to the whole world – and the world was amazed.

Their calloused fists gripped hammers, loudly battered at the wall.
And could the blind night not tell hammer from human at all?

'O quickly crush the cold stone lest death's rust consume the maid!'
Thus – beating at the wall – one brother to the others said.

But all their strivings were in vain, in vain their instruments and arms.
They gave their bodies to the dream that had enticed them with its
charms.

Their ribs collapse; bones crumble; hands – are dust, and faces –
pale . . .
One day they died and passed into the same night, one and all.

And yet their dead shadows – O my God! – would not let the
hammers go.
The hammers just sound different now, time alters in its flow.

Ahead they sound – on all sides pound – and all around they thunder.
And could the blind night not tell where a shade became a hammer?

'O quickly crush the cold stone lest death's rust consume the maid!'
Thus – as he beat the wall – one addressed all the other shades.

But all at once their strength gave out, and shadows can't resist the
dusk!

I powymarły jeszcze raz, bo nigdy dość się nie umiera . . .

I nigdy dość, i nigdy tak, jak tego pragnie ów, co kona! . . .
I znikła treść – i zginął ślad – i powieść o nich już skończona!

Lecz dzielne młoty – Boże mój – mdłej nie poddały się żałobie!
I same przez się biły w mur, huczały śpiżem same w sobie!

Huczały w mrok, huczały w blask i ociekały ludzkim potem!
I nie wiedziała ślepa noc, czym bywa młot, gdy nie jest młotem?

'O, prędzej skruszmy zimny głaz, nim śmierć Dziewczynę rdzą
powlecze!' –
Tak, waląc w mur, dwunasty młot do jedenastu innych rzecze.

I runął mur, tysiącem ech wstrząsając wzgórza i doliny!
Lecz poza murem – nic i nic! Ni żywej duszy, ni Dziewczyny!

Niczyich oczu ani ust! I niczyjego w kwiatach losu!
Bo to był głos i tylko – głos, i nic nie było, oprócz głosu!

Nic – tylko płacz i żal i mrok i niewiadmość i zatrata!
Takiż to świat! Niedobry świat! Czemuż innego nie ma świata?

Wobec kłamliwych jawnie snów, wobec zmarniałych w nicość cudów,
Potężne młoty legły w rząd na znak spełnionych godnie trudów.

I była zgroza nagłych cisz! I była próżnia w całym niebie!
A ty z tej próżni czemu drwisz, kiedy ta próżnia nie drwi z ciebie?

And so they died away again, because we never die enough:

Never enough, and never just quite as the dying man wanted.
Their substance vanished – no trace left – and so their story's ended.

But the brave hammers – O my God! – did not succumb to feeble grief.
They beat against the walls themselves – bronze echoed on itself.

They banged by night, by blazing light, and dripped with human sweat.
And could blind night not tell what's left of hammers that are not?

'O quickly crush the cold stone lest death's rust consume the maid!'
Thus – beating at the wall – one hammer to the others said.

The wall fell down, a thousand echoes shook the hills and dales!
But on the far side: just a void. No living soul. No girl.

Nobody's eyes or mouth; no bed-of-roses destiny.
There'd been a voice, and just a voice, and nothing else you see.

Nothing – but grief and loss and tears and ignorance and night.
Such is the way of this evil world. Why isn't it put right?

Confronted with the dream's clear lie, with wonders wasted on a void,
The mighty hammers lay down in rows, as if well employed.

Sudden silence horribly fell. All Heaven became a vacuum.
Why do you mock the vacuum that has never ever mocked you?

Notes

CHAPTER ONE: PROLOGUE: WORDS AFTER SPEECH

1. Harold Bloom, 'Freud and the Sublime', in *Freud, a Collection of Critical Essays*, ed. Perry Meisel (Englewood Cliffs, NJ: Prentice Hall, 1981) p. 224.
2. T. W. Adorno, *Aesthetische Theorie* (Frankfurt a. M.: Suhrkamp, 1970) p. 9.
3. Henri Bergson, *Creative Evolution*, trs. Arthur Mitchell (London: Macmillan, 1954) pp. 300–1.
4. I examine the theme of the *Gesamtkunstwerk* at greater length in 'Cinema, Symbolism and the *Gesamtkunstwerk*', published in *Comparative Criticism Yearbook 1982*, ed. E. S. Shaffer (Cambridge: Cambridge University Press, 1982), and in my book *The Story of the Lost Reflection* (London: Verso/New Left Books 1985).

CHAPTER TWO: ARCHAEOLOGY: THE ROMANTIC ROOTS OF SYMBOLISM

1. F. W. Bateson, 'Notes on Blake's Poems', in *Songs of Innocence and Experience, a Casebook*, ed. M. Bottrall (London: Macmillan, 1970), p. 182.
2. Cf. C. Gallant, *Blake and the Assimilation of Chaos* (Princeton, NJ: Princeton University Press, 1978) pp. 16–17.
3. See Jonathan Wordsworth, *William Wordsworth: The Borders of Vision* (London: Oxford University Press, 1983).
4. Whenever Wordsworth states, in a characteristic double negation, that something is 'not unworthy' (for instance), the intertextual nature of his work becomes patent: on each such occasion he implicitly quotes, and polemicises with, those for whom the low-born have no dignity. His use of this form, however, indicates the extent to which he himself has internalised the view he rejects.
5. For further reflections on the use of negation in Romantic and post-Romantic poetry, see the section 'Symbolism, Femininity and Negation' in Ch. 4.
6. Some of the instances of synaesthesia in Shelley's work are listed in Glenn O'Malley's 'Shelley's "Air-Prism": The Synesthetic Scheme of "Alastor"', in *Shelley: Modern Judgements*, ed. R. B. Woodings (London: Macmillan, 1968) pp. 72–86.
7. See Leavis's essay on Shelley in *Revaluation* (Harmondsworth: Penguin, 1972) p. 194.

8. Shelley, *Poetical Works*, ed. Thomas Hutchinson, corrected G. M. Matthews (London: Oxford University Press, 1970) p. 578.
9. Ibid., p. 259, ll. 214–17.
10. Shelley's flight from self is the theme of Christopher Small's *Ariel Like a Harpy: Shelley, Mary and 'Frankenstein'* (London: Gollancz, 1972). See esp. ch. 7, 'The Pursuing Shadow', pp. 156–70.
11. Earl R. Wasserman, *Shelley: A Critical Reading* (London and Baltimore: Johns Hopkins University Press, 1971) p. 12.
12. Leavis, *Revaluation*, p. 206.
13. Shelley, *Poetical Works*, p. 15, ll. 1–15.
14. Ibid., p. 621.
15. G. Wilson Knight, 'The Naked Seraph: An Essay on Shelley', in *The Starlit Dome* (London: Methuen, 1959) p. 187.
16. See J. Hillis Miller, 'The Critic as Host', in Harold Bloom *et al.*, *Deconstruction and Criticism* (London: Routledge, 1979).
17. *Shelley's Prose Works*, II (London: Chatto and Windus, 1912) p. 223.
18. Ibid., p. 260.
19. This is one of the main themes of Milton Wilson's *Shelley's Later Poetry: A Study of His Prophetic Imagination* (New York: Columbia University Press, 1959).
20. *Shelley's Prose Works*, II, 247.
21. For Eisenstein, unlike Pudovkin, the juxtaposition of two images yields not their sum but a totally new element.
22. Paul de Man, 'Shelley Disfigured', in Bloom *et al.*, *Deconstruction and Criticism*, p. 64.
23. Ibid.
24. John Addington Symonds, *Shelley* (London: Macmillan, 1887) pp. 172–3.
25. *A Defence of Poetry*, in *Shelley's Prose Works*, II, 7.
26. Ibid., p. 5.
27. See Timothy Webb's excellent study *The Violet in the Crucible: Shelley and Translation* (London: Oxford University Press, 1976) p. 176.
28. Ibid., p. 39.
29. Ibid., pp. 303–4.
30. Franz Kafka, *Briefe an Milena* (Frankfurt a. M.: Fischer, 1952) p. 203.
31. T. W. Adorno, 'Parataxis', in *Noten Zur Literatur* (Frankfurt a. M.: Suhrkamp, 1965) p. 184.
32. W. Waiblinger, *Hölderlins Leben, Dichtung und Washnsinn* (Hamburg: Ellerman, 1947).
33. M. Walser, 'Hölderlin zu entsprechen', in *Was zu bezweifeln war* (Berlin und Weimar: Aufbau, 1976) p. 328.
34. See Michael Hamburger's essay 'Georg Trakl', in his *A Proliferation of Prophets* (Manchester: Carcanet, 1983) p. 195.
35. See his article in the *Hölderlin Jahrbuch 12* (1961–2) p. 41.
36. E. H. Gombrich, 'The Evidence of Images', in *Interpretation*, ed. C. S. Singleton (Baltimore: Johns Hopkins University Press, 1969) p. 62.
37. Wassily Kandinsky, *Concerning the Spiritual in Art*, trs. Sadleir and retrs. Golffing, Harrison and Ostertag (New York: George Witterborn, 1955) p. 58.
38. See Werner Kirchner's essay on 'Die Völker schwiegen, schlummerten . . .'

and on 'Der Frieden' in his *Hölderlin: Aufsätze zu seiner Homburger Zeit* (Göttingen: Vandenhoeck und Ruprecht, 1967).

39. All numbers in brackets refer to the numbers accorded the poems in Emily Dickinson, *The Complete Poems*, ed. T. H. Johnson (London: Faber and Faber, 1976).
40. See R. W. Franklin's *The Editing of Emily Dickinson, a Reconsideration* (Madison, Milwaukee and London: University of Wisconsin Press, 1967).
41. Thomas H. Johnson, 'Establishing a Text: The Emily Dickinson Papers', in *Studies in Bibliography*, V (1952–3), quoted in Franklin, *Editing*, p. 130.
42. For close comparison of the two versions of this poem, see David Simpson's *Irony and Authority in Romantic Poetry* (London: Macmillan, 1979), ch. 1.

CHAPTER THREE: THE WORD UNHEARD

1. T. W. Adorno, *Noten zur Literatur I* (Frankfurt a. M.: Suhrkamp, 1975) p. 102.
2. I owe the notion of the disguised indicative to Dr Michael Long of Churchill College, Cambridge.
3. The interrelationship of these three images in the *fin de siècle* is analysed in my 'Cinema, Symbolism and the *Gesamtkunstwerk*', *Comparative Criticism Yearbook 1982*, pp. 219–20.
4. Cf. 'Question Forms in the "Duino Elegies"', a lecture delivered in Cambridge in 1976 by J. H. Prynne of Caius College.
5. See Pauline Kael's review of that film in her *Reeling* (Boston, Mass. and Toronto: Little, Brown, 1976) p. 92.
6. One is wary of opposing 'style' to 'feeling': the opposition smacks of stale Romanticism. Nevertheless I think the distinction valid in the case of early Eliot. The intensity of 'Prufrock', 'The Portrait of a Lady', 'Gerontion' and 'La Figlia che Piange' makes the poems contemporary with them seem mannered and evasive.

CHAPTER FOUR: NATURE'S DOUBLE NAME: THE POETRY OF BOLESŁAW LEŚMIAN

1. Leśmian, *Poezje*, ed. Jacek Trznadl (Warsaw: PIW, 1975) p. 244.
2. Leśmian, *Szkice literackie*, ed. Jacek Trznadl (Warsaw: PIW, 1958) p. 31.
3. E. Canetti, *Masse und Macht* (Munich: Carl Hanser, 1973), esp. the last chapter, on the survivor.
4. W. Kubacki, 'Komentarz do Leśmiana', in *Twórczość*, 1949, ii, 52.
5. Leśmian, *Szkice literackie*, p. 142.
6. Ibid., p. 143.
7. S. Freud, 'Vermischte Schriften aus den Jahren 1923–8', in *Gesammelte Schriften* (Vienna: Internationaler Psychoanalytischer Verlag, 1934), p. 395.
8. Leśmian, *Poezje*, p. 113.
9. Ibid., p. 173.
10. Ibid., p. 128.
11. W. Benjamin, 'Das Kunstwerk im Zeitalter der technischen Reproduzierbarkeit', in *Schriften*, I. ii (Frankfurt a. M.: Suhrkamp, 1974);

quoted as trs. in *Illuminations*, trs. Harry Zohn (London and Glasgow: Fontana/Collins, 1973) pp. 232–3.

12. K. Irzykowski, *X Muza* (Warsaw: Wydawnictwa artystyczne i filmowe, 1977) p. 65.
13. Leśmian, *Szkice literackie*, p. 59.
14. T. W. Adorno, 'Aufzeichnungen zu Kafka', in *Versuch, das Endspiel zu verstehen* (Frankfurt a. M.: Suhrkamp, 1973) p. 164.
15. Leśmian, *Poezje*, pp. 262–3.
16. T. W. Adorno, *Philosophie der neuen Musik* (Frankfurt a. M., Berlin, Vienna: Ullstein, 1972) p. 139.
17. M. Bakhtin, *Twórczość Franciszkạ Rabeleis'go a kultura ludowa średniowieczna i renesansowa* (Polish trs. of Bakhtin's study of Rabelais) (Cracow: Wydawnictwol literackie, 1975) p. 118.
18. Ibid., p. 115.
19. Adorno, *Philosophie der neuen Musik*, p. 128.
20. Leśmian, *Poezje*, p. 226.
21. Ibid., p. 107.
22. Ibid., p. 222.
23. T. W. Adorno, *Minima moralia* (Frankfurt a. M.: Suhrkamp, 1978) p. 156; quoted from the New Left Books trs. by E. F. N. Jephcott (London, 1974) p. 120.
24. Leśmian, *Poezje*, p. 123.
25. R. Barthes, *Sade. Fourier, Loyola* (Paris: Editions du Seuil, 1971) p. 35.
26. Bergson, *Creative Evolution*, pp. 300–1.
27. See the following section of this chapter.
28. P. N. Furbank, *Reflections on the Word 'Image'* (London: Secker and Warburg, 1970) pp. 42–3.
29. T. W. Adorno, 'Wörter aus der Fremde', in *Noten zur Literatur* (Frankfurt a. M.: Suhrkamp, 1982) pp. 216–32.
30. See Rochelle Stone, *Bolesław Leśmian* (Berkeley, Calif., and Los Angeles: University of California Press, 1976).
31. For more on Norwid's doctrine of silence, see Jerzy Peterkiewicz's *The Other Side of Silence. The Poet at the Limits of Language* (London: Oxford University Press, 1970). For Leśmian's fascination by the Ukraine, see M. Pankowski's *Leśmian. La revolte d'un poète contre les limites* (Brussels: Université Libre de Bruxelles, 1967) p. 38.
32. The best-known example of the 'peasant-mania' was the marriage between the Cracovian poet Lucjan Rydel and a peasant girl. The wedding-feast provided the starting-point for Stanisław Wyspiański's great play *Wesele* (The Wedding).
33. Adorno, 'Wörter aus der Fremde', *Noten zur Literatur* (1982) p. 218.
34. Walter Jackson Bate, *John Keats* (Cambridge, Mass.: Belknap Press of Harvard University Press; London: Oxford University Press, 1963) p. 450.
35. Christopher Ricks, *Keats and Embarrassment* (Oxford: Clarendon Press, 1974) pp. 58–9.
36. M. Głowiński, 'Poezja przeczenia', in *Pamiętnik literacki*, LXVII. ii(1976) 130.
37. A. Sandauer, 'Filozofia Leśmiana', in *Lyrika i logika* (Warsaw: PIW, 1971) p. 31.
38. Bergson, *Creative Evolution*, pp. 300–1.

39. Cf. Edmund Bergler, 'A New Approach to the Theory of Erythrophobia', in *Psychoanalytic Quarterly*, XII (1944), quoted in Ricks, *Keats and Embarrassment*, p. 88: 'The exhibitionistic tendency that was warded off is smuggled into the symptom: by blushing the erythrophobe makes himself really conspicuous, i.e. exhibits himself.' Neologisms can be interpreted as textual blushes of this kind. Bergler's remarks also lend a new meaning to Eliot's 'the roses had the look of roses that were looked at' (*Burnt Norton*): roses are red because the look elicits from them a blush.

40. T. Skubelanka, 'U źródeł stylu erotykow Leśmiana', in *Studia o Leśmianie* (Warsaw: PIW, 1971) p. 146.

41. This may remind one of Leśmian's 'Migoń and Jawrzon' (*Poezje*, pp. 264–5). Migoń dons an invisible helmet and does battle with Jawrzon for the love of a girl. The sun rises after their nocturnal struggle to reveal both of them dead and the helmet hanging on a bush.

42. John Keats, *The Complete Poems*, ed. John Barnard (Harmondsworth: Penguin, 1976) p. 505.

43. E. Goffman, 'Embarrassment and Social Organization', in *American Journal of Sociology*, I. XII (1956), 264–75, quoted in Ricks, *Keats and Embarrassment*, p. 2.

44. A. Sandauer, 'Pośmiertny triumf Młodej Polski', in *Poeci czterech pokoleń* (Cracow: Wydawnictwo literackie, 1977), pp. 11–12.

45. Leslie A. Marchand, *Byron: A Biography*, 2 vols (London: John Murray, 1957) p. 886. See also Sandor Feldman, 'Blushing, Fear of Blushing and Shame', in *Journal of the American Psychoanalytic Association*, X (1962), quoted in Ricks, *Keats and Embarrassment*, p. 86: 'In the course of the analysis of blushers I have found that it is not so much the masturbation itself as the masturbatory fantasy which is the essential stimulus for shame and blushing.' Thus the genesis of the blush appears to be linked to the replacement of the fantasised mental image before one by the real image of another person: with the overruling of fantasy by reality, in short.

46. Bergson, *Creative Evolution*, p. 304.

47. G. K. Chesterton, *The Victorian Age in Literature* (London: Williams and Norgate; New York: H. Holt, 1913) p. 172.

48. For further reflections on and examples of these neologisms, see E. Olkuśnik, 'Słowotworstwo na usługach filozofii', in *Studia o Leśmianie*.

49. Proust, *À la recherche du temps perdu*, I: 'Du côté de chez Swann' (Paris: Gallimard, 1954) p. 188.

50. Ibid., p. 191.

51. W. Gralewski, *Stalowa tęcza* (Warsaw: P. I. W., 1968) p. 211.

52. Ibid.

53. Leśmian, *Klechdy sezamowe* (Warsaw: Czytelnik, 1978) p. 13.

54. G. Josipovici, *The World and the Book* (London: Macmillan, 1971) p. 289.

CHAPTER FIVE: FLOWERS OF NOTHINGNESS: THE 'SPÄTWERK' OF PAUL CELAN

In the following chapter the separate volumes of Celan's verse are referred to by abbreviations: *NR = Die Niemandsrose*, *AW = Atemwende*,

FS = Fadensonnen, LZ = Lichtzwang, SP = Schneepart, and *ZG = Zeitgehöft.*

1. See H.-G. Gadamer, *'Wer bin Ich und wer bist Du?'* (Frankfurt a. M.: Suhrkamp, 1973) pp. 123–9.
2. See Marlies Janz, *Vom Engagement absoluter Poesie: Zur Lyrik und Aesthetik Paul Celans* (Frankfurt a. M.: Syndikat, 1976) pp. 195–200, for her powerful critique of Gadamer's omission of the poem's allusions to the communist and socialist movement in Germany.
3. Peter Szondi, *Eden,* in: *Celan-Studien* (Frankfurt a. M.: Suhrkamp, 1972) pp. 113–25.
4. This metaphor is suggested by Celan's own definition of the function of poetry, in 'Ansprache anlässlich der Entgegennahme des Literaturpreises der Freien Hansastadt Bremen', *Ausgewählte Gedichte* (Frankfurt a. M.: Suhrkamp, 1970), p. 128:

> Das Gedicht kann, da es ja eine Erscheinungsform der Sprache und damit seinem Wesen nach dialogisch ist, eine Flaschenpost sein, aufgegeben in dem – gewiss nicht immer hoffnungsstarken – Glauben, sie könnte irgendwo und irgendwann an Land gespült werden, an Herzland vielleicht.

> (The poem, since it is one of the forms through which language manifests itself and is thus dialogic by nature, the poem can be a message in a bottle, surrendered in a faith, not always nourished by any particularly strong hope, that it could be washed ashore somewhere and sometime – perhaps upon the heart's shore.)

5. Susan Stewart, *Nonsense: Aspects of Intertextuality in Folklore and Literature* (Baltimore and London: Johns Hopkins University Press, 1979) p. 116.
6. Susan Bassnett-McGuire, *Translation Studies* (London: Methuen, 1979) p. 102.
7. Henriette Beese, *Nachdichtung als Erinnerung. Allegorische Lektüre einiger Gedichte Paul Celans* (Darmstadt: Agora, 1976) p. 215.
8. Bernhard Böschenstein, 'Lesestationen im Spätwort. Zwei Gedichte aus Celans "Lichtzwang"', in *Leuchttürme* (Frankfurt a. M.: Insel, 1977) p. 298.
9. Celan, 'Der Meridian', in *Ausgewählte Gedichte,* p. 144.
10. George-Michael Schulz, *Negativität in der Dichtung Paul Celans* (Tübingen: Niemeyer, 1977) p. 215.
11. 'Engführung', in *Ausgewählte Gedichte,* pp. 67–74.
12. See Celan's version of Mandelstam's 'Horse-Shoe Finder', in *Der Hufeisenfinder* (Leipzig: Reclam, 1978) p. 93.
13. The juxtaposition of the neologism and the 'nologism' (itself a neologism) encapsulates the equivocal status of Celan's word coinages: they denote both a new thing beyond the range of our current tongue, and the place of nothing.
14. Peter Horst Neumann, *Zur Lyrik Paul Celans* (Göttingen: Kleine Vandenhoeck-Reihe, 1968) p. 10.
15. Ibid., p. 9.

Index

212

2/03 -1/18